STUDIES IN THE SOCIOLOGY OF SPORT

Edited by
Aidan O. Dunleavy, Andrew W. Miracle, and
C. Roger Rees

Refereed Proceedings of the
2nd Annual Conference of the
North American Society for the Sociology of Sport
Fort Worth, Texas, November 1981

Texas Christian University Press
Fort Worth, Texas 76129

Manufactured in the United States of America

Library of Congress Cataloging in Publication Data

North American Society for the Sociology of Sport.
  Conference (2nd: 1981: Fort Worth, Tex.)
  Studies in the sociology of sport.

  1. Sports — Social aspects — Addresses, essays, lectures.
I. Dunleavy, Aidan O. II. Miracle, Andrew W.
III. Rees, C. Roger.
GV706.5.N67   1981   306'.483   82-16807

ISBN 0-912646-78-0

TABLE OF CONTENTS

FOREWORD ix
  (Barry D. McPherson)

I SPORT, CULTURE, AND SOCIETY
Introduction 1
  1 Some Sociological Clues to Baseball as "National
    Pastime" (G. Brandmeyer and L. Alexander) 3
  2 Social Climbing: A Case Study of the Changing Class
    Structure of Rock Climbing and Mountaineering in
    Britain (P. Donnelly) 13
  3 Gender Variations in Game Attraction Factors of
    Native American Youth (A. Cheska) 29

II THE FORMAL ORGANIZATION OF SPORT
Introduction 51
  4 Weber's Theory of Bureaucracy and the Study of
    Voluntary Sport Organizations (W. Frisby) 53
  5 Modes of Integration in Voluntary Sport
    Organizations (M. Yerles) 73
  6 The Rise to Leadership in Major League Baseball:
    Playing Background and Early Career Influences
    (E. Kjeldsen) 85
  7 Quantity or Quality: Non-Linear Relationships
    Between Extent of Involvement and International
    Sporting Success (J. Colwell) 101

III INVOLVEMENT IN SPORT: PROCESS AND OUTCOME
Introduction 119
  8 Female Sport Involvement: A Preliminary
    Conceptualization (B. Brown) 121

9 The Theoretical Notion of Reciprocity and
Childhood Socialization into Sport (C. Hasbrook) . . 139

10 Sportsmanship: Variations Based on Sex and
Degree of Competitive Experience (M. Allison) 153

11 Feminism and Patriarchy in Physical Education
(M. Duquin) 167

IV PERCEPTIONS OF SPORTS INVOLVEMENT

Introduction 181

12 The Social Stigma of High Risk Sport Subcultures
(B. Vanreusel and R. Renson) 183

13 Attitudes Toward the Participation of Women in
Intercollegiate Sports: Evidence From a
Metropolitan Area Survey (R. Woodford
and W. Scott) 203

14 Reference Group Theory and the Economics of
Professional Sport (S. Lerch) 221

V EFFECTS OF PARTICIPATION IN SPORT

Introduction 237

15 The Athlete as Scholar in College: An Exploratory
Test of Four Models (H. Nixon) 239

16 Intercollegiate Athletic Participation and Academic
Achievement (S. Messner and D. Groisser) 257

17 Sport and Racial Integration: The Relationship
of Personal Contact, Attitudes and Behavior
(D. Chu and D. Griffey) 271

VI IMPACT OF SPORT PARTICIPATION ON YOUTH

Introduction 283

18 Sex Differences in Orientations Towards Games:
Tests of the Sports Involvement Hypothesis
(N. Theberge, J. Curtis and B. Brown) 285

19 Are Children's Competitive Team Sports
Socializing Agents for Corporate America?
(G. Berlage) 309

20 Youth Sport Involvement: Impact on Informal
   Game Participation (W. Podilchak) 325
21 The Behavior of Youth Football Coaches
   (P. Dubois) 349

VII CURRICULUM ADVANCES IN THE SOCIOLOGY OF SPORT

Introduction 361
22 A National Survey: Sociology of Sport Within
   American College and University Physical
   Education Professional Preparation Programs
   (D. Southard) 365
23 Sociological Kinesiology: Perspectives on Program
   Development (A. O. Dunleavy, G. E. Landwer,
   and C. R. Rees) 373
24 Notes on Teaching Sociology of Sport (M. Melnick) 377
25 Sport and American Society: A Course for
   Kinesiological Science Majors and General
   University Students (L. VanderVelden) 385
26 Sport Sociology: A Humanistic Perspective
   (D. Hellison) 393
27 The Use of Sport in Society VTR's in The Sport
   Sociology Curriculum (J. Bryant) 397

FOREWORD

The publication of this volume is a significant development for the field of study known as the Sociology of Sport. The twenty-seven papers in this book represent some of the presentations at the 2nd Annual Conference of the North American Society for the Sociology of Sport (NASSS) in November, 1981.

Whereas the first conference in 1980 attracted about one hundred participants and included papers by many of those in North America who were already strongly identified with the field, the 2nd Conference stimulated over a twofold increase in the number of participants and, more importantly, attracted many new scholars to the field. For example, over one-third of the papers in this volume were written by recent (or about to be) Ph.Ds who intend to devote their career to this field. In addition, another one-quarter of the papers are by sociologists who have only recently developed an interest in sociological phenomena pertaining to sport. The remaining papers are by established scholars in the field. Thus, whereas the 1st Conference was a successful pilot study, the 2nd Conference provided evidence that NASSS was a viable organization that could host an "annual" conference. More importantly, this Conference demonstrated that there is a critical mass of scholars in North America who are actively committed to explaining sport phenomena from a sociological perspective. Hence, a debt of gratitude is owed to the editors of this volume for taking the risk and time to organize a successful and stimulating conference. The quality of the program, as represented by the papers in this volume and companion volume (Foundations in the Sociology of Sport-Human Kinetics Press, 1983), will serve as a model for future conferences and will, no doubt, be recognized in later years as a significant turning point in the development of both NASSS and the field of Sociology of Sport.

The papers in this volume represent one expression of the state of the art in this dynamic and emerging field of study. As an indication of the increasing maturity of our sub-discipline, all of the papers selected for inclusion in this volume either utilized existing sociological theories or were based on a theoretical rationale unique to a specific problem. In addition to the six "professional" papers concerned with the teaching of Sociology of Sport (Part VII), the twenty-one "substantive" papers raise new questions, introduce new approaches to answering old questions, and alert scholars to significant, but as yet unstudied social phenomena pertaining to play, games or sport.

This publication may be used as a discrete reader to introduce students to the Sociology of Sport or, more ideally, as a supplementary reader to complement one of the basic textbooks in the field. It may also be used in conjunction with the companion publication (Foundations in the Sociology of Sport) which includes the papers written by the invited speakers at the 2nd Conference. In addition, this book should serve as a valuable resource, not only for emerging or established scholars, but also for undergraduate and graduate students who seek to become more involved in this field of study. That complete answers or explanations for interesting questions are not provided in the papers should only serve to stimulate the creative thinker to search for more complete or innovative answers. As a result of this search, additional unique questions and partial explanations will be derived. Hopefully, these will be presented at future NASSS conferences.

In summary, the papers in this book epitomize the high scholarly standards to which NASSS aspires, as well as the diversity in subject matter and approaches to the search for knowledge that are essential for the continued vitality of any field of study. These articles should function as a catalyst for the future development of the field in that more questions are raised than answers are provided. Thus, by this cyclical process of reading, critiquing, thinking, and creating the depth and quality of understanding of social phenomena in a sport context will continue to evolve. This volume represents a major, but incomplete, step toward this utopia. Therefore, as you read, consider how the ideas in each paper can be further developed to advance the theoretical and substantive knowledge of the field. You are also encouraged to actively utilize either the NASSS Newsletter or the annual meeting as a forum for the exchange of ideas pertaining to scholarly or professional matters.

Barry D. McPherson, President
North American Society for the
Sociology of Sport

SPORT, CULTURE, AND SOCIETY

Section I

SPORT, CULTURE, AND SOCIETY

The chapters in this section present perspectives on issues relative to the relationships among sport, culture, and society. While no small set of brief essays could possibly examine fully the intricate connections of sport, culture, and society, these pieces do manage to articulate basic questions pertinent to this configuration: 1) Does sport reflect or reinforce cultural values? 2) Do changes in sport effect changes in social values, or do changes in social values effect changes in sport? 3) Are sex-specific attitudes toward sport participation universal or do they vary cross culturally?

Brandmeyer and Alexander address the role of baseball in contemporary U.S. sports. They assess the notion that baseball essentially reflects 19th century pastoral traditions and thus is no longer congruent with the cultural realities of modern urban society. Central to the argument is the assumption that sport is an element of expressive culture involved in a continuous evolutionary process. The authors present evidence that while the role of baseball may have changed during the past 100 years, it remains an integral part of the culture which reinforces important cultural values.

Donnelly offers a case study of the democratization process, as it transpired in rock climbing and mountaineering in Great Britain. In doing so, he follows in the path of Dunning and Sheard's study of the democratization of Rugby football. The central question involves the relationship of social class membership and attitudes toward sport. Do changes in one produce changes in the other? If so, what is the primary or causal direction of the change? Donnelly's piece is especially important because he attempts to document the change process, rather than simply to provide a set of statistical correlations.

Cheska analyzes games and play of Indian boys and girls in the southwestern region of the United States. In addition to providing some general information about the recreational interests of these youth, she attempts to describe gender-specific variations. That is, what is different about the game playing of Indian boys when compared with the game playing of Indian girls. She also contrasts the game playing of Indian youth with game playing by non-Indians. Cheska clearly demonstrates cultural variation in attitudes toward sport, while finding some gender-specific tendencies in both the Indian and non-Indian studies she analyzes. The essay raises several interesting points for future investigation. For example, how can one explain the apparent lack of variation in attitudes toward sport among peoples from such dissimilar cultural traditions as the Athabaskan, Pueblo and Piman? Does this result from convergent evolution and the acculturation pressures from a more or less monolithic superordinate culture?

Chapter 1

SOME SOCIOLOGICAL CLUES TO BASEBALL AS "NATIONAL PASTIME"

Gerard A. Brandmeyer and Luella K. Alexander
University of South Florida

The sports sociology literature reveals a certain ambivalence about the place of baseball in American sports culture. This ambivalence is evident in Allen Guttmann's very thorough, 8700-word essay (1978) on baseball as "national pastime." Guttmann recognized (1978:114-116) that it is specious to portray baseball as passé due to its primitive-pastoral roots since these origins have no claim on the consciousness of the current generation of fans, many of whom find satisfaction in baseball's singular, and very modern, propensity to generate statistics (1978:100). Still, Guttmann concluded his essay on an uncertain note: baseball "has had its day in the sun," he observed, though "it will not decline and disappear" (1978:116).

George Grella (1975:556) was also cognizant of the overworked rural connection when he pointed out that baseball took hold in the small towns and, we would add, urban neighborhoods of the U.S., at a time, the late nineteenth century, when most Americans were no longer farmers, but not yet suburban in residence. Baseball quickly caught on not merely as a game but as a means for expressing local ties and loyalties in competition with rival towns or neighborhoods. These games were more than casual, leisure-time activities in the daily life of these communities because victory meant, in innumerable personal encounters, bragging rights, just as much as does, though on a smaller scale, the outcome of the annual October renewal in Dallas of the Texas-Oklahoma football rivalry. In fact, many a semi-professional, or even professional, ballplayer picked up walking-around money by hiring out as a mercenary in these ball field skirmishes (Pittman, 1981) under the disguise of an assumed name when necessary.

The cosmopolitanization of modern consciousness has eclipsed this traditional function of baseball in American life. To some degree, town baseball has been displaced, at least in the life of smaller communities, by the institutionalization of various high school sports. In this respect, we would share Guttmann's judgment that baseball has lost its place in the sun. But whenever baseball is being pictured as a fading star in the galaxy of American sports, it is invariably compared to football and occasionally to the three other major North American team sports, namely, hockey, soccer, and basketball. Equally invariably, the evidence cited reflects changes in game attendance records and TV ratings. Let us attempt to add some perspective to our understanding of these data. In comparison with these other team sports, organized professional baseball, drawing upon the enthusiasm for town ball, spread to literally hundreds of American communities by the 1920s. This baseball empire began to recede in the 1950s,[1] succumbing to the inroads of television which made baseball, particularly when played in decaying minor league ballparks, seem too dreary and slow for this new entertainment age. Yet, it is a mistake to read into this development evidence of the passing of professional baseball. What is the basis for judgment? None of the other professional team sports, in comparison, has ever developed such a foothold at the grass roots of American life as was represented by the nationwide network of minor league baseball clubs. If they had, is there the slightest doubt that they too, as professional enterprises, would have drifted into insolvency in the same way as did minor league baseball?

At the major league level, disregarding the post-strike or second season phase of 1981, baseball continues its long-term trend of growth at the turnstiles. In this respect, baseball compares favorably with any of its rival professional team sports.

Routinely disparaged as too slow and meandering for television tastes,[2] baseball has at least been able to hold on to major network contracts and even gain expanded coverage in recent years. Professional basketball is barely able to retain its contract with CBS in the face of unfavorable ratings, even suffering the indignity of late-night taped-delay broadcasts of major play-off games. Neither soccer nor hockey has fared that well in the U.S., both having lost major network exposure in recent years.

That leaves football and here the comparison with baseball, while consistently favorable to football, is contaminated by the fact that public opinion polling typically does not separate interest in professional football from college football interest. Still, the margins of difference are too wide to leave room for doubt. Football is more appealing on TV, except to the elderly, the poor, and the least educated.[3]

What is to be made of TV ratings data? While fans of all these games, at least those who attend games at the stadium, protest that a great deal of their game is lost in translation on TV, all legitimate sports events, as opposed to the "trash" or pseudo-sports staged solely to attract week-end TV audiences, are at risk of being found boring on TV. The reason is not difficult to ascertain. We are conditioned to expect novelty on television and all sports events, whatever their differences, are in danger of seeming too repetitive, even stereotyped, by television standards.

Perhaps expectations from television programming are extravagant; nonetheless, every major team sport is subject to the fickle taste of the TV public as the following discussion will attest.

First, all competitive sports events are vulnerable to turning one-sided; a hopelessly one-sided game will begin to lose an audience, whether on TV or at the stadium (Altheide and Snow, 1979:222). In the case of baseball, the score does not even need to become 9 to 1 by the fourth inning; the essential pace of the game, whether due to mythic pastoral origins or not, comes across as far too dilatorious on television. Even the fan who understands and appreciates the time-consuming nuances of baseball begins to hear voices lodged somewhere in his TV-nurtured head, pleading "Why don't they get on with it?"

As incompatible as baseball seems with the demands of TV, the game, once understood, at lest remains intelligible. That much cannot be said for hockey or basketball on television. With regard to hockey, much of the action around the goal mouth, resulting in perhaps half the game's scoring, occurs in such a tangle of sprawling bodies, amidst the hyperactivity of the tiny puck, that the TV viewer often cannot make sense out of what is taking place. As for basketball, perhaps the poor TV ratings are partly due to the same visibility factor which detracts from hockey on television. So often, baskets are scored through quick inside moves, obscured in the massing of bodies under the basket, so that the viewer finds himself missing the point or, to be precise, the points. Then there is the diluted worth of each basket, especially in professional basketball, where baskets are scored with such frequency as to seem meaningless (Ingham and Loy, 1973:13). This scoring inflation tends to modify somewhat during play-offs when defense is played with concentration and persistency. Then the pro game can become quite well attuned to TV tastes. If basketball has too much scoring, then soccer and hockey seem to offer too little scoring for the impatient audience. Play in these two sports, each of which revolves around goal tending, often seems too circular and purposeless. In hockey the puck is forever being dumped into the opposition's end by the offense, only to be controlled and cleared by the defense; the effect of this repeated sight on the viewer can be hypnotic. This, along with goal mouth chaos, spelled the death of hockey as a popular national TV sport in the U.S.

Finally, there is football which does seem to remain more lively and absorbing on TV than do these other games. But football can become monotonous too; just recall the morning-after comments which follow most Super Bowl games. When defense gains the upper hand, reducing contests to an exchange of punts followed by three downs of offensive futility, the TV appetite for excitement becomes demanding (Ingham and Loy, 1973:13). This is likeliest to happen in crucial, championship games where chancing flashy plays is too risky. College football, on the other hand, seems more varied, colorful, and enthusiastic, with the cast of exciting new phenoms changing often enough to satisfy the craving for novelty.

What is unintelligible in football is line play, but this is less crucial to TV enjoyment, with the average viewer satisfied to watch the ballcarrier, the quarterback, and the ball in flight, leaving the linemen to carry out their jousting, mostly obscured beyond the range of primary camera attention.

Any sport, then, once admitted to the exalted heights of prime-time network programming is vulnerable to the appearance of having "had its day in the sun" because, sooner or later, there must be some slippage in audience ratings. Ratings losses mean revenue losses to the networks and, according to "media logic" as discussed by Altheide and Snow (1979:222), the impression of decline is hard to withstand, especially in a society which treats TV ratings with such importance.

To summarize, we contend that for two reasons reports of the demise of professional baseball are an exaggeration: first, at the major league level, pro baseball remains, by and large, a thriving financial concern. Only at the minor league level has baseball lost ground, and there is no basis for comparison here with other team sports in the U.S., since none of the others relied extensively on minor league operations for apprenticing players. Secondly, TV ratings are a precarious basis for judging the viability of competitive sports because the logic, assumptions, and concerns of TV, where programs are essentially a means for drawing public attention to commercial messages , are fundamentally incompatible with the problematic character of sports events (Altheide and Snow: 1978: 190).

The historical position of baseball as this nation's first successful, professionally organized team sport enabled the game to become an American tradition. Beyond its historical roots, one may recognize in baseball's institutional properties, especially its structural components, a conservative microcosm of American social life.[4] As societal microcosm, baseball peculiarly fulfills Peter Berger's (1974:499-500) three conservative imperatives, those of order, continuity, and triviality, which he considers intrinsic to every human community.

Berger's first imperative comprehends society as "the imposition of order upon the flux of human experience" (1974:500). Baseball, as does all sports, satisfies this imperative, but baseball seems particularly to accentuate order, especially through its complex of geometric relationships as symbolized in the shape of the diamond, the reaction of the players to the movement of the ball, and the fact that, after all these years, no field alterations are required to insure that the runner and the thrown ball arrive at first base within a fraction of a second of each other time after time (Angell, 1962:302-3). Baseball is, in Eitzen's terms, an "island of stability" (1981:61).

If stability is the essence of baseball as physical form, then perhaps "decency," James Michener's term (1981:92), best expresses its moral forms. Writer Ben Yagoda explored this aspect of baseball in a *Sports Illustrated* essay on the ethics of baseball rules in which he asserts that baseball "deserves" national pastime status because of its rules which constitute "admirable . . . moral philosophy." In reading the baseball rule book "one finds a consistent code of justice, personal accountability and equality, and even a kind of grace." (Yagoda, 1979:8).

Here are just a few of Yagoda's illustrations from the rules of baseball, recognizing that in all games rules are in the forefront to demand fairness and codify goals and tasks. But to Yagoda, baseball's rules show an especial esteem for order and fairness, respectively, through the "numerical scheme of threes and nines" and the fact that each player is accorded the same number of chances to bat.

The rules reflect a moral order with prohibitions against the brutal in the form of the beanball. Deception is also frowned upon as evidenced in the infield fly rule. In pursuit of fairness, some rules are vey positive. Only the first two foul balls are recorded as strikes because it would seem unfair to call a batter out for hitting a pitch foul. Baseball even reflects the improbable in the dropped third strike regulation which, according to baseball legend, resulted in a turning-point in the 1941 World Series.

Even baseball's statistics reveal the game's ethical sensitivity in their balance and gravity. How a batter reaches base is reported in his batting average. Should he reach base due to a fielding error, the batter is still "charged" with an at bat while not being credited with a hit. Yagoda has much more to say. Suffice it to note that "the game cares" (1979:10) in his mind.

Baseball, in the summer of 1981, persuasively illustrated Berger's observation (1974:500) that social life has a low and short tolerance for disorder. The parties to the strike finally sat down to serious bargaining only when it appeared that a longer strike would undermine the legitimacy, not to mention the financial rewards, of post-season championship play. If the strike had can-celled the entire season, advanced ticket sales and media contracts for next season would have been in jeopardy. Thus a settlement was reached. Judging from a post-strike decline of nearly 20% in game attendance from levels achieved in the pre-strike phase, many fans seem unwilling to forgive this break with the tradition of an ordered and predictable baseball season, with its hastily con-cocted scheme for determining league champions.

The imperative of continuity is closely related to that of order. It is rooted in the necessity both to explain the past and to relate the past to the present. We know of no sport better suited than baseball for enabling one to recall and respect its past. The nature of baseball play is responsible for its rich sense of continu-ity. Role performances among baseball players are so discrete and individualized as to be thoroughly observable and intelligible, once understood.

Agonistic activity is more personalized than in other team sports. Chicago Cub pitcher Charlie Root versus Babe Ruth in the legendary "called" home run episode at Wrigley Field in the 1932 World Series has no counterpart in the annals of American team sports. The fact that baseball play is so discrete and so indivi-dualized gives one time to digest the event, to commit the details to memory before the next pitch. The discrete and individualized form of play also accounts for baseball's incredible variety and volume of statistical data. These data, in turn, facilitate recall of past events and encourage verification of the accuracy of recall.

Obviously, baseball's heritage is easily transmitted from generation to generation, with batting averages and home run records appropriately adorned and embellished in the language of legend. Just as the strike was an assault on baseball order, so was it a disruption of the statistical continuity of the game. Henceforth, 1981 will be blemished in baseball memory as the Year of the Asterisk. None of the data generated in 1981 reflecting the category "fewest," as in fewest errors by a shortstop in a season, will be accepted as valid. This is an unforgivable consequence of the strike for those who care.

The last of Berger's three imperatives (1974:501) is that triviality is one of the fundamental requirements of social life. Fan and critic alike can agree that baseball fulfills this imperative perhaps better than does any other game. With his imperative of triviality, Berger recognizes that our attention span is limited and that we can tolerate only a moderate amount of excitement. No game that is played, as is professional baseball, day in and day out for seven months of the year, eight months if one considers spring training, can require full attention and high emotional involvement from its public, unless that public has a great deal of time on its hands.[5]

Baseball, as a game of rituals and routines, fits in with the requirements of daily life in that it asks of its admirers, at least most of the time, no more than the "dim awareness" (Berger, 1974:501) they can spare. Of course, there are exceptional occasions: special rivalries, e.g., Yankees vs. Red Sox; key games in September; play-offs and World Series; and decisive moments in any game. For the most part, though, baseball is quite suited to being a daily game precisely because it does not demand the full attention and high emotional involvement that, for example, soccer does.

CONCLUSION

Just as baseball was once accepted unquestioningly as America's "national game," so it is more often portrayed today (Eitzen, 1981:61) as pastoral, rural, inner-directed, simple, stable, harmonious, and calm; that is, in terms that tie baseball in some way to the past. Perhaps it was as much the excellent essay of Murray Ross on baseball as pastoral (1973:102-12) and the portrayal by Marshall McLuhan, in *Understanding Media*, of baseball as belonging "to the now passing mechanical age" (1964:239-40) that account for the current rather nostalgic view of the game. Regardless, a sociological perspective suggests otherwise. Baseball, once established, both fits and reflects the realities of social life too well to be eclipsed at the center of the American sports scene. In a society in which professional sports have become year-round, multi-million dollar business, baseball can never again overshadow other team sports as it did in the pre-television era. Nevertheless, we ought to recall Allen Guttmann's observation: "Once a game is part of a culture, it's there to stay." (1978:100).

NOTES

[1]In 1950 there were 58 minor leagues with 446 clubs drawing 34,534,588 fans. By 1960 there were but 22 leagues and 152 clubs attracting 10,660,811 fans. Robert J. Sparks, an official of the National Associaton of Professional Baseball Leagues, in reporting these data by letter, notes that "there is no doubt that television was the serpent as far as baseball was concerned."

[2]This discussion of major team sports and television in the U.S. reflects a perspective similar to that revealed in James Michener's account of sports and the media (1976:355-415).

[3]The data referred to here are drawn from a *CBS-New York Times* poll taken from September 22nd to 27th, 1981 and reported on by Ray Gandolph during *CBS Morning* on Monday, October 5th. Of the 1478 adults interviewed by telephone, with a sampling error of plus or minus 3%, 48% indicated a preference for football while 31% said they would rather see baseball. Some percentages: men prefer football by 57% to 27%; women prefer it 40%-35%; persons in the $40,000 plus income bracket prefer it 64%-20%; and college graduates prefer it 61% to 19%. Those in the under $10,000 category prefer baseball 40%-31%; those lacking a high school diploma prefer baseball 38%-34%. Among age groups, only the 60 years and older group preferred baseball to football.

[4]Ingham and Loy note that although one can discern social change in sports, "the sport order is essentially conservative in nature" (Ingham and Loy, 1973:16).

[5]The phrase "time on its hands" may help explain baseball's appeal to the elderly, as evidenced in the *CBS-New York Times* poll cited above. Old age tends to increase social isolation and baseball, available as it is on a daily basis, provides meaning (Brandmeyer,

1976) to those who enjoy it. Though we have seen no data on this point, anecdotal accounts suggest that older fans were highly represented among those who reported missing baseball a great deal during the 1981 player strike.

REFERENCES

Altheide, David L. and Robert P. Snow
1978 "Sports vs. the mass media." Urban Life 7:189-204.
Altheide, David L. and Robert P. Snow
1979 "Media sports." Pp. 217-235 in David L. Altheide and Robert P. Snow. Media Logic. Beverly Hills, CA: Sage.
Angell, Roger
1962 The Summer Game. New York: Viking.
Berger, Peter L.
1974 "Sociology and freedom." Pp. 495-503 in Brigitte Berger (ed.), Readings in Sociology: A Biographical Approach. New York: Basic Books.
Brandmeyer, Gerard A.
1976 "Reflections on baseball as a leisure career: The private life world of the fan." Unpublished manuscript. Department of Sociology. University of South Florida.
Eitzen, D. Stanley
1981 "The structure of sport and society." Pp. 59-62 in Ian Robertson (ed.), The Social World. New York: Worth.
Grella, George
1975 "Baseball and the American dream." The Massachusetts Review 16:550-567.
Guttmann, Allen
1978 "Why baseball was our national game." Pp. 91-116 in Allen Guttmann. From Ritual to Record. New York: Columbia University Press.
Ingham, Alan G. and John W. Loy
1973 "The social system of sport: A humanistic perspective." Quest 19:3-24.
McLuhan, Marshall
1964 Understanding Media: The Extensions of Man. New York: McGraw-Hill.
Michener, James
1976 Sports in America. New York: Random House.
Michener, James
1981 "Interview with James Michener." Playboy 28:65-92.
Pittman, Robert
1981 "When a strike was a strike." St. Petersburg Times, Sunday, August 2:D1.
Ross, Murray
1973 "Football and baseball in America." Pp. 102-112 in John T. Talamini and Charles H. Page (eds.), Sport and Society: An Anthology, Boston: Little. Brown.
Yagoda, Ben
1979 "Viewpoint." Sports Illustrated 50 (April 16):8 and 10.

Chapter 2

SOCIAL CLIMBING: A CASE STUDY OF THE CHANGING CLASS STRUCTURE OF ROCK CLIMBING AND MOUNTAINEERING IN BRITAIN

Peter Donnelly, McMaster University

There are two basic approaches to the study of democratization in sport—the credulous and the skeptical. In the former, the mass consumption of and participation in sport in 'post-industrial' society are taken to be indications that sport has become 'classless' and that opportunities to participate are available to all regardless of social background. In the latter, while it is acknowledged that a certain amount of democratization has occurred in sport, the particularisms and inequalities that still exist are emphasized. Evidence for the skeptical view is abundant (e.g., Collins, 1972; Gruneau, 1976; Kenyon, 1966; Loy, 1969; Lüschen, 1969; and Webb, 1969), and note has been taken of exceptions to the principle of democratization (e.g., polo), differences in 'style' of involvement (e.g., elite clubs vs. public courts in tennis), the abandonment of democratized sports by the upper classes (e.g., soccer), and the partial democratization or 'bourgeoisification' of many sports (cf., Gruneau, 1976: 110).

Unfortunately, the majority of studies conducted so far only permit the *process* of democratization to be inferred. They are based on the presumption that at some earlier point in time the participants in a particular sport derived from upper class origins. If the present participants are found to be from the middle or lower classes then the process of democratization is assumed to have occurred. As a consequence, the studies provide no insights into the actual process although there have been several attempts to describe the process theoretically (e.g., Dunning and Sheard, 1979; Gruneau, 1975).

Both Gruneau, and Dunning and Sheard emphasize that democratization should be studied as a *process*. Gruneau (1975) suggests that this "gradual process" is, in part, a result of the rationalization and professionalization of sport — the need for a broader base of athletic recruitment in order to serve the purposes of modern business enterprises and for reasons of national prestige; Dunning and Sheard (1979) base their analysis on Elias' theory of sociogenesis in which social processes are determined by social structures ([con]figurations).

Despite the wealth of work on the topic surprisingly few case studies have attempted to determine the actual mechanics of democratization. The one outstanding exception in this regard is Dunning and Sheard's study of the development of rugby football in England. They have shown how social conditions resulted in the rapid democratization of rugby in South Wales and Northern England during the Nineteenth Century, eventually leading to the split between the amateur and professional games in the North, and how the subsequent democratization of the amateur game in England has been a long-term process that is still continuing. Their study has demonstrated the difficulty of making generalizations regarding the process of democratization since differing regional conditions have led to differing rates of democratization in the same sport.

However, Dunning and Sheard's study remains something of an exception, and there is an apparent need for further case studies of this type in order to delineate more precisely the manner in which sports democratize. The present study is an attempt to meet this need. At first glance, climbing appears to support the credulous model of democratization in sport. It is a sport with elite origins that now has participants drawn from almost the entire range of the social spectrum. However, closer analysis reveals certain anomalies and indicates that a number of costs are, or were, involved for lower class participants. In addition, rationalization and professionalization do not appear to have had any significant impact on the democratization of climbing since the sport had spread to the working class before there was any significant business involvement in the sport and before national prestige became attached to the ascent of the world's highest mountains. Thus, although both social (con)figurations and rationalization/professionalization appear to have been involved in the democratization of rugby, it is possible that other reasons must be sought in order to account for the democratization of climbing.

A NOTE ON METHODOLOGY

Attempts to determine the social status of long-dead participants in a sport are fraught with difficulty. As Dunning and Sheard found, it is impossible to determine precisely the class composition of sports during the Nineteenth Century, but informed guesses and generalization from the available surviving data (e.g., club records) can provide close approximations.

In the case of climbing, the only available substantial data on the social class of participants is to be found in Mumm's (1923), *The Alpine Club Register*, which provides capsule biographies (including, where possible, school, university and occupation) of members of the Alpine Club (British) from 1857 to 1890. While it is possible that these individuals were unrepresentative of climbers as a whole during the second half of the Nineteenth Century, it is also highly unlikely. To this may be added my own, somewhat unrepresentative data on the social class of climbers collected during the 1970s. There is no actual data at all for the period between 1890 and the early 1970s. However, climbing is an extremely literate sport, and in the mass of literature there are numerous references to the social class or occupation of participants at all periods of the history of climbing. These three sources, incomplete as they may be, form the basis for the present study. Because the largest body of climbing literature is in English and because climbing as a sport was a British invention, this analysis deals primarily with the democratization of British climbing. The analysis is organized into three significant periods: 1850-1914 (the beginnings); 1919-1939 (the interwar period); and 1945-the present day (the postwar period).

THE BEGINNINGS: 1850-1914

In one of his essays, Roland Barthes suggested that climbing was a bourgeois invention, and, in fact, the appreciation of mountain scenery and the subsequent origins of mountaineering as a sport did coincide with the rise of the bourgeoisie during the first half of the Nineteenth Century. But, we should remember Dunning and Sheard's caution that, "the middle class was internally differentiated, for example in terms of property ownership, into the 'grand' and 'petit' bourgeoisie; occupationally, into business, professional and clerical sections; and in prestige terms, into 'upper middle,' 'middle middle' and 'lower middle' strata" (1979: 131). The founders of climbing as a recreation, and eventually as a sport, were primarily from the new industrial and intellectual upper middle classes of the mid-Nineteenth Century.

The mountains of the Alps (the birthplace of climbing) had become familiar to Englishmen by 1850, and they were beginning to be climbed by young university graduates, primarily from Oxford and Cambridge, for recreational reasons rather than for scientific or unique tourist experiences. It is clearly no accident that these graduates would have been among the first to have been influenced by the growing movements of athleticism and 'muscular Christianity' in the public schools.

Data concerning their social class are abundant, particularly in *The Alpine Club Register*. They were primarily professional men, barristers and clergymen, who were able to take long summer vacations, subsequently some of the new industrial elite joined them. It should not be assumed that these were *all* extremely wealthy individuals with large amounts of disposable income.

They were not in the same class (literally or metaphorically) as the 'Grand Tourists' who had ventured abroad for periods ranging from six months to several years. The cost of reaching the Alps from England decreased enormously as the railway network began to spread across Europe. The opening of the Paris-Geneva line between 1850 and 1856, greatly reduced both the time and cost involved in a journey that had previously taken several days by horse-drawn coach.

Within 20 years the sport began to show the first signs of incipient democratization. The key to this shift was apparently the advent of guideless climbing, although whether this was a cause or an effect is not apparent. The trend was signalled in 1870 with the publication of the Rev. A. G. Girdlestone's, *The High Alps Without Guides*. There are so many class-related themes associated with the issue of guideless climbing that the topic warrants an entire paper. They include the following:

1) The cost of climbing with guides.
2) The 'master-servant' relationship. Because guides were charged with the safety of their clients and because they had grown secure in the knowledge that they were needed if their clients were to travel in the mountains, many guides had developed a manner that the new generation of middle middle class climbers considered domineering. Their domestic servants and those in the service occupations with whom they came into contact would never be so bold. The older, more elite climbers were far more secure in their social status and were also imbued with Rousseau's 'noble savage' ideas — they could live with the relationship, while the new generation began to resent it.
3) Amateurism-professionalism. The amateur-professional distinction became an issue with the concurrent growth of organized sport and growing class consciousness.

However, climbing represented something of a unique case. Rather than competing against professionals, the amateurs competed alongside professionals in a modified 'master-servant' relationship in which they played a relatively minor role (the guides generally led the way, cut the steps, and tugged on the rope when the client was having difficulties). This situation was acceptable for a time because it coincided with three major views of amateurism — one was able to display wealth (Veblen, 1953), demonstrate 'near-competence' (Stone, 1972) and not be mistaken for a professional (Polsky, 1969). But, as the amateurs grew in competence and confidence, they began to realize that most of the guides were not actually that good. They found themselves in the apparently ludicrous position of paying, taking orders from, and playing a secondary role to an individual who was quite definitely a social inferior and quite often an inferior in climbing skills. Thus, conflict was engendered between the need to demonstrate one's amateur status and the situation of having to hire someone to perform a task at which one was more capable.

The issue, which became a major debate during the 1870s and 1880s (e.g., Grove, 1870; Mathews, 1880; Dent, 1885), was resolved in several ways. The older and upper middle class climbers tended to retain the *status quo*. Arguing that safety was paramount and that guides must be natural climbers since they were born and raised in the Alps (it is interesting to note that Darwin's, *Origin of Species* first appeared at the end of the 1850s), they argued strongly against guideless climbing. However, these were also the individuals who could afford to hire the best guides for the entire season. The more competent and middle middle class climbers opted for two changes which were often combined. The first was a redefinition of the guide-client relationship into a more traditioinal servant-master relationship. Clients began to take a more assertive role in route finding, climbing and decision making which either resulted in a rather egalitarian relationship, or in the demotion of the guide to pack-carrier and step-cutter. The second was a great increase in the number of guideless ascents.

As noted previously, it is not completely clear whether the incipient democratization of climbing resulted in the shift to guideless ascents, or whether the shift to guideless ascents permitted the democratization. While there is more evidence for the former, it is possible that the relationship is circular, with democ-ratization leading to guideless ascents which permitted more democratization. *The Alpine Club Register* indicates that the new middle class climbers were manufacturers, engineers, business-men, and even more clergymen. But the change did not occur without resistance. While there was no way for the old order to prevent others from climbing in the Alps, they did snap up all of the best guides each summer and they could control membership in the Alpine Club.

A final change during this period made climbing even more socially accessible. During the last decades of the Nineteenth Century, British Alpine climbers had taken to climbing in Britain during the off-season in order to train for the Alpine season. This move rendered the British mountains acceptable as places in which to practice the sport of climbing and thus available to those who could not afford to visit the Alps on any regular basis.

By 1914, climbing was well-established as an upper middle and middle middle class sport in Britain, and there were the first signs of lower middle class involvement.

THE INTERWAR PERIOD: 1919-1939

The most marked characteristics of this period in Britain were the mass unemployment of the Depression and the signifi-cant growth of Labour activism that resulted from the success of the Russian Revolution and the subtle changes in the social order that were a consequence of the First World War. These were to have a significant impact on the democratization of sport.

In the former, mass unemployment created a new leisure class, particularly among young unemployed workers who had no family responsibilities. This resulted in a marked increase in par-ticipation in inexpensive and accessible sports. There is a ten-dency in democratization literature to suggest that the working class was 'given' access to, or 'allowed' to participate in certain sports. This type of patronizing explanation completely denies a great deal of the working class activism that was involved in taking or winning concessions and also ignores the fact that once a certain level of development is achieved and once an activity is considered meaningful in the social milieu of the working class, there is very often nothing to prevent working class participation in a sport.

It was inevitable that, in the interwar period, climbing in Britain would spread to the lower middle classes. Bédarida described the 'petit' bourgeois of this period as follows: ". . . they made desperate and absurd efforts to ape their betters, in their house, furnishings, dress, reading habits and general way of life, and to be recognized by them — without ever succeeding" (1979: 208). Although there was no chance of them ever joining groups such as the Alpine Club, only partially because of an inability to afford foreign holidays, they began to climb regularly in Britain, form their own climbing clubs, and join middle class organizations such as the Ramblers' Federation. However, it was a combination of mass unemployment and Labour activism that led to the most significant change in the class structure of climbing during this period.

Access to most of the mountain wilderness areas in Britain was restricted until after the Second World War. The land was in private ownership, and used for hunting, primarily grouse shooting. Although an Access to Mountains Bill had been introduced in Parliament as early as 1888, the power of private landowners precluded its passage. Polite lobbying by middle class groups was futile.

The Peak District is one of these mountain regions, bordered on the East, West and South by the major industrial centers of Northern England. A tradition of hill walking had begun to develop among the working classes of these centers and the growing unemployment of the 1920s and 1930s had expanded the numbers of those taking to the hills. Increasing radicalism led to an obvious resentment against the feudal restrictions and to inevitable confrontations.[1] While the middle and lower middle class Ramblers' Federation and the Footpaths Preservation Society had been lobbying politely and unsuccessfully for greater access, the growing frustration of the working class resulted in a call for civil disobedience (cf., Barnes, 1932):

> . . . the idea of a 'mass trespass' seems to have first arisen at one of the camps organized by the British Workers' Sports Federation, held in the village of Rowarth in 1931. This organization had been set up on the initiative and under the influence of the Young Communist League . . . and it presented the question of access to the hills in open class terms (Cook, 1974: 31).

Several mass trespasses were organized, occasionally ending in violence (which was inevitably exaggerated in the newspapers) and arrests. The middle class Ramblers' Federation condemned the movement in no uncertain terms — 'not only were there Reds under the bed, they were also under the heather!' But the trespasses brought the problem of access to public attention and gained a great deal of sympathy for the cause. The Access to Mountains Bill was finally passed by the Attlee Government shortly after the Second World War.

It was inevitable that some of the hill walkers would take up rock climbing: it was a more exciting and challenging pursuit and the only additional expense involved was the purchase of a rope. By 1939, climbing had begun to democratize to at least the more 'respectable' elements of the working class in the North of England (Byne and Sutton, 1966).

A parallel movement occurred in Scotland where access was less of a problem, but where mass unemployment and Labour activism in the industrial centers around Glasgow (e.g., the 'Clydeside Reds') produced numbers of working class climbers during the 1930s. At least three working class climbing clubs were founded in the Glasgow district at this time, the most famous of which was the Creagh Dhu Mountaineering Club based in Clydeside and drawing its membership from young, frequently unemployed and extremely left-wing workers in the shipbuilding industry. These climbers overcame the cost of travel by developing the art of hitch-hiking, an activity that was not to become respectable until its use by servicemen during the Second World War, and they slept in the rough in caves and barns throughout the Highlands of Scotland. A larger club, the Lomond Mountaineering Club, went so far as to hire a bus to take members to club meets and actually ran two bus trips to the Alps before the War.

THE POST-WAR PERIOD: 1945 TO THE PRESENT

The post-war period was again marked by changes in the social order, and by a growing prosperity. The most significant changes in Britain were those that affected working class life. After the mass unemployment of the 1930s, the principle of full employment was first introduced in 1940 and fully implemented by the first majority Labour Government in 1945. In addition, there was a marked levelling in wages that had its greatest effect at the bottom of the pay scale, an enormous increase in the Welfare State, a reduction of the working week to 44½ hours, and universal paid holidays (usually two weeks). While such changes in North America have had the effect of bourgeoisification, the working class in Britain in the 1950s

> was still deeply imbued with its own exclusive class culture and with the conviction of belonging to a distinct community that was quite apart from the middle-class universe. It was the feeling of having a status rather than an ideology . . . (Bédarida, 1979: 213).

Studies by Hoggart (1957) and Zweig (1952) emphasized this point, and the cultural distinction was to have a marked effect on climbing.

There was a significant increase in the number of working class climbers in the post-war period, partly as a continuation of the trend that had started before the war, but also because of the relative affluence and security that affected the working class for the first time, the large number of people who were exposed to climbing as a part of their wartime training in the services, and the publicity attached to the successful ascent of Everest in 1953, the announcement of which coincided with the coronation and marked the growing optimism of the 'new Elizabethan Age.' Almost every child in Britain was taken on a school trip to see the film of the Everest Expedition.

The influx of working class climbers had an enormous influence on increasing the standards of climbing and the difficulty of the climbs that were being completed. This was partially a result of improved equipment such as nylon rope that resulted from wartime research, but also because the working class climbers were isolated from middle class influences regarding the conduct of climbing. Working class climbers formed their own clubs, often because of restricted access to the established clubs, and violated all of the norms of excessive safety and non-competition that had previously existed.

The 'pushiness' of the 'lower orders' is a traditional rallying cry of the upper and middle classes who find their traditional power and position in jeopardy, and the new order in climbing did not pass without criticism and attempts to rationalize the new standards that were being achieved. The superiority of the new working class climbers was considered to be somehow innate.[2] That is, because they were involved in manual work, their strength and natural training must give them an unfair advantage, and, because the two best known climbers of the 1950s (Joe Brown and Don Whillans) were both short in stature, shortness (more a characteristic of the working than other classes) was declared to be an asset in climbing.

By the late-1950s, the working class was beginning to achieve a certain social cachet in Britain, probably as a result of their rising consumer power. 'Kitchen-sink' drama was the order of the day (John Osborne's "Look Back in Anger" was first performed in 1956), working class novelists and actors began to appear for the first time, and regional accents were 'in.' Working class heroes were needed, and the newspapers dubbed Brown and Whillans "the climbing plumbers."

The rapid social changes in post-war society led to another change in climbing. In the period between 1959 and 1963, a period that rock-critic Nick Cohn terms the "interregnum' (between Elvis Presley's 'sell-out' and the rise of the Beatles), youth culture began to become somewhat more significant than working class culture. With the publication of the Robbins Report in 1963 and the implementation of its recommendations, a far more significant proportion of the British population began to become involved in some form of post-secondary education, and the colleges and universities became the centers of youth culture.

This appears to have resulted in a shift in the recruitment of climbers, with far more climbers in the 1960s and 1970s coming from the colleges and universities than from the working class.[3] The working class influence from the 1950s persisted throughout the 1960s. It became mandatory in the subculture of climbers, regardless of one's class background, to drop 'h's, wear a flat cap (a working class symbol), drive a mini van, wear dirty and torn clothes, be chauvinistically and uncompromisingly 'British' when in the Alps, and to drink long and loud.

By the 1970s, youth culture had come to the fore and resulted in a relative embourgeoisement of climbing. However, the recent class polarization in Britain that is a result of 'Thatcherism' is causing yet another change. Growing unemployment is again creating a new leisure class, and both the number of climbers and the difficulty of climbs being completed are increasing.[4]

CONCLUSION

It is apparent from this brief analysis of democratization in climbing, and the comparison of these results to Dunning and Sheard's findings regarding rugby, that democratization is an extremely complex process that cannot be adequately considered in "classes to masses" type statements. Several conclusions are possible when the two studies are compared:

1) Sports vary in terms of their accessibility to the process of democratization. When a sport is dependent upon organization into leagues and clubs, it is relatively simple to control access on an ascriptive basis (e.g., rugby). When sports such as climbing become physically (transportation and leisure time) and materially (financially) accessible, it is impossible to prevent participation on an ascriptive basis once the sport comes to have meaning within a particular social milieu.

2) The rate of democratization varies both within and between sports. Dunning and Sheard found different rates of democratization within rugby because of differing regional social conditions. While it would have been impossible for climbing ever to have experienced the rapid democratization that occurred in rugby in the North of England, differing rates of democratization were also apparent in climbing because of different social and geographical conditions.

3) The actual mechanics of democratization may vary by sport and at different stages in the democratization process. Four systems suggest themselves here. The first is *recruitment*, in which lower class participants are encouraged to become involved as the forces of rationalization affect a sport (e.g., rugby in the North of England). The second is *modelling*, an essentially middle class phenomenon in which the middle middle class imitates the upper middle class, and the lower middle class imitates the middle middle class as changing social conditions bring a sport within physical and material range (e.g., climbing). The third, which might be termed *acquisition*, is the process by which the working classes in Britain and Europe became involved in climbing. Rather than becoming involved by *recruitment* or *modelling*, the working classes *acquired* climbing as a result of mass unemployment. This is evidenced by the fact that whenever and wherever the working class became involved in

climbing they tended to bring an entirely new set of values to the sport which resulted in a significant increase in standards. They did not model their involvement on middle class climbers, and the changes that they wrought were, in every case, initially denigrated by middle class climbers. Of course, with the decline of working class culture and the embourgeoisement of the working class, *acquisition* ceases and *modelling* becomes the norm. The fourth system involves democratization through the doctrine of *good works*, in which a sport is introduced to the lower classes in the belief that "it will be good for them." Examples of this latter type are numerous, ranging from the missionary type of 'muscular Christianity' to industrial sports clubs, and from Outward Bound and outdoor education programs to sport programs for delinquents and employee fitness programs. Of course, what is 'good' for the lower classes is often also good for the upper and middle classes (i.e., sport as social control; increased industrial productivity and decreased absenteeism).

4) As suggested by Gruneau (1976), democratization and embourgeoisement may be seen as complementary processes that result in the bourgeoisification of sport — the re-creation of sport as a middle class phenomenon.

NOTES

[1]"As early as 1923 the *Manchester Evening Chronicle* had contained an amazing Wild West style 'wanted' notice. It showed two photographs of walkers on Kinder Scout, and underneath it read: 'Kinder Scout Trespassers, £5 reward will be paid for the name, address and occupation of any of the persons represented in the photos. Apply Cobbett, Wheeler & Cobbett, Solicitors, 49 Spring Gardens, Manchester.' Grandfather William Cobbett, the early nineteenth century radical, must have been squirming in his grave at the role his offspring were playing" (Cook, 1974: 30-31).

Of the 149,712 acres of the Peak District, 109,500 were privately owned, 39,000 acres were owned by local authorities, and there were only 1,212 acres with adequate public access.

[2]The comparison with attempts in the United States to account for the apparent superiority of black athletes is obvious.

[3]There was some overlapping here because an increasing number of working class students were beginning to appear, but it was not a very significant overlap.

[4]When I was conducting research for this project in England during the Summer of 1981, I was told several times that, "Thatcher is good for climbing — she provides grants (i.e., unemployment benefits) to climbers."

REFERENCES

Barnes, P. A.
  1932 Trespassers Will Be Prosecuted. Pamphlet campaigning for public access in the Peak District.
Bédarida, F.
  1979 A Social History of England 1851-1975. London: Methuen.
Byne, E. and G. Sutton
  1966 High Peak: The Story of Walking and Climbing in the Peak District. London: Secker and Warburg.
Collins, L. J.
  1972 "Social class and the Olympic athlete." British Journal of Physical Education 3(4).
Cook, D.
  1974 "The battle for kinder scout." Mountain 32 (February).
Dent, C. T.
  1885 "Amateurs and professional guides of the present day." Alpine Journal 12.
Dunning, E. and K. Sheard
  1979 Barbarians, Gentlemen and Players: A Sociological Study of the Development of Rugby Football. New York: New York University Press.
Girdlestone, Rev. A. G.
  1870 The High Alps Without Guides. London: Longmans, Green.
Grove, F. C.
  1870 "The relative skill of amateurs and guides." Alpine Journal 5.
Gruneau, R. S.
  1975 "Sport, social differentiation, and social inequality." In D. W. Ball and J. W. Loy (eds.), Sport and Social Order. Reading: Addison-Wesley.
  1976 "Class or mass: notes on the democratization of Canadian amateur sport." In R. S. Gruneau and J. G. Alpinson (eds.), Canadian Sport: Sociological Perspectives. Don Mills: Addison-Wesley.
Hoggart, R.
  1957 The Uses of Literacy. London: Essential Books.
Kenyon, G. S.
  1966 "The significance of physical activity as a function of age, sex, education, and socio-economic status of northern United States adults." International Review of Sport Sociology 1.
Loy, J. W.
  1969 "The study of sport and social mobility." In G. S. Kenyon (ed.), Aspects of Contemporary Sport Sociology. Chicago: The Athletic Institute.
Lüschen, G.
  1969 "Social stratification and social mobility among young sportsmen." In J. W. Loy and G. S. Kenyon (eds.), Sport, Culture and Society. Toronto: Macmillan.
Mathews, C. E.
  1880 "The growth of mountaineering." Alpine Journal 10.
Mumm, A. L.
  1923 The Alpine Club Register. London: Arnold.
Polsky, N.
  1969 Hustlers, Beats and Others. New York: Anchor.

Stone, G. P.
    1972 Games, Sport and Power. New Brunswick: Transaction Books.
Veblen, T.
    1953 The Theory of the Leisure Class. New York: Mentor.
Webb, H.
    1969 "Reaction to Loy paper." In G. S. Kenyon (ed.), Aspects of Contemporary Sport
         Sociology. Chicago: The Athletic Institute.
Zweig, F.
    1952 The British Worker. Harmondsworth: Penguin.

Chapter 3

GENDER VARIATIONS IN GAME ATTRACTION FACTORS OF NATIVE AMERICAN YOUTH

Alyce Taylor Cheska, University of Illinois

As early as 1565 enthusiastic participation in recreational activities by North American Indians was recorded by Laudonnière (1565). Other observers also noted such enjoyment (Diaz, 1963; Lescarbot, 1609; dePaina, 1676; Catlin, 1884; Mooney, 1890; Culin, 1907). Cheska (1976, 1979) found that in the nineteenth century traditional Indian ball games were played over at least two-thirds of native American lands. Women most commonly participated in doubleball, juggling, shinny, tossed ball and, in a few California tribes, even modified lacrosse; the men most commonly played football (kicking with only the foot), lacrosse, stick ball (rackets) and, at times, juggling, shinny, and tossed ball (Cheska, 1982).[1] Therefore, according to historical references, both Indian men and women participated in traditional Indian ball-oriented recreational activities.

In the late 1800s when Indians were placed under federal jurisdiction and it became mandatory for Indian children to attend government or missionary schools, traditional Indian games were discouraged and became obsolete. In their place, the youth adopted the new games and sports of the white man (Powers, 1973). McCaskill (1937:29) stated, "Indian boys and girls have taken to the sports of the white boys and girls with great enthusiasm. In small rural schools throughout the Indian country boys and girls play baseball, football, basketball and other American games."

It must be assumed, then, that both Indian males and females participated in vigorous recreational sports, first in traditional Indian games and later in games introduced by white contact. In a recent analysis by Blanchard (1981) of the values of sports in the lives of modern Choctaw Indians, he observed that sports participation by Choctaw girls enhanced their personal status. In like manner, this author observed sport participation of Southwestern Indian girls as well as boys. This elicited such questions as: What recreational activities are preferred by these youth? Are there different preferences according to tribe and sex? What factors attract these youth to engage in sports? Are there tribal and/or sex differences in game attraction factors?

This study wishes to move beyond the observation stage to determine the relative importance of sport among the southwestern Indian boys and girls and the selectivity within these activities. It also hopes to show what factors attract these youth to participate in their recreational activities. Because virtually no research exists on differential selection of recreational activities among native American youth, this study may provide data important to cross-cultural analysis of sex differences. It should be noted here that Glassford (1970) collected similar data on a selected population of Alaskan Eskimo and Indian children but has not published these results.

METHOD

Sample

Of the 183 native American respondents, 66% (120) were females and 34% (63) were males, ranging in age from 10 to 21 years with 94% (172) between 13 and 18 years of age. The tribal affiliations of these students were Apache (42), Hopi (34), Navajo (20), Papago (41), and Pima (46), representative of the major Indian groups in the Southwest: Apache and Navajo (Athabaskan), Hopi (Pueblo), Papago and Pima (Piman) (Dutton, 1976).

These native peoples have lived in proximity for at least 500 to 1000 years and are located at present in New Mexico and Arizona. The definition of a native American used in this study is a person with one-fourth or more Indian blood having tribal affiliation.[2]

Ninety-two percent (170) of the youth were born on an Indian reservation and have lived the great majority of their lives in the same location. At the time of the study every respondent lived on a reservation. Most of the students attended boarding high schools (142) and during the nine school months lived in dormitories on the grounds; the rest attended a public high school (34) or a non-boarding Indian high school (8) in major metropolitan areas to which they were transported daily from their reservation homes. The mean high school year of these students was the tenth grade. The average subject belonged to a seven-child (three brothers and three sisters) family whose 1973 average income was reported between $3000-6000, well below the $12,051 national median of all families that year. (The 1973 poverty level for four-member non-farm families in United States was $4540 [U.S. Census, 1974].) It should be noted that the growing and raising of food stuffs on reservation land, plus the common practice of kinship sharing among southwestern Indian families, could indirectly inflate the reported income.

Instrument

A paper and pencil instrument, The Games and Recreation Activities Opinionnaire, modified from Gerald Glassford's (1970) instrument, was administered to 183 native American youth in their schools during the spring, 1974. The subjects were asked, in an open-ended statement, to list in rank order six of their favorite games, hobbies, or recreational activities. They were also asked to judge on a descending four-point scale the importance to themselves of four general game attraction factors (each of which was made up of two to four specific questions): 1) attitudes toward participation (equity, skill, victory); 2) tactics (use of strategies, tricks); 3) involvement (win as a game player, an individual, and a team member); and 4) spectatorship (watching others, "star" performer, teamwork and cooperation).

For each attitudinal statement a response was elicited on a four-point Likert-type scale: very important, quite important, not very important, not important at all. This provided a numerical range from one to four. The lower the score the more important the statement was to the respondents. Gender and tribal differences were then analyzed regarding both recreational preferences and the game attraction.

Statistical Procedures

The statistical treatment of the data was divided into two basic parts. Part one included the comparison and rank ordering of preferred recreational activity choices: 1) preferred recreational activities; 2) preferred activities into the following categories: sports, amusements, games, and crafts; 3) activities according to sex by choice, diversity, and category of participation. Part two was an examination of statistical differences by tribe and sex of game attraction factors on which participation was based: 1) attitudes; 2) tactics; 3) involvement; 4) spectatorship. This included measures of central tendency and analysis of variance between females and males. The .05 level of significance was chosen. Also, the sign test was used to compute the probability of attitude preference (equity, skill, or victory) based on percentage of choice by respondents taken randomly from the sample.

RESULTS

Incidence of Preferred Recreational Activities

The first phase of this study examined the activity choices of these youth. The results were divided into four general findings.

1) *Incidence of preferred recreational activities.* Of the fifty-seven different recreational choices named one or more times by these students, the top ten favorite activities in descending order were basketball, softball, baseball, football, vol-

leyball and dancing, rodeo and running, pow wow, and horseback riding. (See Table 1.)

2) *Comparison of female and male preference choices.* Team sports participation was overwhelmingly preferred over other recreational choices. Of the top six preferred activities, team sports ranked one through four and tied for fifth preference with rodeo, basically an individual sport. Some differences between females' and males' choices were found. For example, softball was preferred mostly by girls (58%), while only 24% of the boys chose softball. Baseball was selected by 56% of the boys and by only 28% of the girls. The two represent variants of the same game. Volleyball was chosen exclusively by the girls (43%), while football was chosen exclusively by the boys (56%). Basketball was the most popular activity with both sexes, with 84% of the girls and 81% of the boys participating in it. (See Table 2.)

3) *Categories of preferred activities.* Participation in sports was greatly preferred by both sexes over the other general recreational activity categories of amusements, games, and crafts. This supports earlier observations of participation in sports by Indian youth. (See Table 1.)

4) *Sex differences by choice, diversity, and category of participation.* Of the 57 named recreational activities, 60% (34) were chosen by both boys and girls. Females chose 51, while males selected only 40 different activities, thus females participated in a 22% greater variety of activities than males. Of the 51 different activities in which the females participated, 23% (17) were exclusive to them, while of the 40 activities in which the males participated, only 15% (6) were exclusive to them. When compared, the females participated in more activities than males by 19% (11). This finding agrees with Sutton-Smith and Rosenberg (1961) who found that girls in the mid-western

Table 1

Nineteen Preferred Recreational Activities of Southwest Teen Age Indian Youth

Activity*	Rank Order of Choice	N	Percent	Categories of Activities			
				Sport	Amusement	Games	Crafts
Basketball	1	154	84.15	x			
Softball	2	84	45.90	x			
Baseball	3	69	37.70	x			
Football	4	57	31.15	x			
Volleyball	5.5	53	28.96	x			
Dancing	5.5	53	28.96		x		
Rodeo	7.5	40	21.19	x			
Running	7.5	40	21.19		x		
Pow Wow	9	37	20.21		x		
Horseback Riding	10	22	12.02		x		
Billiards/Pool	11.5	20	10.93		x		
Soccer	11.5	20	10.93	x			
Swimming	13.5	19	10.38		x		
Basket, bead, leather drawing, crafts	13.5	19	10.38				x
Track/Cross Country	15	16	8.74	x			
Arts & Crafts	16	15	8.20				x
Carnival	17	13	7.10		x		
Miscellaneous	18	11	6.07				
Tennis	19	10	5.46	x			
				9	7	0	2

N = Total number of subjects is 183.

*This list includes the nineteen preferred recreational activities selected by 10 or more students out of a total of 57 such activities named.

Table 2

Comparison of Female and Male Preferred Recreational Activities
Of Southwest Teen Age Indian Youth

Female			Rank Order of Choice		Male		
Activity	N	%	F	M	Activity	N	%
Basketball	101	84.16	1	1	Basketball	51	80.95
Softball	69	57.50	2	2	Football	42	66.66
Volleyball	51	42.50	3	3	Baseball	35	55.55
Dancing	45	39.91	4	4	Running	21	33.33
Baseball	34	28.33	5	5.5	Rodeo	15	23.80
Rodeo	25	20.83	5	5.5	Softball	15	23.80
Pow Wow	24	20.00	7	7	Pow Wow	13	20.63
Horseback Riding	19	15.83	8.5	8	Track/Cross Country	10	15.87
Running	19	15.83	8.5	9	Billiards/Pool	9	14.20
Basket, bead leather drawing, crafts	17	14.16	10	10	Swimming	8	12.69

N = 120

N = 63

United States participated in a greater variety of games than boys.

In comparing all the choices by categories of sports, amusements, games, and crafts, different sports in which girls participated totaled 19 while boys listed 16. In amusements females chose 23, while males listed 20. In games the females played six, and the males played only one. In crafts each group chose three. For girls and boys the combined number of amusements listed totaled 27, exceeding numerically those of sport which totaled 21. However, sports were participated in by a great many more youth as shown by the preference ranking. For example, basketball was played by 84% of the girls, while only 14% of the girls engaged in crafts. The number of different games totaled six and, of crafts, three.

The above evidence shows that females participated in more diverse recreational activities than males, but caution must be taken in reporting these differences because there were almost twice as many females in the study as males, thus affecting the potential for recording diversity.

Gender Variations in Game Attraction Factors

In this second phase of the study, game attraction factors which were thought important in participation by the Indian youth were identified: 1) attitudes toward participation (equity, skill, victory); 2) tactics (use of strategy and tricks; 3) involvement (winning as a game player, as an individual and as a team member); and 4) spectatorship (watching others, outstanding performer, teamwork and cooperation).

The importance of these four factors was compared between sexes to determine, in spite of both sexes preferred participation in similar kinds of recreational activities, i.e., sports, if the reasons for participation were proportionally dissimilar.

Participation based on attitude. Three attitudes were selected to indicate the importance of playing a game. These are 1) equity

— "to play fairly," 2) skill — "to play as well as possible," and 3) victory — "to beat your opponent."

Group means of the three attitudes showed that equity was very important to all of the students ($\bar{x}$ 1.56), while skill was less, but quite important ($\bar{x}$ 1.79), and victory was also quite important ($\bar{x}$ 2.07). In comparison between sexes, only victory was significantly more important for boys than girls (p.<.01). (See Table 3.)

The probability of preference by the girls and boys was statistically determined between any two attitudes by application of the sign test. A sign test yielded the ratio or percentage probability of preference between attitudes based on the percentage of choice by respondents taken randomly from the sample. This allowed an examination of preference between any two attitudes, such as equity to victory, equity to skill, skill to victory.

When a difference was recorded between any two of these selected game attitudes (e.g., equity, victory, skill) the probability that these youth preferred equity over victory was 83%; those preferring equity to skill was 74%; and those preferring skill to victory was 72%. By the use of the sign test to find the importance in game participation of these attitudes, equity was chosen over victory and also over skill. Likewise skill was preferred over victory. The only difference between the girls' and boys' responses was the degree of choice of skill to victory; the boys' preference was 55%, while the girls' was higher at 75%. Where there was a difference in the importance between equity and victory as well as equity and skill, the probable preferences were markedly toward equity; while skill was preferred to victory. Another way of viewing these choices is that victory was less preferred than equity or than skill.

The results of the sign test showed that girls clearly preferred equity to victory 80% of the time, equity to skill 75% of the time, skill to victory 75% of the time. The boys also clearly preferred equity to victory 90% of the time, to skill 75% of the time, and skill to victory a little better than half the time. These

Table 3

Game Attraction Factors Important to Southwest Indian Youth

Code Number	Level of Importance to All Subjects		Level of Importance by Sex				F Score	Level of Significance between Fe and Males[+]
			Female N = 120		Male N = 63			
	Most Often Checked*	Mean#	Most Often Checked*	Mean#	Most Often Checked*	Mean#		
Attitude:								
37 How important is it to you to play a game as WELL as you are able?	2	1.79	2	1.86	1	1.68	2.057	.149
35 How important to you is playing games to BEAT your opponent?	2	2.07	2	2.20	2	2.13	6.725	.010+
39 How important is it to you to play a game FAIRLY as being a good sport?	1	1.56	1	1.62	1	1.46	1.920	.164
Tactics:								
36 In games where you have a winner and a loser would you use a TRICK even though you knew the trick is against the rules to win the game?	3	2.91	2	2.91	2	2.92	.004	.999
41 How much enjoyment do you get when you or your opponent do NOT tell each other the game plays and you try to outsmart your opponent, as in basketball?	2	2.13	2	2.21	2	1.98	2.336	.124

*Level of Importance most often checked by respondents: 1 = very important; 2 = quite important; 3 = not very importan 4 = not very important at all
#Mean is numerical conversion of levels of importance: 1 = 1.00 to 1.75; 2 = 1.76 to 2.50; 3 = 2.51 to 3.25; 4 = 3.26 to 4.00
+Level of Significance at least .05

Game Attraction Factors Important to Southwestern Indian Youth

Code. Number	Level of Importance to All Subjects		Level of Importance by Sex				F Score	Level of Significance between Fe and Males[+]
			Female N = 120		Male N = 63			
	Most Often Checked*	Mean#	Most Often Checked*	Mean#	Most Often Checked*	Mean#		
Involvement:								
31 How important to you are games where you have WINNERS and LOSERS?	2	2.07	2	2.27	1	1.69	15.429	.001+
32 How important to you are games where WINNING or LOSING is completely up to you, as in running a race?	2	1.82	2	1.95	1	1.59	6.336	.012+
33 How important to you are games where you play on a TEAM to beat the other team, as baseball or basketball?	1	1.65	2	1.76	1	1.45	6.215	.013+
45 How important is it to you to be singled out as the most IMPORTANT person helping your team the most to win the game?	2	1.84	2	1.91	1	1.71	2.039	.151+
Spectator:								
43 When you watch a game, how much enjoyment do you get in seeing the INDIVIDUAL who plays much better than his teammates?	2	2.02	2	1.98	2	2.11	1.202	.274
44 When you watch a game, how much enjoyment do you get in seeing teamwork and cooperation by ALL the team members?	1	1.50	1	1.57	1	1.38	3.214	.071
46 Would you rather WATCH other people play a game than play in the game yourself, even if you know how?	3	2.51	2	2.32	3	2.86	10.604	.002+

*Level of Importance most often checked by respondents: 1 = very important; 2 = quite important; 3 = not very importan 4 = not very important at all
#Mean is numerical conversion of levels of importance: 1 = 1.00 to 1.75; 2 = 1.76 to 2.50; 3 = 2.51 to 3.25; 4 = 3.26 to 4.00
+Level of Significance at least .05

Table 4

Probability of Indian Youth's Attitudinal Preference on Measures of
Equity, Skill, Victory

Attitudes	Combined Boys and Girls	Girls	Boys
EQUITY TO VICTORY:			
Number responding	175	112	63
% having preference	54%	39%	43%
% preferring equity	83%	81%	89%
Level of significance	.01	.01	.01
EQUITY TO SKILL:			
Number responding	179	116	63
% having preference	40%	48%	40%
% preferring equity	74%	73%	76%
Level of significance	.01	.01	.01
SKILL TO VICTORY:			
Number responding	177	114	63
% having preference	52%	53%	51%
% preferring skill	72%	75%	55%
Level of significance	.01	.01	--

Total N = 183
Girls N = 120
Boys N = 63
% having preference

Number responding indicates respondents who answered both attitude statements.
% having preference represents % of respondents who marked different level of importance between 2 attitudes.
The remainder assigned the same level of importance to both attitudes.
% preferring _____ indicates % of respondents who marked one attitude more important than the second.
e.g., equity was selected over victory by 83% of respondents; conversely, 17% preferred victory over equity.

responses point to the major importance of playing fairly to these Indian youth.

The attitudes of equity, skill, and victory have been studied by Webb (1969) as components of "professionalism" of attitudes toward play, which in turn parallel increases in rationalization of adolescents toward success value used in Western urban society. Webb suggested that the achievement criteria emphasizes success or victory which skill can produce, but equity or fairness may inhibit success. Results from application of his three-attitude "play scale" supported increasing professionalization over age and between sexes. Thus, there was a decrease by age in importance of equity with a corresponding increase in importance of skill and victory components. The native American adolescents' data indicate the opposite. They considered equity or playing fairly very important, with skill, and victory less so. These results did not support Webb's "professionalization" of attitudes which, over time, increasingly substituted skill for equity and increased importance of victory (Webb, 1969:164). In fact, the native American attitudes seemed in contradiction to those found in white children by Webb. The concept of fair play found in native American youth seemed consistent with expressed tribal values of individual integrity (Kluckhohn, 1967, Allison and Lueschen, 1979). The importance of equity was also reinforced by the young people's attitude toward employing "tricks."

Tactics. The second component in game attraction, tactics, consisted of the employment of strategies to outsmart the opponent and the use of tricks to gain advantage. The subjects were asked how much enjoyment they got in trying to outsmart their opponents. The average response ($\bar{x}$ 2.13) indicated that this tactic was "quite enjoyable." The boys' response ($\bar{x}$ .1.98) appeared a bit more forceful than the girls ($\bar{x}$ 2.21) but was not significant.

The use of tricks to win a game, even though the youth knew these were against the rules, was soundly rejected by both young women and young men as "not very important" ($\bar{x}$ .2.91 and $\bar{x}$ 2.92 respectively, with the average mean of 2.91). This was the most negative response to all the game attraction items; therefore, it must be considered as a vital expression of their moral code. Such an expressed value differs from the seemingly growing attitude among Anglo team players who knowingly bend or break the rules, pushing the advantage against opponents to the point of official sanction. A two-pronged view of moral behavior in interpersonal relations is held by Southwest Indians. One level is reported by Kluckhohn and Leighton (1962). They noted that among the Navajo each individual is controlled not by sanctions from the top of a hierarchy of persons but by lateral sanctions (Kluckhohn and Leighton, 1962:302). The other, concerning Navajo, reported by Ladd (1957:302), indicated that a few proscriptions serve indirectly as behavior guides, not an elaborate system of rules. According to Fox (1961), among the Pueblo peoples (including the Hopi), the strongest force for social conformity is the power of public opinion. An individual tends not to cheat for fear of sanction by gossip, criticism or ridicule if deviation from the norm is discovered (Dutton, 1976).

In summary, the dominant attitude of victory and the lessor role of fair play in Anglo game participants, as observed by Webb (1969), was not preferred by the Indian youth. This point appears to be a basic ethnic difference.

Involvement. The third aspect of game attraction is the phenomenon of individual involvement in the game. Overall, being involved in winning seemed quite important to the Indian youth, both as individuals and as team members. To the question of involvement in games having winners and losers, the youth thought this quite important ($\bar{x}$ 2.07). However, this statistic masks the divergence between the sexes. Specifically, playing such games was significantly more important to boys than to girls (p.<.001). The girls' response indicated that this was quite important ($\bar{x}$ 2.27), while to boys this was very important ($\bar{x}$ 1.69). Likewise, the girls reported that involvement in winning or losing a game was, as an individual, quite important ($\bar{x}$ 1.95), while the boys reported that it was very important ($\bar{x}$ 1.59). The average mean for both sexes showed this was quite important ($\bar{x}$ 1.82).

Also significant was the importance concerning winning and losing as a team member. Playing as a team member to beat the opponent was very important ($\bar{x}$ 1.65), but was significantly more important to boys than girls (p.<.01). The boys considered this very important ($\bar{x}$ 1.45), while the girls thought it quite important ($\bar{x}$ 1.76). For both the boys and girls, these group means were among the lowest of the study, indicating that being involved in game play is of cardinal consequence to the respondents. Eifermann (1970) found that Israeli kibbutz children, who were raised in a cooperative group which resembles to some extent the southwest Indian kinship orientation, most strongly preferred group games which called for cooperation toward the achievement of a common aim within a competitive framework. This seems to be a similar preference as expressed by the native American youth and may also be common in the play of Anglo American youth. More work needs to be done on team membership.

In the case of being singled out as the most important person helping the team to win the game, as a group the youth felt this to be quite important ($\bar{x}$ 1.84). Girls reported this to be quite important ($\bar{x}$ 1.91), while boys considered this to be very important ($\bar{x}$ 1.71); the difference was not significant. Being singled out as the most valuable person at first seems to go against the Indian value of cooperation and orientation toward sharing. However, it appears that being singled out by the team is different from the self-centered egotism of a "prima donna" athlete. It encompasses the attribute of being instrumental in helping the team to win a game; thus it involves the acceptance of personal responsibility for the group's welfare in accord with one's ability. This trait is considered important to native Americans' concept of group welfare. The key or focal point here is the notion that the group bestows prestige on the individual most helpful to the group, not the individual assuming this as a demonstrated right. Kluckhohn and Leighton (1962:301) in describing the Navajo contended, "Personal excellence is thus a value, but personal 'success' in the white American sense is not." Allison (1980) infers this in insisting that succeess for the Navajo athlete must remain in the private realm, not interpreted in expectations of extrinsic reward.

In summary, involvement in games in which there were winners and losers, as individuals, as team members, and the most valuable person on the team were all quite important to girls but were very important to boys.

Spectatorship. The fourth game attraction factor examined was spectatorship. Neither boys nor girls generally showed much interest in watching other people play rather than playing the game themselves ($\bar{x}$ 2.51). Girls reported $\bar{x}$ 2.32, while the boys reported $\bar{x}$ 2.86. Interestingly, when cast in the role of spectator, the girls enjoyed watching others significantly more than did the boys (p. < .002). However, the basic message remains that these youth would rather play than watch. Because teen-agers are physiologically and socially action-oriented, it is no surprise that they preferred to play rather than watch a game that they knew how to play. The statistically greater importance to boys than girls of game playing may indicate that in native American boys, as in Anglo boys, such involvement seems to carry greater status or recognition than for girls. However, in the past decade this attitude of participation has been reinforced for Anglo girls as well as for boys. In the Choctaw youth, Blanchard (1981) points out that sports participation by girls as well as boys is a positive status marker. Further cross-cultural studies of proportional interest between sexes as spectator versus player are needed.

As spectators, students received a great deal of enjoyment from seeing teamwork and cooperation by all the team members ($\bar{x}$ 1.50). Girls reported a mean of 1.57, while boys reported a mean of 1.38. This difference approached significance at .07 with the boys tending to place even more importance on teamwork and cooperation than girls. Of all the attitudinal statements, this was of the highest relative importance for both boys and girls, thus giving added support to the value of cooperation recognized by the native American youth.

As spectators, both girls and boys indicated that they received quite a bit of enjoyment from seeing the individual play much better than his teammates ($\bar{x}$ 2.03). The girls' average was 1.98, while the boys' average was 2.11. However, this was only nominally important to both and considerably less important than seeing teamwork and cooperation. This response, which implies an appreciation of skillful execution and finesse, coupled with the enjoyment of being singled out as the most important person helping the team win a game, may seem incongruous with the value of cooperation and teamwork. However, this is not necessarily so. It may indicate an appreciation for expertise recognized and desired in others and self.

To summarize this game attraction factor, when placed in the role of spectators, the youth received much enjoyment in observing teamwork and cooperation by all team members. They also received quite a bit of enjoyment from seeing the individual who plays much better than his or her teammates singled out as the most important person helping the team to win a game. Overall, however, it must be assumed that these youth would rather be involved in playing the game than in watching.

Tribal Variations in Game Attraction Factors

Examination of the main effects by tribes (Apache, Hopi, Navajo, Papago, Pima) revealed no significant differences for the game attraction factors. While this was also true for females by tribes, the males showed two significant tribal differences. One was the attitude of equity or playing fairly ($p. < .009$). The other was individual involvement in games ($p. < .035$). However, this tribal variation is still within the category of "very important." The over-all tribal attitude concerning individual involvement was quite important ($\bar{x} = 1.82$), but the boys considered personal involvement was quite important ($\bar{x} = 1.59$), while the girls found it only quite important ($\bar{x} = 1.95$). Again the tribal variation remained within the category of "very important" for boys. Because the inter-tribal variations for girls and boys were rather minimal, including the above two factors, an extensive analysis was not warranted. The general conclusion is that tribal variations in game attraction factors were not significant.

Summary of Gender Variations in Game Attraction Factors

An examination of gender variation in game factors which attracted Southwest native American youth to participate in these self-chosen recreational activities showed the following. Three attitudes were selected to indicate the importance of playing a game: equity (to play fairly), skill (to play as well as possible) and victory (to beat an opponent). In general equity was considered very important, while skill and victory were quite important to these youth. By analyzing their probability of preference, equity was preferred to skill and to victory, while skill was more preferred than victory.

Tactics used in a game provided data on values of these youth. The knowing use of a trick, which was against the rules, in order to win a game was soundly rejected by both girls and boys. This was the most negative statistic in the whole survey, implying a strong opposition to cheating in games. The use of strategy was viewed as quite enjoyable. When comparing the responses of girls to boys, no significant differences were found.

The individual's involvement in games where there were winners and losers and, more specifically, the contribution as an individual as a team member, and being singled out as the most important person helping the team to win a game, were all very important to the boys and quite important to the girls. Each condition was significantly more important to boys than to girls.

Both boys and girls would rather play than watch a game. However, when cast in the role as spectator, girls enjoyed watching others play significantly more than did boys. Both sexes greatly enjoyed seeing teamwork and cooperation by all the team members; they also considered watching an individual play better than his or her teammates to be quite enjoyable.

CONCLUSIONS

General conclusions of this study, which examined gender variations in recreational activities and the game attraction factors of southwestern native Indian youth, are as follows.

1) Sports participation was overwhelmingly preferred by both sexes to other recreational choices (e.g., amusements, games, and crafts).

2) More diverse recreational activities were participated in by females than by males.

3) The attitude of fair play (equity) was more strongly preferred by both sexes over playing skillfully (skill) or playing to beat an opponent (victory).

4) The use of tricks which were against the rules to win a game was emphatically rejected, but the employment of strategy in game play was considered quite enjoyable by both sexes.

5) Involvement in competitive games as an individual player, as a team member, and as an outstanding player on the team was significantly more important to boys than girls.

6) Indian youth would rather play than watch a game, but girls, when cast in the role of spectator, were significantly more willing to watch than boys.

7) As a spectator, watching teamwork and cooperation by all the team members was highly enjoyable, but seeing the team's outstanding individual player perform was also quite enjoyable.

In summary, participation by native American females as well as by males has transferred from traditional Indian games to twentieth century modern white sports. Of the 57 different recreational activities chosen by southwestern native American youth, team sports (basketball, softball, baseball, football, and volleyball) were overwhelmingly preferred. The Indian heritage of sports participation by women and men alike continues in the later part of the twentieth century. This study showed that females participated in more diverse recreational activities than males. It was also shown that boys consider it significantly more important than girls to win and to be individually involved in winning, while girls enjoyed watching others playing a game significantly more than did boys.

This study represents an exploratory analysis of sex differences in preference and participation factors in sports by native American youth. It is hoped that it will stimulate further investigations of sex differences in other ethnic groups, so that cross-cultural comparisons can be made.

NOTES

[1]Descriptions of traditional Indian games can be found in Culin, 1907; Baldwin, 1969; and Cheska, 1981.

[2]Definition and identity implications of a native American and a member of a specific tribe in social, economic, political, and legal matters are of utmost importance. Specific tribal regulations vary in percentage of ethnic blood, inter-tribal marriage and descent lines, tribal involvement, geographical location, and self identification.

REFERENCES

Allison, Maria T.
    1980 A Structural Analysis of Navajo Basketball. Ph.D. dissertation. University of Illinois.
Allison, Maria T. & Gunther Lueschen
    1979 "A comparative analysis of Navajo Indian and Anglo basketball sports systems." International Review of Sport 14:75-86.
Baldwin, Gordon C.
    1969 Games of the American Indian. New York: Grosset and Dunlap.
Blanchard, Kendall
    1981 The Mississippi Choctaws at Play. Urbana, IL: University of Illinois Press.
Catlin, George
    1884 Letters and Notes on the Manner, Customs, and Conditions of North American Indians. London: Constable and Company, Ltd. (Reprinted by Dover Publications, Inc., New York, 1973.)
Cheska, Alyce Taylor
    1976 "Ball Games Played by North American Women." In R. Renson, P. P. DeNayer, & M. Ostyn (eds.), The History, the Evolution and Diffusion of Sports and Games in Different Cultures. Brussels, Belgium: B.L.O.S.O.
    1979 "Native American games as strategies of societal maintenance." In E. Norbeck and C. Farrer (eds.), Play Forms of Native North Americans. St. Paul, Minnesota: West Publishing Company.
    1981 "Games of North American Indians." In G. Luschen and G. Sage (eds.), Handbook of Social Science of Sport. Champaign, IL: Stipes Publishing Company, 1981.
    1982 "Influence on foundations of sport in American southwest southwestern American Indian." Paper presented at Annual Conference of the American Alliance for Health, Physical Education, Recreation, and Dance, Houston, Texas.

Culin, Steward
    1907 Games of North American Indians. 24th Annual Report of the Bureau of Amer-
        ican Ethnology. Washington, D.C.: United States Government Printing Office.
de Paina, Father Juan
    1676 "Origin and beginning of the ball game which the Apalachee and Yustage Indi-
        ans have been playing from pagan times up to the year 1676." In Archivo general
        de indias Seville. Escribania de camara legajo 156. III. (Julian Granberry, tran-
        script and translation.) Photostats, Stetson Collection Library, Gainesville: Uni-
        versity of Florida.
Diaz, Bernal
    1963 The Conquest of New Spain. (Translated from Spanish.) Middlesex, England:
        Penguin Books Ltd., 1963. (Originally published in Spanish about 1575 ± .)
Dutton, Bertha P.
    1976 The Pueblos. Englewood Cliffs, N.J.: Prentice-Hall, Inc.
Eifermann, Rifka
    1970 "Cooperation and egalitarianism in kibbutz children's games." Human Relations
        24:579-587.
Fox, Robin
    1961 "Pueblo baseball: a new use for old witchcraft." Journal of American Folklore
        74:9-16.
Glassford, R. Gerald
    1970 Application of a Theory of Games of the Transitional Eskimo Culture. Doctoral
        dissertation, University of Illinois (Reprinted, New York: Arno Press, 1976.)
Kluckhohn, Clyde
    1967 "Expressive activities." In E. Z. Vogt and E. Albert (eds.), People of Rimrock.
        Cambridge, MA: Harvard University Press
Kluckhohn, Clyde and Dorothea Leighton
    1962 The Navajo. New York: Natural History. (Originally published, 1946).
Ladd, John
    1957 Structures of a Moral Code. Cambridge, Massachusetts: Harvard University
        Press.
Laudonniere, Rene
    1869 "History of the first attempt of the French to colonize the newly discovered
        country of Florida." In B. F. French (ed.), Historical Collections of Louisiana
        and Florida. (Richard Hakluyt, translator.) New York: J. Savin and Sons.
        (Originally published, 1565.)
Lescarbot, Marc
    1914 The History of New France. Volume III. (W. L. Grant, translator.) Toronto:
        The Champlain Society. (Originally published, 1609.)
McCaskill, J. C.
    1936 "Indian sports." Indians at Work 3:29-30.
Mooney, James
    1890 "The Cherokee ball play." American Anthropologist 3:105-132.
Powers, William K.
    1973 Indians of the Northern Plains. New York: Capricorn Books.
Sutton-Smith, Brian and B. G. Rosenberg
    1961 "Sixty years of historical change in the game preferences of American children."
        Journal of American Folklore 74:17-46.
U.S. Dept. of Commerce Bureau of the Census.

1974 Household Money Income in 1973 and Selected Social and Economic Characteristics of the Household Series 60, Number 96. Washington, D.C.: Government Printing Office.
Webb, Harry
1969 "Professionalization of attitude toward play among adolescents." In Gerald Kenyon (ed.), Aspects of Contemporary Sport Sociology. Chicago: The Athletic Institute.

THE FORMAL ORGANIZATION OF SPORT

Section II

THE FORMAL ORGANIZATION
OF SPORT

Formalization has been a hallmark of modern sport.
Traditional sport structures have been replaced by organizations
devoted to particular sports. The chapters in this section examine
the nature of such organizations, as well as their effectiveness in
realizing their stated goals.

Frisby is interested in bureaucracy and effectiveness in voluntary sport organizations. Her purpose is to present a rationale
and a framework for investigating this relationship, using
national sport governing bodies in Canada as the basis for testing
her hypotheses. In doing this she provides a review of Weber's
theory of bureaucracy. Weber saw bureaucracies as efficient means
of social organizations, yet potentially destructive of some essential aspects of human personality. Frisby notes the implications of
this dilemma for modern sport and discusses some of the existing
literature on the subject.

Yerlès, without questioning the bureaucratic nature of modern sport organizations, asks whether it is proper to categorize
these organizations as voluntary associations. Her data are drawn
from tennis and volleyball federations in France and Quebec. If
these sport federations are voluntary associations, it is assumed
that they would be marked by consensus and normative integration. Yerles interviewed 40 French and 33 Quebec sport executives using three measures of integration: satisfaction with one's
own role, satisfaction with the operative goals of the federation,
and satisfaction with the overall performance of the federation.
Her conclusion is that consensus and normative integration can-

not be assumed, and that these sport federations appear to have negotiated some degree of social order.

Kjeldsen's work assesses the rationality of sport organizations by focusing on two questions: how do major league baseball teams select managers? And, what factors influence the manager's success? Various measures of career success are used to determine if there are different constructs of career factors associated with the outcomes. Kjeldsen's conclusions are threefold. First, selection of a manager is associated with high visibility of that individual in the sport, which is gained through participation over a long period for high prestige teams in championship competition. Second, successful managers come from the ranks of less regular players who were somewhat less successful in terms of participation on championship teams. Third, high prestige teams tend to select managers from other high prestige teams rather than on the basis of the individual's playing or early managerial record.

Colwell's interest is to measure the success of national Olympic organizations. Specifically, she seeks to account for differential levels of international sporting success achieved by modernized and developing nations. To accomplish this, she reviews previous studies and then examines the influence of the extent of involvement on national success in the 1976 Summer Olympic Games. She finds that the number of events in which a nation competed did influence the level of success. However, since the relationship is curvilinear, she concludes that there is an interaction between extent of involvement and success which determines optimal national performance.

Chapter 4

WEBER'S THEORY OF BUREAUCRACY AND THE STUDY OF VOLUNTARY SPORT ORGANIZATIONS

Wendy Frisby, University of Waterloo

Modern society is highly organized and bureaucratized, a feature which has held the interest of several sociologists for many years. For example, Etzioni stated:

> We are born in organizations, educated in organizations and spend most of our lives working in organizations. We spend much of our leisure time paying, playing and praying in organizations. Most of us will die in an organization and when the time comes for burial, the largest organization of all — the state — must grant official permission (1964:3).

Much of the research on patterns of organizational behavior which has been conducted in numerous disciplines, including sociology, business, economics, industrial psychology, management science and education, has been stimulated by Max Weber's (1958) theory of bureaucracy.

Weber presented a "double message" in his assessment of the effects of bureaucratic structures upon organizational and individual behavior. On the one hand, Weber viewed bureaucracy as an efficient means of social organization and predicted that with the onset of modernity it would invade all facets of social life. This is due in part to its superiority in dealing with the complexities and ever-changing conditions associated with industrialization and urbanization. Authority and control by notables and arbitrary decision making, which are characteristic of patriarchical societies, are superseded by a stratum of expertly trained professionals who rely on rules, procedures and laws to conduct their daily business. An impersonal work orientation emerges to eliminate "all the personal, irrational and emotional elements which escape calculation" that existed in more traditional types of social structures (Weber, 1968).

The ideal type bureaucracy carries out administrative functions according to a specialized division of labor of highly trained professional experts, an objective and impersonal work orientation, a clearcut hierarchy of authority, and a logical means-ends approach to decision making. This type of structure is, according to Weber, the most efficient way of conducting business. In the following excerpt, he explains reasons for the superiority of bureaucracy:

> The decisive reason for the advance of the bureaucratic organization has always been its purely technical superiority over any other form of organization. Precision, speed, unambiguity, knowledge of the files, continuity, discretion, unity, strict subordination, reduction of friction and of material and personal costs; these are raised to the optimum point in the strictly bureaucratic administration (Weber, 1968:973).

For Weber (1968), "unrenumerated honorific service" makes administrative work an avocation and thus the service is performed more slowly, is less precise, less unified, less continuous, less bound to schemata, more formless and requires more compromises between colliding interests and views. In contrast, the ideal bureaucracy:

> offers above all the optimum possibility for carrying through the principle of specializing administrative functions according to purely objective considerations (Weber, 1968:975).

The reason for the transition from traditional authority structures to the modern bureaucratic structure was an economic one; the desire for greater profits. This desire, according to Marcuse (1971), requires the systematic, methodical calculation of probable profit, regulation by a scientific apparatus and the reduction of quality to quantity, or the mathematization of experience. Control is no longer based on kinship relationships, property relationships or political partisanship as it now relies on expert and scientific knowledge.

Yet while Weber viewed bureaucracy as progressive on the one hand and predicted that it would accompany the modernization of society, he was also deeply troubled by its repressive qualities. Accompanying the logic of bureaucratic rationality and its "this worldly" asceticism, Weber saw the destruction of essential aspects of human personality: grace, dignity, personal creativity, spontaneity and ultimate meaningfulness (Mitzman, 1969). Thus, Weber was pessimistic about the future of Western civilization. He saw bureaucratization as a dead-end process leading only to "a cage of bondage" in which men would become mere "cogs in a machine." As roles become more specialized and relations more impersonal, Weber envisioned the alienation of the worker from the forces of production as a universal trend. Thus, Weber's notion of alienation extended Marx's fear of economic alienation to include the work place in general. Weber contended that:

> The modern soldier is equally separated from the means of violence; the scientist from the means of inquiry; and the civil servant from the means of administration (Gerth and Mills, 1946:50).

For Weber, the rationally regulated form of domination found in bureaucracy is paradoxical because organizational coordination and effectiveness can only occur through the impersonal coercion of subordinates. According to Seeman, Weber's concern for the struggle of the individual against large scale organizations reflects only one of several possible variants of alienation. Seeman described five uses of the concept of alienation which have pervaded sociological thought: powerlessness, meaninglessness, normlessness, isolation and self-estrangement. As Weber was primarily concerned with the legitimatization of emerging power structures in modern society, Seeman associated his work with the "powerlessness" dimension of alienation. He defined this dimension as follows:

> the expectancy or probability held by the individual that his own behavior cannot determine the occurrence of outcomes, or reinforcements, he seeks (Seeman, 1959:184).

Thus, Weber presented the double view that bureaucratic rationality is superior and effective, if instrumental goals are being pursued by an organization, while recognizing the alienating effect that it can have for the individual.

Weber's visions pose a number of implications for the modern world of sport. First, there is the change in structure and meaning as more modern sport forms evolve from traditional forms; a topic which has been addressed by Riesman and Denny (1972), Ingham (1978), Luschen (1970), Frey (1978) and Schlagenhauf and Timm (1976). This trend parallels Weber's approach of analyzing the structure of modern society in comparison to more traditional patriarchical societies.

Second, the repressive consequences of bureaucracy can be considered. For example, Page (1973), Sage (1978), Frey (1978), Kidd (1980), among others, have bemoaned the loss of personal autonomy on the part of the participants and volunteers, the intrusion of the law and government into the arena of sport, and the usurpation of expressive values by instrumental values as sport has become more bureaucratic in nature. For example, Kidd (1980) fears that the day to day administration of Canadian amateur athletics will be taken further and further away from the volunteers, and thus further away from the athletes themselves, as the government continues to finance centralized centers such as the National Sport and Recreation Center and Sport Canada. In addition, because medal counts are becoming the sole criteria for acquiring government grants and assistance, the human quality of the competitive experience is being ignored. Thus, according to Kidd (1978), athletes are being treated like assembly line workers with production quotas; the difference being that the athletes are not paid for their labor.

A third line of inquiry that could evolve out of Weber's discussion on bureaucracy is an examination of whether or not a bureaucratic structure is the most effective structure for sport organizations which are in pursuit of instrumental goals such as performance excellence and resource acquisition. This question has received little or no attention in the sociology of sport besides the recognition that bureaucracy is present in both amateur and professional sport organizations (Schlagenhauf and Timm 1976; Ingham 1978; Frey 1978).

The purpose of this paper is to present the rationale and a framework for investigating the relationship between bureaucracy and effectiveness in voluntary sport organizations. To illustrate structural and effectiveness indices within context, special reference is made to Canadian national sport governing bodies (N.S.G.B.'s). Variables indicative of bureaucracy and organizational effectiveness in this type of voluntary organization are discussed, and finally, a set of hypotheses for future testing is presented.

THE NATURE OF CANADIAN NATIONAL SPORT GOVERNING BODIES

As in many countries throughout the world, Canadian N.S.G.B's, which are largely composed of volunteers, play a significant role in the organization of amateur athletics. Through their international, provincial and local affiliates, they involve thousands of athletes, coaches, government officials, parents and volunteers. What makes the Canadian N.S.G.B.'s unique is that the executive board members and paid professionals work in a close liaison with the Canadian federal government. The government, through the Ministry of Fitness and Amateur Sport, provides millions of dollars in support to the various N.S.G.B.'s. Part of the rationale for increased government involvement in amateur athletes in recent years can be gleaned from a policy statement prepared by Campagnola, a former Minister for Fitness and Amateur Sport.

> Athletic excellence demands funding and technical expertise beyond the reach of athletes and most voluntary associations. The systematic coordination of all levels of athletic activity within the bound of any sport demands not only funding and technical expertise, but also the kind of support and planning not generally to be found, for perfectly understandable reasons, within most voluntary structures . . . it can best be expediated by a central staff well placed on the national and international levels (Campagnola, 1979:8).

Broom and Baka (1978) contend that the Canadian federal government has dramatically increased its involvement in amateur sport ever since the 1969 Task Force Report was struck to determine reasons for Canada's dismal performance in international sport. These authors contend that since this report, the National Policy on Amateur Sport has come out unabashedly in favor of sport excellence whereas in the past it was thought to be politically risky to take such a stand unless 'fitness for the masses' was used as a cover. Thus in the 1970's the National Sport and Recreation Center, the Coaching Association of Canada, Student Athletes Grants in Aid and Game Plan Programs were launched. In addition, Sport Canada provided funding for the hiring of full-time personnel such as national coaches, technical directors, executive directors and support staff, for international training camps and competitions and for athlete talent identification systems. All of this has been done for the explicit objective of improving Canada's performance in international competition (Regan, 1981).

Because Sport Canada may control up to 90% of N.S.G.B. funding, it is able to exert a considerable effect on the goals and structures of these organizations. For example, Regan, the current Minister of Fitness and Amateur Sport, briefly discussed the criteria that N.S.G.B.'s must meet to be considered for government funding:

Regardless of their participation base, all sports will be required to meet specific criteria and funding guidelines in determining financial support. Priority consideration will be given to both broad-base sports, such as swimming and soccer, and the more limited-base sports, such as ski jumping, that have a commitment to excellence and continually demonstrate technical, administrative and financial maturity (Regan, 1981:10).

Thus N.S.G.B.'s are encouraged to pursue goals of performance excellence with a business-like approach. Yet, while administrative maturity of the N.S.G.B.'s might aid in the achievement of instrumental performance goals, it may also reduce the power that athletes and volunteers possess in the organization of their competitive milieu.

Historically, administrative hierarchy at the local, provincial and national levels was much less formal and many of the administrative duties, including coaching and officiating, were performed by the athletes themselves (Schrodt, 1981). Volunteers were often ex-athletes or parents of athletes who devoted their spare time to the organization of sport in a spontaneous and informal manner. However, with the increased bureaucratization of sport, decision-making power and authority, especially at the national level, are becoming more and more concentrated into the hands of professionally trained executive members and paid professionals. While this transition may improve organizational effectiveness, it is also "removing the power from the athletes and volunteers," thus resulting in the loss of "player-controlled games to management-controlled big time" (Page, 1973). Using Weber's terminology, the athlete may be becoming a mere cog in the bureaucratic machine. According to several sport sociologists, the consequences of such a shift in power from the athletes and volunteers to the professionals and government officials may include: declining personal autonomy on the part of the athletes (Page, 1973), a concentration on producing winners instead of an emphasis upon the personal and emotional growth of the athlete

(Sage, 1978), abandonment of expressive values achieved through athletic participation (Frey 1978), the depersonalization of relationships (Willey, 1977), and the subordination of the athlete to the major decision makers (Sage, 1978).

Thus, while the main focus of this paper is to discuss the relationship between bureaucracy and effectiveness, careful consideration must be given to the historical context in which voluntary sport organizations emerged and to the effects of a shifting locus of control and power in amateur sport.

To date, little research has been done in the sociology of sport which integrates the concepts of bureaucracy, organizational effectiveness, and the voluntary organization. In fact, voluntary organizations are seldom characterized as being bureaucratic in nature; a quality that is most often associated with governments, big business and professional sport. If bureaucracy is found to exist in voluntary organizations such as the Canadian N.S.G.B.'s, a revision of present conceptualizations of voluntary organizations may be in order. For example, Smith (1972) sees the functions of voluntary organizations as being pluralistic, counteracting the trend toward anomie, personal isolation and alienation that have accompanied the bureaucratization of society, contributing to innovation and social change, perserving cultures and nurturing personal freedom. Smith's statements seem to imply that voluntary organizations are not bureaucratic, an assumption that may not be accurate in the case of Canadian national S.G.B.'s. If it can be established that such organizations are bureaucratic, then one could argue that participation results in consequences opposite to those espoused by Smith. Because bureaucracy is associated with impersonality of work relations, involvement may actually contribute to feelings of anomie, personal isolation and alienation; pluralism of power bases may be restricted through government intervention; innovation would not be encouraged due to a reliance on formal work procedures; the culture-perserving function may be undermined by the pressure for standardization, and finally, personal freedom would be difficult to maintain when roles, duties, decision-making procedures and authority channels are clearly designated.

BUREAUCRACY AND ORGANIZATIONAL EFFECTIVENESS IN VOLUNTARY SPORT ORGANIZATIONS

According to Blau (1974), the most common variables appearing in the research on bureaucracy include: organizational size, complexity, specialization, professionalism, hierarchy of authority, relative size of the administrative component, formalization of rules and procedures, impersonality of work relations, career stability, and the degree of centralization of decision making. In his review of the literature on bureaucracy, Blau concluded that these structural attributes are inter-related and their effects interact on each other. If these same attributes are found to be present to some degree in Canadian N.S.G.B.'s, then the same interaction effects can be expected. It is highly unlikely, however, that these characteristics are present in the N.S.G.B.'s to the degree outlined by Weber, because his ideal types were not meant to represent reality. They were constructed as heuristic devices from which comparative and causal judgements could be made (Rex 1977; Ingham 1979). The question is to determine the extent to which Canadian N.S.G.B.'s and other voluntary sport organizations approximate the structure of Weber's ideal type. In addition, in order to test Weber's assumption that bureaucracy is an effective form of social structure, the correlations between indices of bureaucracy and organizational effectiveness should be examined. To this end, a series of hypotheses are presented in the next section of this paper. Before these are presented, however, the concept of organizational effectiveness is discussed in further detail.

Researchers have long been interested in isolating the variables which predict organizational effectiveness but several problems regarding the measurement of the concept have hindered progress in this direction (Steers, 1977). Part of this problem stems from the use of alternative theoretical orientations regarding the functioning of organizations. More specifically, some researchers have used the goal model to measure organizational effectiveness (Price, 1968), while others have employed the systems model (Yuchtman and Seashore, 1967). With the goal model, effectiveness is measured according to the ability of an organization to achieve desired objectives, while in the systems model, effectiveness is measured in terms of the organization's ability to acquire scarce resources. While it is beyond the scope of this paper to discuss these models in detail, it would be useful to include measures of both models in a study on the relationship between bureaucracy and effectiveness in voluntary sport organizations. This strategy would assist in examining the controversy in the organizational effectiveness literature regarding whether the goal and systems models are contradictory (Campbell, 1976) or complementary methods (Webb 1974; Molnar and Rogers 1976) of measuring organizational effectiveness.

Returning to the case of Canadian N.S.G.B.'s, international performance excellence is an explicit objective of all the national sports governing bodies which have teams competing in Olympic and World Championships. Therefore, present world rankings of Olympic sports could be used as an indicator of effectiveness. However, the fact that performance excellence is a goal that is common to all these organizations and thus forms a standardized basis for comparison is not the only rationale for its inclusion as an index of effectiveness. Weber closely linked achievement and the pursuit of instrumental goals to his theory of bureaucracy. This is most evident in his writings in *The Protestant Ethic and the Spirit of Capitalism* (1958). Similarly, in sport, Luschen (1970) and Seppanen (1981) have reported that unequal success levels around the world can not only be explained by the material basis of the economy but are also related to the asceticism, achievement orientation and inner worldly tradition commonly associated with Protestantism. In addition, Riesman and Denney (1972) suggest that the emphasis placed on winning in modern sport is related to the social struggle for success. This struggle in turn evokes a more scientific and technological approach to sport. Wohl (1975) predicts that modern sport will continue to become more intellectual and rationalized and will place an increasingly greater emphasis on success. Thus the selection of performance excellence as one indicator of organizational effectiveness is in line with the assumption that the goals of modern sport will continue to become more instrumental in nature.

With the systems model, effectiveness is assessed according to the ability of the organization to secure scarce resources. This model evolved over dissatisfaction with the goal model in which effectiveness is measured as an end point instead of being conceptualized as a dynamic process (Katz, Kahn and Adams 1980; Yuchtman and Seashore 1967). Because N.S.G.B.'s and other voluntary sport organizations must continually struggle to obtain funding, their ability to acquire funds from the government and other sources could be a second measure of effectiveness. The use of the goal and systems model is intended to examine the controversy existing in the literature on organizational effectiveness in which these two models are either regarded as alternative views on organizational performance or as complementary tools for analyzing organizational action.

In sum, Weber's theory of bureaucracy provides a framework for investigating the structure and meaning of modern amateur sport by focusing on the historical and cultural context in which organizational structures emerge and examining the effects of structure on the attainment of instrumental objectives and resource acquisition, while considering the consequences of a shift in power as control is taken out of the hands of the worker, or in this case, the participant. However, little consideration has been given to Weber's assertion that a bureaucratic structure is positively related to certain indices of organizational effectiveness.

Below are a series of hypotheses and the rationale for expected relationships between indices of bureaucracy and organizational effectiveness in voluntary sport organizations. Variables indicative of bureaucracy include: formalization, centralization, impersonality of work relations, professionalism, specialization, career stability, organizational size, the proportion of clerical staff, and the emphasis placed on science and technology. The ability of the organization to achieve performance objectives and its ability to acquire scarce resources are indicative of the goal model and the systems model of organizational effectiveness respectively. One might expect that there is a positive relationship between these two measures of effectiveness. That is, organizations with teams which rank high in world rankings are expected to be more successful in acquiring scarce funding resources than are organizations with teams with moderate or low world rankings.

HYPOTHESES REGARDING BUREAUCRACY AND ORGANIZATIONAL EFFECTIVENESS

1. The Greater the Extent of Formalization, the Greater the Organizational Effectiveness

Formalization refers to the extent to which work activities are guided by written rules and procedures (Hall, 1972). Thus in sport organizations, the greater the proliferation of written documents including constitutions, job descriptions, records on performances and policy statements, the greater is the formalization. White (1980) contends that the aim of increased formalization is to achieve social order and stability through the patterned regulation of human behavior. Glisson and Martin (1980) add that although formalization is often associated with red tape, it assures a minimum of fairness and consistency in treatment and may also reduce work uncertainty. In addition, a formally established system of procedures and rules is thought to ensure continuity even with frequent changes in personnel, a common occurrence in voluntary organizations.

2. The Greater the Decentralization in Authority and Decision Making, the Greater the Organizational Effectiveness

Although Weber (1968) stipulates that bureaucracy coincides with the concentration of the material means of management in the hands of the master, empirical research has most often demonstrated a positive relationship between a decentralized structure and effectiveness. For example, Aiken and Hage (1966) reported a positive relationship between decentralization and program innovation while Negandhi and Reimann (1973) found that decentralized business firms experienced greater employee retention and profitability. A decentralized authority structure is associated with participative decision making, a process which is designed to involve and clarify members' responsibilities in contributing to goal attainment. In national sport governing bodies, this variable can be operationalized according to the degree to which decision making is concentrated with the paid personnel versus being distributed to other groups in the organization such as the national executive board, the subcommittees, the national coaching staff and national team athletes.

3. The Greater the Impersonality of Work Relations, the Greater the Organizational Effectiveness

An impersonal orientation is important to the bureaucratic organization because, according to Weber, it helps to prevent personal feelings from distorting rational decision making. Weber contrasted the impersonal approach with the ways of the old order in which those in power were moved by "personal sympathy and favor, by grace and gratitude" (Weber 1968). Along with formalization, impersonal work relations are designed to:

> eliminate from official business all purely personal, irrational and emotional elements which escape calculation (Weber, 1968:975).

Work relations become more impersonal when objective facts, such as statistical records, are used as a basis for decision making. In the case of the N.S.G.B.'s, attempts have been made in recent years to design objective criteria for national team selection and athlete talent identification. Thus various tactical, physiological and psychological tests have been employed by the N.S.G.B.'s to improve the objectivity of the athlete selection process (Sport Canada, 1978 Mid Quadrennial Review). These tests are also useful for pointing out weaknesses that may effect team performance. Therefore, it is expected that the more an N.S.G.B. relies on objective statistical information as a basis for national team selection, the more impersonal work relations are a necessary condition for organizational effectiveness.

4. The Greater the Professionalism of Major Decision Makers, the Greater the Organizational Effectiveness

For Weber, the evolution of bureaucratization was an inevitable response to the patriarchical society in which authority was based on kinship ties and the possession of property. Instead, important social roles are allocated according to the technical competence which is superior to "arbitrary decision making by notables." Blau (1974) found that the degree of professionalism is inversely related to the degree of centralization. He explained that because professional qualifications allow one to see the implication of one's work and make a person more self directing, decision making can be more dispersed throughout the organization. Conversely, in the absence of a professionally trained staff, coordiantion can more likely be achieved through a centralized hierarchy of authority. Thus, to investigate the relationship between professionalism and effectiveness, careful consideration must be given to the interaction effect between professionalism and the type of decision-making structures.

Indicators of professionalism in amateur sport would include specific training in business or sport administration, experience in occupations which require administrative expertise, or participation and certification in athletic or coaching roles which require leadership and other organizational skills.

5. The Greater the Specialization, the Greater the Organizational Effectiveness

Specialization implies a high division of labor in which work responsibilities are divided into more narrow areas for each individual to concentrate on. According to Weber (1968), a high degree of specialization promotes expertise among personnel by narrowing the range of duties on the job. Specialization is thought to lead to increased effectiveness because it allows each member to maximize his or her contribution to goal-directed activities (Steers, 1977). The number of board positions, paid positions and subcommittees with specific responsibilities would be indicative of the degree of specialization.

6. The Greater the Career Stability of the Organizations, the Greater the Organizational Effectiveness

Although formalized work procedures are designed to offset continual changes in personnel, career stability is an important variable to consider in voluntary associations in which elective positions are often held for one or two-year terms. In contrast, Weber's bureaucracy is characterized by formal employment, salaries, pensions, promotions, elected rather than appointed officials, and positions are often held for life. Because consistency may be difficult to achieve with a large turnover rate, as new incoming members require training and socialization in their new positions, it is expected that the more careers approximate Weber's description of the official in bureaucracy, the more effective the organization will be.

7. The Greater the Organization Size, the Greater the Organizational Effectiveness

Blau (1974) contends that organizational size and the degree of specialization of roles and functions are strongly related. In his study on the structure of small bureaucracies, Blau found that small undifferentiated agencies operate at high cost while an increase in size and differentiation is associated with reduced operating costs. While effectiveness will not be operationalized in terms of operating costs in this study, it is still expected that increased size will allow the organization to diversify and more effort will be directed toward goal attainment and resource acquisition.

8. The Greater the Proportion of Clerical Staff, the Greater the Organizational Effectiveness

Again, Blau (1974) found a positive relationship between the proportion of clerical staff among the total staff and reduced operating costs. Clerical staff maintain channels of communication which are important as differentiation of roles increases. Furthermore, clerical staff help to reduce the work load of major decision makers so that they can concentrate on matters affecting the organization's effectiveness.

9. The Greater the Emphasis Placed on Science and Technology, the Greater the Organizational Effectiveness

Just as bureaucracy rests on the specialized knowledge of the professional, its advance is also dependent on the acquisition of new technology and scientific information (Weber, 1968). Both Wohl (1975) and Ingham (1978, 1979) have commented on the significant role that science and technology play in modern sports forms. For example, Ingham notes that the bureaucratic nature of modern sport is reflected in the elaborate and calculative system of formal rules, an instrumental, national profit and performance-oriented action system and an "intellectualized strategy" which necessitates growth of technology and the sport sciences (Ingham, 1979). The presence of research committees and methods of keeping up with training methods and strategies used in other countries indicates how strong an emphasis organizations are placing on science and technology.

CONCLUSION

In conclusion, the purpose of this paper was to apply Weber's theory of bureaucracy to the study of voluntary sport organizations. More specifically, a line of inquiry, which has received little attention in the sociology of sport, was developed through the formulation of hypotheses regarding the relationship between variables indicative of bureaucracy and organizational effectiveness. The subsequent investigation of these relationships is designed to perform three functions: one, to examine the extent to which Weber's theory of bureaucracy holds for voluntary sport organizations; two, to extend the literature on voluntary organizations from an organizational perspective; and three, to examine the structure and meaning of sport in our modern society.

REFERENCES

Aiken, M. and J. Hage
    1966 "Organizational alienation: a comparative analysis." American Sociological
        Review 31:497-507.
Blau, Peter
    1974 On the Nature of Organizations. New York: John Wiley.
Broom E. F. and R. S. Baka
    1978 Canadian Governments and Sport. CAHPER Sociology of Sport Monograph
        Series, Ottawa.
Campagnola, Iona
    1979 Partners in the Pursuit of Excellence: A National Policy on Amateur Sport.
        Ottawa: Ministry of Fitness and Amateur Sport.
Campbell, J. P.
    1976 "Contributions research can make in understanding organizational effective-
        ness," Pp. 29-45 In S. L. Spray (ed.), Organizational Effectiveness: Theory,
        Research, Utilization. Kent, OH: Kent State University Press.
Etzioni, Amitai
    1964 Modern Organizations, Englewood Cliffs, NJ: Prentice-Hall, Inc.
Frey, James H.
    1978 "The organization of American amateur sport: efficiency to entropy." American
        Behavioral Scientist 21:3:361-378.
Gerth, H. H. and C. W. Mills
    1946 From Max Weber: Essays in Sociology, New York: Oxford.
Glisson, C. A. and P. Y. Marten
    1980 "Productivity and efficiency in human service organizations as related to struc-
        ture, size and age." Academy of Management Journal, 23:21-37.
Hall, Richard M.
    1972 The Formal Organization. New York: Basic Books.
Ingham, Alan G.
    1978 "American sport in transition: the maturation of industrial capitalism and its
        impact upon sport." Unpublished doctoral dissertation, Univeristy of
        Massachusetts.
    1979 "Methodology in the sociology of sport, from symptoms of malaise to Weber
        for a cure." Quest 31:2:187-215.
Katz, Daniel, Robert L. Kahn, and J. Stacy Adams
    1980 The Study of Organizations. San Francisco: Jossey-Bass.
Kidd, Bruce
    1978 The Political Economy of Sport, CAHPER Sociology of Sport Monograph
        Series, Ottawa.
    1980 'The Canadian state and sport: the dilemma of intervention." Paper presented at
        the 2nd Annual Conference of the National Association for Physical Education
        for Higher Education, Brainerd, Minnesota.

Lüschen, Gunther
1970 "Sociology of sport and the cross-cultural analysis of sport and games." In G. Luschen (ed.), The Cross-Cultural Analysis of Sport and Games. Champaign, IL: Stipes Publishing Company.

Marcuse, Herbert
1971 "Industrialization and capitalism. In O. Stammer (ed.), Max Weber and Sociology Today. Oxford: Basil Blackwell.

Mitzman, Arthur
1969 The Iron Cage: An Historical Interpretation of Max Weber. New York: Alfred A. Knopf, Ltd.

Molnar, J. J. and David C. Rogers
1976 "Organizational effectiveness: an empirical comparison of the goal and system resource approaches." Sociological Quarterly 17:401-413.

Negandhi, A. and B. Reimann
1973 "Task environment, decentralization, and organizational effectiveness." Human Relations 26:203-214.

Page, Charles H.
1973 "Pervasive sociological themes in the study of sports." In J. Talamini and C. H. Page (eds.) Sport and Society: An Anthology, Boston: Little Brown: 14-37.

Price, J. L.
1968 Organizational Effectiveness: An Inventory of Propositions. Homewood, Ill.: Irwin.

Regan, Gerald
1981 A Challenge to the Nation: Fitness and Amateur Sport. Ottawa: Ministry of Fitness and Amateur Sport.

Rex, J.
1977 "Value relevance, scientific laws and ideal types: the sociological methodology of Max Weber." Canadian Journal of Sociology 2,2:151-166.

Riesman, David and Reuel Denney
1972 "Football in America: a study in culture diffusion." In E. Dunning (ed.), Sport: Readings From a Sociological Perspective. Toronto: University of Toronto Press.

Sage, George
1978 "American values and sport: formation of a bureaucratic personality." Leisure Today 49:8:10-12.

Schlagenhauf, Karl and Waldemar Timm
1976 "The sport club as a social organization." International Review of Sport Sociology 11:2:9-30.

Schrodt, Barbara
1981 "Changes in the governance of sport in Canada." Unpublished paper in the files of the author.

Seeman, M.
1959 "On the meaning of alienation." American Sociological Review 24:783-791.

Seppanen, Paavo
1981 "Olympic success: a cross-cultural perspective." In G. Lüschen and G. Sage (eds.), Handbook of Social Science of Sport. Champaign, IL: Stipes Publishing Company.

Smith, D. H., R. D. Reddy, and B. R. Baldwin
1972 Voluntary Action Research. Toronto: Lexington Books.

Steers, Richard M.
1977 Organizational Effectiveness: A Behavioral View. Calfornia: Goodyear Publishing Co.

Webb, Ronald R.
   1974 "Organizational effectiveness and the voluntary organization." Academy of
         Management Journal 17:663-677.
Weber, Max
   1958 The Protestant Ethic and the Spirit of Capitalism. New York: Charles Scribner's
         Sons.
White, Terrence H.
   1980 "Formal organizations." In R. Hagidorn (ed.), Sociology. Toronto: Holt, Rine-
         hart and Winston of Canada.
Willey, D. L.
   1977 Bureaucracy, Sport and Physical Education. Bulletin of Physical Education 8
         (3):27-32.
Wohl, A.
   1975 "The influence of the scientific-technical revolution on the shape of sport and
         the perspectives of its development." International Review of Sport Sociology
         10:1:19-34.
Yuchtman, E. and Seashore, S. E.
   1967 "A system resource approach to organizational effectiveness." American Socio-
         logical Review 32:891-903.

Chapter 5

MODES OF INTEGRATION IN VOLUNTARY SPORTS ASSOCIATIONS

Magdeleine Yerles, Université Laval

The question of integration of members within their organization, the subject of this paper, is in fact a huge topic and a major problem for any organization, i.e., how to secure a minimum of predictability in the behavior of members. The brief overview of the problem which is presented here must be viewed in its proper context, i.e., as an attempt to direct attention to a sociological analysis of this issue within voluntary sport associations.

"Common sense" sociology, as well as the current literature in the sociology of sport organizations (Bratton, 1970), leads toward the expectation that amateur sport agencies rely heavily on integration based upon consensual norms for securing a minimum of cooperation. Some arguments can be invoked in support of this expectation. First, membership in voluntary associations is, by definition, based on free will and this holds true, as well, for members in executive positions. These officials especially should be integrated and feel part and parcel of their federation. Second, since amateur sport federations are designed to serve the common interest of their members and can be classified into Blau's and Scott's category (1962) of mutual benefit associations, it seems reasonable to expect executives to show an acknowledgement of this common interest and to reach a high level of consensus about organizational goals. Third, since it might be assumed with Hoyle (1971) that amateur sport agencies fall into Etzioni's normative-moral category (1961), executives are expected to express a deep commitment to their federation and strong cooperation toward goal achievement. Finally, given the large amount of freedom afforded voluntary members, consensus may be thought of as a crucial factor for the very existence of amateur sport governing bodies.

These expectations, however, rest upon two major postulates concerning the fundamental organizational problem of integration and participation. First, the integration of members within their sport federation is here conceived of as normative integration, that is, members subscribe to the values preached within the organization, they obey existing norms defining their roles and they enact their roles according to the expectations of their partners. Second, participation is conceived in terms of cooperation, never in terms of conflict.

Research efforts have brought these postulates into serious question, namely through the work of Crozier and Friedberg (1977). These two authors do not deny that normative integration may occur at times, especially when abetted by strongly held common values and shared principles of functioning, obedience to ritualistic functions, and a convergence of role expectations. But they offer strong evidence to the effect that integration within organizations can be realized through contract, that is through a complex process of implicit or explicit bargaining. However, Crozier and Friedberg (1977) do not clearly express any proposition concerning voluntary associations.

This paper questions the assumption of normative integration within sport federations, and some evidence is presented that, within these voluntary associations, integration is not necessarily reached through consensus about organizational goals and shared satisfaction with organizational performance.

METHOD

Data were collected by means of interviews with 40 French sport executives involved in tennis and volleyball federations, and a similar sample of 33 Quebec sport executives. Three traditional measures of integration were used — satisfaction with one's own role, satisfaction with the operative goals of the federation, and satisfaction with the overall performance of the federation. Pertinent statements were rated on three-point scales. For the second measure, the two sometimes competing objectives of mass participation in sports and the development of an athletic elite, were opted for as operative goals. These two issues were selected on the basis that uncertainty as to how they will be solved is still very high in France and Quebec. Consequently, if volunteers participate through normative integration, they ought to concur with current policies as they perceive them. On the other hand, if statements vary by categories of actors and levels in the hierarchy, they will lead toward a line of interpretation closer to Crozier's view of integration. The third measure — satisfaction with the overall performance of the federation — was also asked in order to prevent any confusion in the respondents' mind as to policies and performance. The findings discussed below examine the relationships between the three measures of integration and the following four variables: organizational role, hierarchical level, type of sport federation and country.

RESULTS

General Level of Satisfaction

Table 1 presents the overall results on measures of integration for all the respondents. As the table indicates, results for the first measure of integration — satisfaction with role — would seem to support the explanatory line of normative integration, i.e., role requirements do not appear to be a major source of dissatisfaction that might possibly lead to a high turnover of executives. Only one executive indicated a low degree of satisfaction implying possible resignation. The other officials either disliked one or two particular subtasks (20.3 percent) or enjoyed all aspects of their role (78 percent).

Table 1

Overall results on measures of integration

of sport executives*

Measures	Degree of satisfaction or agreement					
of	High		Moderate		Low	
integration	N	%	N	%	N	%
Satisfaction with role	46	78.0	12	20.3	1	1.7
(N = 59)						
Agreement with policies	32	50.0	13	20.3	19	29.7
(N = 64)						
Satisfaction with federation performance	24	39.3	18	29.5	19	31.2
(N = 61)						

* Despite the small number of cases, percentages were computed
  in all tables for comparative purposes.

For the second measure of integration—degree of agreement with mass/elite policies — the executives are about equally divided into those who agree with current policies (50 percent), and those who either are uncertain (20.3 percent) or who express marked opposition to the policies (29.7 percent). It appears that for a substantial number of members participation in the organization is hardly attributable to their enthusiasm for current policies.

As to the last measure of integration — how satisfied are sport officials with the overall performance of their federation? — the degree of dissatisfaction increases since only 39.3 percent of sport executives expressed a high degree of satisfaction.

These first results draw an overall picture of sport officials being unambiguously enthusiastic about their role but rather lukewarm about the operative goals and the performance of their federations.

Organizational Role

The positions of president, secretary, treasurer, technical advisor, referee and coach vary in terms of social roles associated with modes of secondary involvement, i.e., coaches belong to the category of direct producers of sport whereas other volunteers and appointed personnel belong to the category of indirect producers (Loy, McPherson, and Kenyon, 1978:17-18). For the following analysis — the relationship between role and general level of satisfaction — the corps of technical advisors was retained as a category of indirect producers mainly in charge of policy implementation. Volunteers other than coaches were classified in another category of indirect producers mainly in charge of policy-making.

Among the categories of sport officials, coaches show the widest gap between satisfaction with their role and the two other measures of integration. If 78.6 percent among them are highly satisfied with their task, only 17.6 percent and 12.5 percent, respectively, agree with current policies and are satisfied with the overall performance of the federation. Direct producers of sport,

who are directly responsible for bringing results up to expectations, are obviously dissatisfied with both policies and outcomes.

Among indirect producers, technical advisors whose task is
mainly policy implementation show a high degree of agreement
with the policies they help implement (86.7 percent) and are less
critical of the overall performances of their federation than coaches
or policy-makers. However, their position as appointed staff is a
peculiar one in voluntary sport associations.

Finally, there is a near even split among policy-makers
between those who agree with current policies (51.6 percent) and
those who either mention their uncertainty (19.4 percent) or who
depart from these policies (29 percent). Criticism is heavier
within this category of indirect producers when the overall performance of their federation is concerned since only 44.8 percent
are highly satisifed with performance. Looking closer to the volunteers interviews, a diversity of opinions appears that seems to
rest more upon the organizational level of action than upon the
role in itself.

The Organizational Level of Action

As already observed, satisfaction with one's own role runs
high among sport officials, and this tendency holds true whether
it be at the national, regional or local levels.

At the national level, sport officials are seldomly critical of
the policies they set up. (The term "national level" is used to des-
ignate the highest level in the hierarchy both in France and in
Quebec.) In fact, 90 percent of them express support for these
policies, and the same percentage is satisfied with the performance
of their federation, i.e., the results of their own policies.

At the regional level, sport officials are divided as to their
judgements of current policies (45.5 percent agree with the policies; 31.8 percent pronounce themselves against the policies) and
of the federation performance with 40 percent of their members
either uncertain or unwilling to judge the performance.

At the local level, the tendency shifts toward widespread criticism of current policies (50 percent) and dissatisfaction as to federation performance (57.1 percent).

The observed cleavages are close to, and probably not independent from, cleavages by categories of roles. Indeed, direct producers mainly work at a local level of action, and in this sample, appointed staff mainly belong to regional or national boards. The probability is high of an interdependent influence of organizational level and specialization of roles upon modes of integration.

Type of Sport Federation and Country

Sport federations are not self-sufficient, and Crozier and Friedberg (1977) as well as several authors belonging to the structural contingency perspective show that organizational boundaries are not environmentally insulated. Technological, economical, social and cultural constraints interfere with and modify the internal functioning of these organizations. Since tennis and volleyball federations are faced with different contingencies such as the size of the organizations, the degree of stability of the respective environments, and the exposure to the public eye, it is reasonable to expect differences between sport federations with respect to the level of satisfaction of their executives. Furthermore, since France and Quebec differ with respect to such factors as the degree of centralization of decision-making processes, the degree of social criticism toward national governing bodies, the mean age and the socio-economic status of sport executives, differences between countries come as no surprise.

Comparing first the two French federations, volleyball officials are rated lower on the three measures of integration than their tennis counterparts. This difference between sport officials is most obvious for agreement with current policies and satisfaction with federation performance. As to the two Quebec federations, the same observation can be made, with the exception of satisfaction with task. When results are broken down by countries, the main difference between the two countries appears in the third measure of integration, where only 22.9 percent of

Table 2

Attitudes of sport officials toward their

federation priorities with respect to mass/elite

policies in four sport organizations

Attitudes toward mass/elite objectives	Sport organizations									
	FFT[a]		FFVB[b]		FQT[c]		FVBQ[d]		Total	
	N	%	N	%	N	%	N	%	N	%
Agree with	11	61.1	5	29.4	7	70.0	9	47.4	32	50.0
Uncertain	6	33.3	3	17.6	-	-	4	21.0	13	20.3
Depart from	1	5.6	9	53.0	3	30.0	6	31.6	19	29.7
Total	18	100.0	17	100.0	10	100.0	19	100.0	64	100.0

[a] FFT: French tennis federation
[b] FFVB: French volleyball federation
[c] FQT: Quebec tennis federation
[d] FVBQ: Quebec volleyball federation

Table 3

Satisfaction of sport officials with the overall

performance of their own federation

in four sport organizations

Degree of satisfac-tion	Sport organizations									
	FFT		FFVB		FQT		FVBQ		Total	
	N	%	N	%	N	%	N	%	N	%
High	6	33.4	2	11.8	6	75.0	10	55.6	24	39.3
Intermediate	6	33.3	7	41.2	2	25.0	3	16.7	18	29.6
Low	6	33.3	8	47.0	-	-	5	27.7	19	31.1
Total	18	100.0	17	100.0	8	100.0	18	100.0	61	100.0

French sport officials declare themselves to be highly satisfied with their federation's overall performance, whereas 61.6 percent of Quebec respondents rate high on this measure. The greatest variability in answers is thus observed in French federations.

CONCLUSION

To sum up the results of this study, some descriptive evidence has been presented that normative integration is not the only integrative force at play within voluntary associations such as sport organizations. Integration of sport executives was assessed in terms of satisfaction with their role, satisfaction with current operative goals and satisfaction with overall performance of their federations. While they are unambiguously satisfied with their role, sport executives express disagreement with current policies and dissatisfaction with the performance of their federation.

From a comparative perspective, major cleavages on measures of integration appear between officials at different levels of action, between incumbents of various roles, between sport federations and between countries. National sport executives rate high on the three measures, whereas local sport officials strongly disagree with current policies and the overall performance of their federations. Coaches are strongly opposed to policies and very critical of overall policy outcomes, whereas appointed personnel agree with current policies and are fairly satisfied with performance; volunteers' attitudes vary by hierarchical level of action. Tennis sport executives show a higher degree of satisfaction than their volleyball counterparts; these results hold true within and between countries. In addition, in both countries, top executives working at the national level show a very high degree of satisfaction on the three measures of integration; in both countries coaches rate much lower than either volunteers or appointed staff on agreement with current policies and satisfaction with performance; French regional executives show the greatest variability on the three measures of integration.

These results converge toward those of Heinilä (1979) who found some variation in the "norm source" of Finnish sport leaders' activity according to their organizational membership and individual variation in the acceptance of opposition as being legitimate. Consensus and normative integration cannot be assumed in sport organizations except at the most general level of goals. The question remains whether other voluntary organizations might show the consensus which is often assumed to be a basic characteristic of their voluntariness. Since other complex organizations were found to have high dissent, this study gives further credence to a postulate of negotiated order. It certainly puts into question the usefulness of the concept of voluntary organizations and the inclusion of sport federations thereunder.

REFERENCES

Blau, Peter M. and W. Richard Scott
    1962 Formal Organizations. San Francisco, California: Chandler Publishing Co.
Bratton, Robert
    1970 Consensus on Association Goals among Executive Members of Two Canadian Sports Associations. Unpublished Ph.D. Thesis, University of Illinois.
Crozier, Michel and Erhard Friedberg
    1977 L'acteur et le système. Paris: Seuil.
Etzioni, Amitai
    1961 A Comparative Analysis of Complex Organizations. New York: The Free Press.
Heinilä, Kalevi
    1979 "The value orientations of Finnish sport leaders." International Review of Sport Sociology 14: 59-74.
Hoyle, Eric
    1971 "Organization theory and the sociology of sport." Pp. 82-93 in Ralph Albonico and Karl Pfister-Bintz (eds.)., Soziologie des Sports. Basel: Birkhaüser.
Loy, John W., McPherson, Barry D. and Gerald S. Kenyon
    1978 Sport and Social Systems: A Guide to the Analysis, Problems, and Literature. Reading, Mass.: Addison-Wesley.

Chapter 6

THE RISE TO LEADERSHIP IN MAJOR LEAGUE BASEBALL: PLAYING BACKGROUND AND EARLY CAREER INFLUENCES

Erik K. Kjeldsen, University of Massachusetts

Ever since Grusky (1963) noted the association between position and field leadership in major league baseball there has been continuing discussion as to the basis for that association (Loy, Curtis and Sage, 1979). However, the search for prospective leaders by sport executives and the conventional wisdom regarding what "makes" a good leader go back well before that time. This investigation builds on that tradition by examining the playing background of major league managers and the circumstances and accomplishments of their first year or so as a manager with the expectation that these experiences are in some way related to later career success as managers. The underlying theory to be tested might be specified in the following manner:

$$
\begin{array}{ccc}
\text{Playing} & \text{Selection as} & \left(\begin{array}{c} \text{Performance} \\ \text{as a} \\ \text{Manager, Yrs. 1 \& 2} \end{array} \right) \\
\text{Background} & \xrightarrow{} & \text{a Manager} \\[2em]
& \text{Nature of} & \left(\begin{array}{c} \text{Winning \%,} \\ \text{Championships,} \\ \text{Yrs. Mgd.} \end{array} \right) \\
\xrightarrow{} & \text{Career as} & \\
& \text{a Manager} &
\end{array}
$$

While such a theory can hardly be "proven" beyond its logical validity, strong and significant statistical association between
and among available measures of accomplishment at the various
points in the time sequence can serve as evidence supporting the
theory. Lack of such statistical evidence would not "disprove" the
theory; rather, it would turn the investigation to qualities which
are measurable but less available, or to qualities of the playing
career and early managerial career which are less subject to objective measures (i.e., symbolic interactionist approaches).

Kjeldsen (1981) determined that the disproportion of managers by position was a factor of the selection process rather than
of the retention process. That is, managers were *not* selected pro-
portionately from the positions and weeded out by lack of success
until the disproportion existed. They were, instead, initially
selected at a differential rate from the positions. Hence, whatever
causes players to be disproportionately identified as prospective
managers by position played is a factor of their pre-managerial
career. The most logical characteristics at which to look are factors
associated with the playing career (of which playing position is
only one). However, it must be recognized that there may be
other possible sources of such selection such as social affiliations,
administrative contributions to the team (e.g., the "Company
Man") or other characteristics of organizational life better examined through a qualitative methodology. In examining both the
selection and the retention process, this study will confine itself
to utilizing as independent variables the available, measurable
qualities of the playing and early managerial careers of major
league managers.

METHOD

Subjects for the Investigation

Data concerning the playing and managerial careers of the
subjects of this investigation were taken from the *Encyclopedia of
Baseball* (Turkin and Thompson, 1978). This source gives a wide
selection of data concerning each player/manager, but does not

necessarily give every facet of their playing lives. Perhaps more data could be culled from the files in Cooperstown. The study is, therefore, limited in this regard. Data were collected for every manager who led a team between 1901 and 1968 (the most structurally stable period for major league baseball). This totaled 252. Of these, 171 (68%) had appeared as players in the major leagues. These players served as the study group in the present investigation. Background data on the non-player/managers were not available, and they were dropped from this investigation.

To facilitate comparison with players who never became managers, a control group of one hundred (100) was randomly selected from the all-time roster. Given that ex-player/managers were found to have had rather lengthy playing careers (Mdn = 14.2 years) and the fact that random selection of a control group would produce a very high percentage of players with one year careers,[1] the control group was limited to those with careers in the major leagues of at least five years. This process produced a baseline of performance with which the playing careers of major league managers could be compared.

Analysis of Data

The data were analyzed using the sub-programs of the Statistical Package for Social Sciences (SPSS) (Nie, et al.: 1975). Descriptive statistics were generated for the managers and the control group of non-manager players and their differences were examined by the t-test.

Next, discriminant function analysis was used to identify characteristics of the playing career which discriminated between those players who were selected as managers from those who were not selected.

Discriminant function analysis was also used to identify characteristics of the playing and early managerial career which discriminated between those managers who were more "successful" on a variety of criteria and those who were less successful according to those criteria.

RESULTS

Descriptive Analysis

The comparison between managers and non-managers by position (i.e., pitchers vs. non-pitchers) on the characteristics of their playing careers is shown in Table 1. Using the .10 level of significance as a criterion, we see that the ex-pitcher managers differed from those ex-pitchers in the non-managerial control group on five of the six measures.

Ex-pitchers who achieved managerial status had longer careers, played in more games, played for higher prestige clubs, played on more championship teams and had a superior winning percentage. In short, they were superior players on the best teams and had longer careers than those ex-pitchers who failed to achieve managerial status. For the non-pitchers we see a similar situation except for one notable difference. Persons selected for managership from those positions also had longer careers and played in more games; they were also participants in more championships and played on higher prestige teams. However, their performance (as measured by their batting average) was not superior to comparable players who were not selected to positions of managership.

This description would seem to undermine the conventional wisdom of the utility infielder becoming a manager as he studies the moves of his mentor during his extended career in the dugout. It appears to lend weight to the idea that general managers and owners turn for their managers to established players of high visibility achieved as a result of their participation in championship competition and on high prestige teams.

It is interesting to note the difference in performance for pitchers and non-pitchers. Apparently only the highly successful from pitching positions are selected to be managers, while players from non-pitching backgrounds need not be outstanding performers (as measured by their batting average, at least). Perhaps this implies that there are multiple ways in which non-pitchers

Table 1*

Comparison of managers and non-managers by position
according to their playing characteristics

Playing Career Data	Pitchers			Non-Pitchers		
	Mgrs (15)	Non-Mgrs (39)	Diff	Mgrs (156)	Non-Mgrs (61)	Diff
Length of Career (yrs.)	15.4	8.2	7.2^c	13.3	9.9	3.4^c
Games Played	471.0	228.0	243.0^c	1283.0	922.0	361.0^c
Games/yr.	29.9	26.5	3.4	88.3	88.8	0.5
Performance	0.5	0.5	0.1^a	0.3	0.3	0.0
Prestige of Clubs	3.0	2.2	0.8^c	2.6	2.3	0.3^b
Championship Tennis	2.0	0.7	1.3^b	1.9	0.8	1.0^c

a = $p. < .10$

b = $p. < .05$

c = $p. < .01$

* = Values rounded to one decimal place

Table 2

Discriminant Function Analysis
Managers vs. Non-Managers on playing data

Pitchers

Mgrs (15)   Non-Mgrs (39)
Function: Lambda = .497, $X^2 = 35.58$ (2) < .000

     CARLEN   .936
     PLAPRES   .454

Cases: 79.6% correct

Non-Pitchers

Mgrs (156)   Non-Mgrs (61)
Function: Lambda = .837, $X^2 = 37.95$ (4) < .000

     GAMES   -1.427
     GAMES/YR.   1.221
     PLAPRES   -.263
     CHAMP   -.239

Cases: 70.5% correct

can demonstrate their potential to be good managers in comparison to those available to pitchers.

Discriminant Function Analysis

Another approach to understanding the qualities which distinguish groups is discriminant function analysis. This form of analysis, when used in a stepwise mode, permits the selection of measures in order of their power to discriminate between groups, and it ceases to add variables when such addition would not increase that discriminating power. This capability reduces the redundancy which otherwise appears due to high intercorrelation between measures such as that found in the previous analysis between career length and number of games played.

Table 2 shows the results of such an analysis for the previously presented data. In the present data significant functions distinguishing managers from non-managers can be identified for both pitchers and non-pitchers. For the fifteen managers from pitching backgrounds a function consisting of length of career (CARLEN) and prestige of clubs played for (PLAPRES) shows a Wilks Lambda of .497 and a chi-square which is significant well beyond the .01 level ($X^2 = 35.58$, df = 2, p.<.000). In predicting individual cases by this function, 79.6% of the predictions placed the player in the correct category. Hence, it may be said that, in comparison to other pitchers, those selected to be managers had significantly longer careers and played for higher prestige teams. Addition of the other measures found to be significant by the t-test did not add significantly to the predictive power of this discriminant function.

For the 156 non-pitcher managers, a significant function ($X^2 = 37.95$, df = 4, p.<.000) was identified which distinguished them from the 61 non-managers in the control group. This function demonstrated a Lambda of .837 and consisted of games played, games per year, prestige of clubs played for and number of championships in which the player participated. Managers in this category participated in more games, played for higher prestige clubs and participated in more championships than did non-managers from these positions. Interestingly, once the number of games played had been taken into account, games per year showed up as a discriminating measure in spite of being a non-significant difference according to the original t-test. Managers, in fact, showed a somewhat lower games per year average (88.3 vs. 88.8). This difference, while theoretically interesting, is not of much practical value in identifying prospective managers due to the very small difference in the raw data. This function, when used as a basis for predicting the individual cases, successfully classified 70.5% of the 217 players in this analysis.

Once having identified the factors associated with selection to a managerial position, it becomes logical to seek the qualities, if any, distinguishing successful managers from less successful managers. But what factor should be selected as the criterion of success? While winning percentage and championships won are traditional indicators of success in sport, perhaps prestige of teams managed (see Loy and Sage, 1978) and longevity as a manager, each in their own way, indicate a form of success. Rather than choose among them it was decided to examine each singly and then to attempt to identify managers high in multiple measures as a roster of "super-star" managers in order to see if they share some unique construct of playing and/or early qualities.

In order to avoid spuriously high measures of association it was necessary to develop measures of "later career" success not inclusive of the achievement of the first year(s) in the league. Hence reference is made to later career performance or later career prestige to distinguish these measures from overall career averages.

Given the low number of ex-pitcher managers (15) and the relative lack of success of these managers (Kjeldsen, 1981) it was decided to confine the analysis of success as a manager to the non-pitchers only.

Later career performance (LCPERF) as a criterion variable. The winning percentage of each manager was calculated exclusive of his first year as a manager and exclusive of any year in which he replaced another manager during the season. It did, however, include seasons during which he was replaced by another manager. On the basis of these winning percentages, managers were divided into a more successful group ($+.520$, $N = 38$) and a less successful group ($-.520$, $N = 118$). Table 3 shows the findings for these groups.

A significant discriminating function (Lambda $= .754$, $X^2 = 43.00$, df $= 4$, p. $< .000$) was identified by the analysis which was successful in predicting 73.7 percent of the cases in the two groups. The single most powerful distinguishing quality between the successful and the less successful on later career winning percentage is winning percentage in the first year of managing. A higher number of games played and having managed a championship team during the first two years as a manager also distinguished between greater and lesser success on this criterion variable. The analysis indicated that the number of championships participated in was also useful in this distinction; however, this influence operated in a negative direction. This direction or distinction is not reflected in the raw data (successful mgrs $= 1.9$ championships, less successful managers $= 1.8$ championships) and may only emerge after the discriminating qualities of the other factors is taken into account.

Later career championships (LCCHAMP) as a criterion variable. In this analysis managers who won three or more league championships in their later career (i.e., after their first two years) were identified as the high success group ($N = 9$) and those who won two or less as the lower success group ($N = 147$). A significant function (Lambda $= .884$, $X^2 = 18.58$, df $= 7$, p. $< .01$) was identified which consisted of seven factors. The most powerful statistical discriminator was length of playing career. However, this is not apparent in the raw data as the difference between the groups is only one year (14.3 to 13.3 in favor of the more successful managers). Successful managers were initially hired by teams of higher prestige (2.89 vs. 2.21 on a scale 1-4) and performed better in their first year as a manager (.543 vs. .476). Interestingly, their performance record as a player was inferior (.247 vs. 267) and they

played in a lesser number of games (1165 vs. 1291) and participated on a lesser number of championship teams (189 vs. 1.92).
They were also hired at a somewhat younger age (34.9 yrs. vs. 38.9
yrs.). The most effective discriminators, given the closeness of the
raw data on some of the selected factors, appear to be performance
in the first year of managership, batting average as a player and the
prestige of the team which first hires him. It is also interesting to
note that managers successful on championships won were also
highly successful on the other dependent variables (winning % =
.544 vs. .391, prestige of clubs managed = 3.09 vs. 2.03 and
number of years managed = 25.7 vs. 6.2). Sorting out the temporal (hence the causal) connections among these career variables
is impossible; therefore, they are not considered as potential
explanatory variables.

   *Later career prestige of teams managed (LCPRES) as a criterion
variable.* The prestige of teams played for and/or managed was
determined by a scaled ordering of franchises on the basis of championships won during the period of the study (range = 1 to 4, with
4 equaling high prestige). This resulted in a bias toward teams with
a long history of success on the field based on the assumption that
this is the "stuff" of which prestige in major league baseball is
made. It resulted in classifying all "expansion" teams in the lower
prestige category. While there may be other ways to represent
prestige, the ordering had a certain face validity to it. Managers
were classified as managers of higher success if they had a later
career average prestige score of 2.5 (N = 51) or higher; scores lower
than 2.5 (N = 105) were placed in the lower success category. A
significant function was identified which discriminated among
managers in these categories (Lambda = .752, X^2 = 43.54, df = 2,
p. < .000). The most powerful determinant of later career prestige
is the prestige of the first team which hires the manager (raw
data = 2.9 vs. 1.9). Playing performance also discriminates
between these groups but the raw data on batting average do not
differ sufficiently to be effective in practical terms (.273 vs. .263).
However, on the basis of these two factors, 76.9 percent of the cases

were correctly predicted. Hence, the function does have predictive power.

Number of years managed (YRSMGD) as a criterion variable. The raw number of years managed was also used as an indicator of success as a manager. Those who managed ten years or more in the major leagues were considered the success group (N = 39) and the remainder (N = 117) as the less successful group. Needless to say, such "durability" was highly associated with the other dependent measures (rs of .44, .28 and .76 on LCPERF, LCPRES and LCCHAMP respectively). Data for the playing and early managerial career appear in Table 4. A highly significant discriminant function was identified (Lambda = .852, $X^2 = 24.17$, df = 6. p. < .001) which successfully classified 74.4 percent of the cases in the groups. The length of the career and the number of games played are the most powerful statistical predictors. Years played is positively associated with durability while total games played is negative in its association. This seems contradictory at first glance and implies that games per year should be a better predictor. In fact, games per year is lower for the durable managers (80.2 vs. 91.0). However, this must be combined with a lengthy career before there is predictive power for number of years managed. Championships managed in the first two years and managerial performance in the first year are also positively associated with durability, while championship teams played on and age at first job are lower for managers of greater longevity.

An attempt was made to identify a discriminating function for the number of teams managed. However, managers who led four or more teams could not be distinguished from managers of lesser number of teams by any discriminant function. Therefore, this measure was dropped from further analysis. However, there was a trend toward these managers being more regular players (GAMSYR = 99 vs. 87) and being more likely to have been hired by higher prestige teams and to have managed a championship team during their first two years of employment as a manager.

Prestige of first club (MPRSFST) as a criterion variable. What qualities does a hiring club look for when there is no managerial record to go on? Discriminant function analysis was used in an attempt to answer that question. For non-pitchers, a significant discriminant function was identified which consisted of only one measure from the playing career — that is, average prestige of clubs played for. No other playing career characteristic discriminated between those non-pitchers who were hired by high prestige teams in their first job and those who were hired by low prestige teams. Table 5 shows that, by itself, prestige of teams played for correctly placed sixty-six percent of the cases in the study group (Lambda = .926, X^2 = 11.83, df = 1, p. < .001). Apparently, the prestige of the teams a player played for was more influential in selection to leadership than any measure of achievement and/or experience.

A similar analysis was carried out for the pitchers. A discriminating function was identified; however, it failed to achieve signficance at the .05 level. Since this lack of significance may be due to the low number in the group of pitcher-managers (15), and since the function correctly predicted 73.3 percent of the players in the group, the results will not be disregarded. Length of career (− 1.02), prestige of team played for (− 1.26), and championship teams played on (1.04) were identified as the components of the function. Hence, pitchers selected to manage high prestige teams in their first jobs (N = 6) had shorter careers (14.5 yrs. to 16.0 yrs.), played on teams of lower prestige (2.67 to 3.2) and played on more championship teams (2.5 to 1.67) than pitchers selected to manage teams of lower prestige (n = 9). These findings are surprising when compared to those for non-pitchers and must be regarded tentatively due to the low number. However, they appear to reinforce the pattern that pitchers are selected to managerial positions on criteria different from those applied for non-pitchers.

DISCUSSION

This study attempted to examine the playing and early managerial career characteristics which are associated with selection to and success in positions of managership in major league baseball. Tests of the significance of found differences were used initially to examine differences between players who were selected as managers and those who were not to become managers. This analysis revealed that managers were players with long careers who had played with high prestige clubs and who had participated in more championship competition than non-managers. In addition, pitchers who became managers had superior performance records in comparison to those who were not selected to managerial positions. This was not true for non-pitcher managers. These findings appear to support a visibility model of managerial selection for non-pitchers and visibility plus achievement model for pitchers. That is to say, for non-pitchers, participation over a long period of time on high prestige teams in multiple championships seems to be related to selection to managership to a degree greater than personal achievements as a performer. Such a pattern of participation may be hypothesized to lead to higher than average visibility to the baseball executives who select people to management. Pitchers, on the other hand, apparently seem to have to add a quality performance component in order to be selected as a manager.

The visibility model was supported for both pitchers and non-pitchers by the multi-variate approach of discriminant function analysis. Measures of career length and prestige (pitchers) and the above two plus participation in championships (non-pitchers) identified those who would become managers.

The assessment of success is a much more complex process. As a global concept, managerial success includes many criteria, and there is serious question as to whether there is an adequate global indicator of success. Hence, this analysis was restricted to an examination of the separate criteria in general usage for the evaluation of a manager, (i.e., winning percentage, number of championships won, prestige of teams managed and length of career as a manager). Significant discriminant functions were identified which distinguished the more successful from the less successful according to these criteria. Unfortunately, (but understandably) these discriminant functions were different for each of the success criteria making it impossible to identify any set of core characteristics which contribute to overall success as a manager. Three variables, however, showed consistent directions of influence for three of the four criteria. The extent of the career (either number of games played or length of career), the number of championship teams played on and the managerial performances in the first year of managing all contributed to the performance (LCPERF and LCCHAMP) and longevity (YRSMGD) criteria. A long playing career and high performance in the first year of managing were both associated with success as a manager; while, surprisingly, successful managers played on a lesser number of championship teams than did managers of lesser success.

Each of the success criteria demonstrates an interesting construct of measures which are associated with it. For example, performance in the first year of management is the best predictor of later career performance. The second strongest predictor is championships won in the first year of management. It appears that successful managers are successful from the beginning of their careers rather than improving with age. That this is also related to longevity as a manager is demonstrated by their positive association with number of years managed.

An across dependent variable analysis seems to reveal some support for the marginal player hypothesis. A consistent set of relationships seems to indicate that successful managers (i.e., high performing and durable managers) tend to be those who had long playing careers but played in a lesser number of games (i.e., a non-regular status), players who played on a lower number of championship teams and players who were somewhat lower in their batting average in comparison to the less successful managers.

A most interesting set of findings emerge when we examine prestige of teams managed as a dependent variable. Later career prestige is best predicted by prestige of the team which first hired the manager and the prestige of the first team is best predicted by the prestige of the teams the person played for. In each case little

else contributed to the prediction of subsequent levels of prestige.
Player performance level contributed to some degree to the understanding of later career prestige but average prestige of teams
played for was the sole predictor of prestige level of the first job.
This pattern supports the findings of Loy and Sage who also used
organizational set theory to explain the job prestige of college
football and basketball coaches.

Table 3

Discriminant Function Analysis
Success: LCPERF Dependent

Function: Lambda = .754, X^2 = 43.00 (4) p. < .000

GAMES	.323
CHAMP	-.381
CHFST	.430
MPRFST	.788

Cases: 73.7% correct

Table 4

Discriminant Function Analysis
Success: YRSMGD Dependent

Function: Lambda = .852, X^2 = 24.17 (6) p. < .001

CARLEN	1.176
GAMES	-1.180
CHAMP	- .363
CHFST	.573
AGEFST	- .272
MPRFST	.393

Cases: 74.4% correct

Table 5

Discriminant Function Analysis
MPRESFST Dependent

Function: Lambda = .926, X^2 = 11.83 (1) p. < .001

PLAPRES	1.000

Cases: 66.00 correct

SUMMARY

Discriminant function analysis has been demonstrated to be a useful tool in examining factors which distinguish the various stages of a career in the management of professional baseball. It has provided insight into the selection of a player to a managerial career and into the career factors which distinguish the more successful from the less successful. In general, it lends weight to several theoretical concepts. First is the importance of visibility, through participation over a long period for high prestige teams and in championship competition, for selection as a manager. Second, it tends to support the concept that successful managers come from the ranks of less regular players who were somewhat less successful in terms of participating on championship teams. Third, it provides consistent support for the idea that high prestige teams tend to select their managers from other high prestige teams (either former managers or ex-players) rather than on the basis of either their playing and/or early managerial record.

Further research is still to be done with this data. The technique of path analysis seems potentially fruitful for analyzing the sequential paths followed by managers as they proceed through the stages of their career, and the development of some multimeasure criterion of success may enable us to develop a roster of super-star managers (see Kjeldsen, 1981) and to seek those playing and early managerial characteristics which distinguish them from less successful managers (if any). Additionally, these analyses for professional baseball await extension to other sports to determine if there are common patterns across the spectrum of sports. Finally, such findings from a quantitative approach need to be compared with findings which emerge from a variety of qualitative orientations.

NOTE

The modal career for an initial random selection was one year as a player. This supports Rosenberg's findings (1980) regarding the careers of professional athletes. Such a comparison group would be invalid since it would produce data reflective of players generally unsuccessful as major league players. Since the managers were apparently drawn from those who were successful as players (at least in terms of longevity), the criterion of five years as a major league player was established for selection into the comparison group.

REFERENCES

Grusky, O.
    1963 "The Effect of formal structure on the management recruitment: a study of baseball organization." Sociometry 26: 345-53.
Kjeldson, E.
    1981 "Centrality and leadership recruitment: a study of their linkage." Review of Sport and Leisure6(2): 1-20.
Loy, J. W., J. E. Curtis, and J. N. Sage
    1979 "Relative centrality of playing positions and leadership recruitment in team sports." Pp. 257-84 in R. S. Hutton (ed.), Exercise and Sports Sciences Reviews, Vol. 6, 1978. Philadelphia: Franklin Institute Press.
Loy, J. W., and G. H. Sage
    1978 "Athletic personnel in the academic marketplace." Sociology of Work and Occupations 5 (4): 446-69.
Nie, N. H., et al
    1975 SPSS Manual, 2d. Ed., New York: McGraw-Hill.
Rosenburg, E.
    1980 "Gerontological theory and athletic retirement." Paper presented at Second Annual Conference of the North American Society for the Sociology of Sport, Denver, CO, October, 1981.
Turkin, H., and S. C. Thompson
    1979 The Official Encyclopedia of Baseball. Garden City, N.Y. Doubleday.

Chapter 7

QUANTITY OR QUALITY: NON-LINEAR RELATIONSHIPS BETWEEN EXTENT OF INVOLVEMENT AND INTERNATIONAL SPORTING SUCCESS[1]

Jane Colwell, University of Western Ontario

Originally talent was a sufficient condition to be successful in international sporting competitions. A simple comparison of the performances of individual athletes was a reasonably precise measure of success. Today a variety of economic, political and social conditions influence the level of athletic achievement reached. International sporting success is now a product of many complex interacting influences, and attempting to define or to account for international sporting success is a complex task requiring consideration of these interactions.

A myriad of factors have been used as independent variables by researchers attempting to account for the differential levels of success achieved by different nations. The selection of these variables often appears to have been made on an ad hoc basis with few theoretical linkages outlined between the dependent and independent variables.[2] Similarly, the selection of the dependent variables(s) appears to have frequently been made with no statement of the theoretical definition or of the rationale behind the choice of operational definition. This paper explores the dependent measures used in previous studies to determine if there are different kinds of international sporting success which have been examined. Detailed consideration is given to the influence of the extent

TABLE 1

OLYMPIC YEAR, AND OPERATIONALIZATION OF

THE DEPENDENT VARIABLE USED IN PREVIOUS

STUDIES

STUDY (YEAR)	OLYMPIC YEAR(S)	THEORETICAL CONCEPT	OPERATIONAL MEASURE SELECTED
Snyder (1936)	1936	Winners	Ideal/real scores of medal points adjusted for population
Jokl (1964)	1896-1960	Athletic Efficiency	Individual standings - point allocation system based on individual rank and number in event
Ibrahim (1969)	1896-1968	Olympic Achievement	Total number of points based on medal winners (3-2-1)/population
Seppanen (1970)	1896-1968	Success Sports Achievement	Coefficient of success; actual/expected medal points (3-2-1); points/ population;
Ball (1972)	1964	Overall olympic performance; national team success;	Total points based on medal winners (3-2-1)
Novikov & Maximenko (1972)	1964	Sports Achievement	Jokl's point allocation system - individual standings;
Levine (1974)	1972	Olympic Games Success	Total number of medals
Grimes, Kelly & Rubin (1974)	1972	National Olympic Performance	Total number of medals
Sutphen (1976)	1956-1972	Success Performance	Snyder's success index: Medal pts/population;
Shaw & Pooley (1976)	1972	National Success	Total points based on top 6 places (6-5-4-3-2-1)
Kiviaho & Makela (1978)	1964	Success Superior performance	Absolute success based on top 8 places; relative success adjusted for population;
Gillis (1980)	1896-1976	Olympic Success	Success index= proportion of points earned for proportion of total population;
Colwell (1981)	1976	International Sporting Success	TOTRANK = Summed ranking over entire Olympic Program ADJRANK = Average rank achieved for only events entered REALRANK = summed ranking for only events entered MEDAL = Total # of medals won.

of involvement of nations at the 1976 Summer Olympic Games and the level of national success achieved. The first section presents the dependent variable selection in previous studies and summarizes the operational and theoretical definitions. This is followed by an analysis of the influence of the extent of involvement on national success for the competing nations as a whole and as distinguished by the United Nations Conference on Trade and Development.

DEPENDENT MEASURES USED IN PREVIOUS STUDIES

This section relates, chronologically, the operational and theoretical definitions of "success" which have been used to date. A variety of dependent measures have been used, and the terminology for the dependent variable is almost as varied as the methods of calculating the nation's level of performance in the Olympic Games (Table 1).

In an early study examining the "winners" of the Olympic Games, Snyder (1936:372) focused on determining the "real position of excellence" of the competing nations. He believed that the absolute scores, generated by the Associated Press based on medal counts, were not representative of the "respective relative positions of excellence" (1936:372) of the competing nations. Snyder assumed that given equal opportunity and training, the total score of points achieved by a nation should be in proportion to their population. In order to compare the actual points won to those expected, based on the size of the population, he calculated a ratio of the total points awarded and the total population of the competing nations. This coefficient was then multiplied by the population of each nation to determine the expected number of points for that nation. By dividing the actual earned score by this ideal score he generated a percentage of the ideal number of points actually achieved by a nation. The shift in rankings was quite interesting. The smaller northern countries exceeded their ideal or expected scores by as much as five times, while the United States only gained 64.8% of their expected score and fell from second position to fourteenth position. The explanations offered by Snyder for this phenomenon are not very satisfactory, but even at this early stage, the intervening influence of population size was demonstrated. His use of a gross adjustment for population size, without due consideration given to the quality (e.g. health, stature) or distribution (e.g., age, sex) of the population is problematic. Further consideration of the theoretical implications of this operational adjustment to the dependent variable are required.

Jokl (1964) used the term "athletic efficiency" in his study. He devised a point allocation system for each individual performance in accordance with the number of participants in each event. Ibrahim (1969) was concerned with the operational measurement of "Olympic achievement." However, he restricted his study to an examination of the achievement of the medal winners, or only the top three positions in each event. He made a gross adjustment to the total number of points a nation received based on the "achievements" of the medal winners adjusted for the size of the population of the nation. Theoretically, this measurement of "Olympic Achievement," which excludes the performances of the majority of the competitors (those who didn't win medals) is highly suspect. Adjusting his dependent measure for the size of the population of the nation, without considering the total number of athletes representing the nation also raises more questions than it answers. For example, what factors influence the proportion of the population which become elite athletes? Seppanen (1970) was also interested in adjusting the scores for the populations of the nations. He measured "success" using a coefficient of actual versus expected points achieved, by dividing the per mille of total points a nation received by the per mille of the world population.

The 1972 study by Ball was indicative of a study with a more sociological approach and greater explanatory value. He focused on what he termed "Overall Games success." The only explanation offered regarding the theoretical basis for selecting this dependent variable was that it was to be measured in terms of overall national team performance. To operationalize this concept he used a 3-2-1 (Gold, Silver, Bronze) point system based on medal counts. "Overall Games success" was a simple summation of the point counts for the medals awarded. The performances of other competing athletes were not examined.

Novikov and Maximenko (1972) returned to the concept of sport achievement. They operationalized the "level of achievement" of the participating nations based on Jokl's (1964) system of point allocation. The use of the term "level of achievement" and the measurement of the concept based on individual performances suggests that the independent variables include factors such as motivation, reward structure, basic physiological potentiality and previous levels of performance attained. This is not the case. Rather, the independent variables draw upon aggregate data sources which use the nation as the unit of analysis.

Sutphen (1973) also used an adjustment factor to generate a measure of the percentage ideal score realized in an effort to determine the "real position of excellence of each country vis a vis all others." Using medal winnings, he employed Snyder's (1936:372-374) method to generate an ideal score for each country. This index (medal point score total for all nations competing/Total population) is multiplied by the population of each country to generate an ideal number of points expected based on the size of the population. A percentage of the ideal versus the actual points received by the medal winners from each nation is then calculated. This is a preferable measure to the gross adjustment based on raw population scores because it accounts for the population in proportion to other nations represented, and the actual level of performance in proportion to the performance of other nations. However, no consideration is given to the size of the team representing the nation, in proportion to its population, and the study only examines medal winning nations. Grimes, Kelly and Rubin (1974) also restricted their study to medal winners. Their concept, "National Olympic Performance," was measured by the total number of medals won.

Levine (1974) emphasized that the Olympic Games competitions were no longer competitions between individuals, but between nations. He measured the extent to which Olympic success is *not* just a random factor associated with competing individuals by focusing on the differences between nations to isolate characteristics of Olympic success. He selected the total number of medals won as his operational measure of "Olympic Games success." There was no theoretical explanation offered for the selection of this concept or its operational measure.

Pooley *et al*, (1975) and Shaw and Pooley (1976) used the top six places (6-5-4-3-2-1) to determine their measure of "national success." This increased the sample size in their studies, but few explanations were offered for the implications of using this measure of success as opposed to medal winners. Kiviaho and Makela (1978) made the distinction between absolute success and relative success measures. Absolute success was measured by the points received for the top eight finishers (8-7-6-5-4-3-2-1). Relative success took this raw score and adjusted it for the nation's population. No details were given as to how this adjustment was performed. They demonstrated that different independent variables are important in explaining the variation in each of these measures.

Gillis (1980) used an index of success relativized for population. She used the top six finishers (6-5-4-3-2-1) for each event, adjusted for the total number of points awarded, divided by the ratio of the nation's population to the total population represented. Colwell (1981) used three measures of international sporting success. TOTRANK, a measure of a nation's performance over the entire program of Summer Olympic events, considered both the level of performance and the extent of involvement of athletes from the competing nations. A second measure ADJRANK, was a calculated average (from REALRANK total rank standing) of the competing athletes for each nation, with no bonus or penalty for the range of sports or events entered. This is a measure of the effectiveness of performance. A third dependent measure, MEDAL, is a summation of the number of medals won by athletes from each nation, and is conceptualized as a measure of international sporting success only among the successful (i.e. medal winning) nations.

This brief overview of the dependent measures used in previous studies highlights the diversity of measures of "success" which have been investigated. Various researchers expressed concern for the influence of the size of the competing teams on the measures of success they used. A range of manipulations to the absolute success scores was made in an attempt to adjust the measure of success. Indeed it appears that the stress has been placed on generating operational measures, with few attempts to arrive at a theoretical understanding of the concept prior to constructing an operational definition. Another severe limitation of many of the previous studies is that the samples have been restricted (by the dependent variable selection) to only successful nations. This choice of medal counts or top rankings as the measure of success appears to be one of availability for most researchers and not one which has been theoretically justified. The external validity of studies restricted in this way must be questioned.

Colwell (1981b) has the only study to include all competing nations. Her findings suggest that some of the factors found to be important in accounting for different levels of "medal-winning" are not as important when all competing nations are analyzed. This highlights the limitations of the dependent variable selection of many of the previous studies.

Kiviaho and Makela (1978) illustrated that absolute success and relative success (adjusted for population) are explained by different factors. Colwell's findings (1981b) support this. Her comparisons between overall success as measured by TOTRANK and success adjusted for the extent of involvement (ADJRANK) illustrate that there are different kinds of success. The extent of involvement was shown to influence strongly the level of success achieved as measured by different dependent variables. The relationship between extent of involvement and international sporting success is examined in more detail in the next section.

EXTENT OF INVOLVEMENT AND INTERNATIONAL SPORTING SUCCESS

International sporting success, or success of any kind, is related to the effective use of resources to achieve some established goal. Several factors may intervene between the resources available and the attainment of international sporting success. These factors may be classified broadly as factors within the control of the social system (e.g. number of athletes sent to a competition), and factors outside the control of the social system (e.g. size of the country). A researcher may choose to ignore these factors and select an absolute measure of international sporting success, such as number of medals won by each nation. Conversely, a measure taking into consideration certain factors which may influence the level of success achieved, may be selected as the dependent variable for relative success.

Factors within the control of the system which affect the performance of nations, and which might be considered as relative success measures include the extent or range of involvement. For international sport the system controls to a large extent which sports are developed to an elite level, and the extent (e.g., number of events) and range (e.g., number of sports) of involvement in international sporting competitions. Obviously the size of the team competing in any competition increases the chances of achieving some measure of success. Additionally, the number of events and the number of sports competed in influence the nation's chances for success as measured by absolute overall standards. Therefore, some measure of the effectiveness of the performance of the athletes from each nation, regardless of the extent of involvement, might also be considered as a measure of international sporting success. Lenk (1976:150) has cautioned that there is "no just and precise assessment of national athletic superiority." It is thus important that the variety of dependent variables used in recent studies be examined and possible intervening factors identified. This study focuses on the relationship between the extent of involvement in the 1976 Summer Olympics and the level of national success achieved.[3]

To assess the importance of the degree of involvement on the dependent measures of success, the nature of the relationship between absolute performance as measured by REALRANK (summed rankings of individual performances for all events competed in) and Z (the number of events not competed in) was examined to determine if there is a straight linear increase in REALRANK as the number of events competed in increases.[4] The bivariate correlation for NEVENTS and REALRANK ($r = .77$) suggests that this is the case, but an examination of the plot (Figure 1) of this relationship reveals a possible curvilinear relationship. An analysis was therefore made to determine the amount of variance in REALRANK which could be accounted for by a 2-factor model based on number of events not competed in. Eighty-one percent of the variance in REALRANK can be accounted for in this way compared to 62% using a linear relationship between success and number of events.

To examine this curvilinear relationship graphically, the parameter estimates from this analysis were substituted into a quadratic equation which is solved in order to find the coordinates of the vertex of the parabola. This point and the intercepts are then used to fit the curve to the data.

Inspection of the plot of the quadratic equation (Figure 1) suggests that the vertex of the parabola represents a "point of minimal" returns which is reached before increasing the number of events "payoffs" in an improved overall level of performance. In other words, the highest point on the parabolic curve represents a nation which has increased the number of events entered (decreased Z) and has shown a concomitant increase in the REALRANK scores. After this point, the curve suggests that any further increased involvement will not lead to an improvement in overall performance (reduced REALRANK).

To determine if all nation groups fit the patterned relationship suggested by Figure 1 another plot of the relationship between REALRANK and Z was made using separate codings for

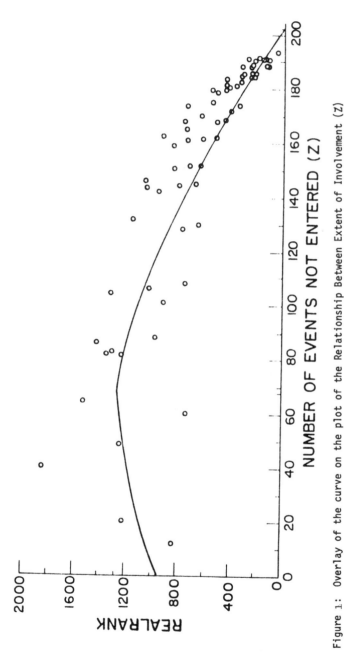

Figure 1: Overlay of the curve on the plot of the Relationship Between Extent of Involvement (Z)
and International Sporting Success (REALRANK)

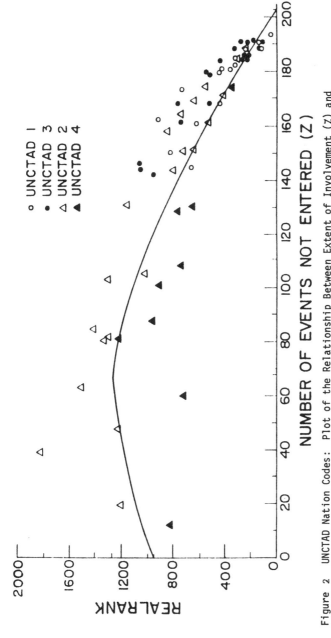

Figure 2 UNCTAD Nation Codes: Plot of the Relationship Between Extent of Involvement (Z) and

International Sporting Success (REALRANK)

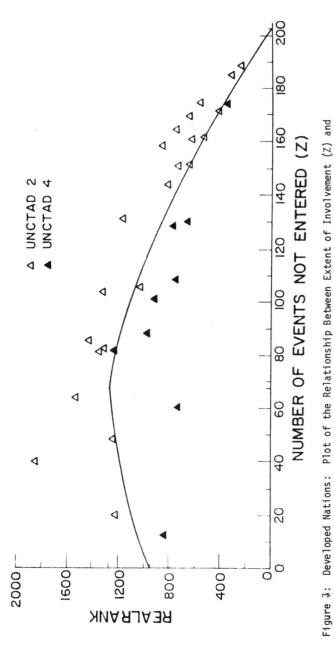

Figure 3:   Developed Nations: Plot of the Relationship Between Extent of Involvement (Z) and
International Sporting Success (REALRANK)

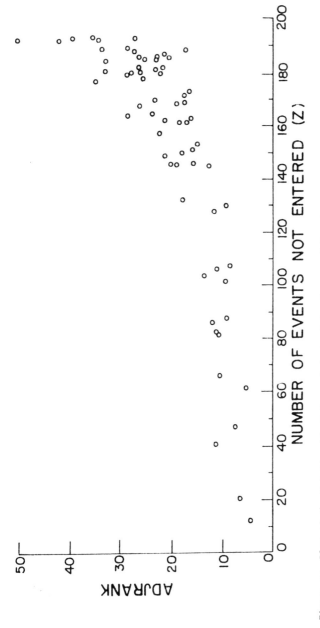

Figure 4:   Plot of the Relationship Between Extent of Involvement (Z) and International
            Sporting Success (ADJRANK)

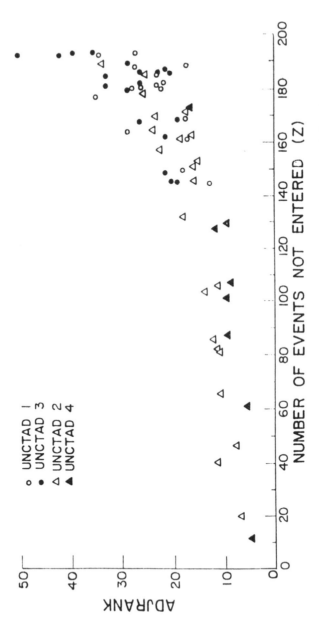

Figure 5: UNCTAD Nation Codes: Plot of the Relationship Between Extent of Involvement (Z) and

International Sporting Success (ADJRANK)

the UNCTAD nation groups (Figure 2). The developed nations (UNCTAD 2) exhibit a range of involvement (Z) and a range of success (REALRANK) which quite closely follows the parabola. Only a few nations have passed the "point of minimal returns" where greater investment is accompanied by greater accomplishments. One nation, Canada, at the extreme peak of the plot, appears to have made a considerable investment in the number of events and has not shown the improvement in overall performance (reduced REALRANK) during this Olympiad as suggested by the curve. This may be due to the privilege given to the host nation of entering an athlete into each event. Nations do not have to exercise this option, but in previous studies the host nations have been eliminated from the analysis. The greater number of events entered by Canada results in a slight advantage using the TOTRANK measure of success, but, as indicated in Figure 3, it does not necessarily result in improved levels of performance.

The socialist nations, as a group, also appear to illustrate this pattern. All of the nations in the UNCTAD 4 group (▲) (Figure 3) fall below the predictive curve, including those with limited involvement to date. The greater effectiveness of the socialist systems in achieving international sporting success is thus graphically illustrated. The German Democratic Republic stands out as a nation which has achieved the point where continued expansion in the level of involvement is associated with an improvement in overall performance. The Federal Republic of Germany and the United States have also passed the point of minimal returns, as suggested by the curve, and are increasing their level of involvement concomitantly with performance improvement.

The two groups of developing nations (UNCTAD 1 and UNCTAD 3) have limited involvement in the Olympic Games and are clustered on the lower right hand side of the curve (Figure 2). The Latin American developing nations (●) show an almost direct linear increase in REALRANK with increased involvement (reduced Z). In contrast, the other developing nations (○) have an initial linear increase followed by a dispersion of the nations away from the predictive curve. Yugoslavia (YUG) is an example of a nation which is successfully increasing involvement while improving overall performance level. (Nations falling under the predictive curve can be conceptualized as performing more effectively than other nations).

The theoretical problem of interpretation affiliated with the REALRANK measure was considered and a plot of the relationship between ADJRANK (REALRANK/#events) and Z was made (Figure 4). A curvilinear relationship, as suggested by Figure 1, was found. The average rank attained improves with increased involvement (decrease in Z), followed by a flattening of the curve where the average rank is maintained through increased involvement.

To assess if the different nation groups are consistent for this pattern, another plot (Figure 5) was constructed using the UNCTAD categories of nations. Similar patterns to that found in Figure 4 emerged. The developing nations (○, ●) have a higher average rank (ADJRANK) and more limited involvement. As the number of events entered increases, the average rank decreases. The developed nations (UNCTAD 2, ▲) exhibit a full range of involvement and success, which follows the general pattern of improved performance with increased involvement, followed by a leveling off. The socialist nations (UNCTAD 4, ▲) show their greater performance level by a lower ADJRANK at all levels of involvement.

This analysis, comparing absolute success (REALRANK) and extent of involvement (Z), demonstrates that the relationship is not linear but rather curvilinear. The predictive ability of the model is increased by 19% when a curvilinear relationship is specified. Figures 1 to 3 illustrate this relationship and demonstrate the position of the different nation groups (UNCTAD categories) along the predicted curve.

The number of events competed in clearly influences the level of international sporting success achieved by nations competing in the 1976 Summer Olympic Games. The relationship between extent of involvement and success is not linear but rather curvilinear. This suggests that any explanatory models attempting to account for differential levels of international sporting success must allow for curvilinearity. This is particularly true for studies examining all competing nations. Is it the quantity of athletes or the quality of performance which determines national sporting success? It appears that there is an interaction between extent of involvement and success which determines optimum national performance.

NOTES

[1]The financial and technical assistance of the Department of Kinesiology, University of Waterloo is acknowledged.

[2]One exception is Colwell (1981), who presented a conceptual framework with economic, political and social dimensions which outlined in propositional format the theoretical importance of each of the independent variables and their relationship to international sporting success.

[3]The findings reported in this paper are one section of the dissertation findings presented in Colwell (1981b). The reader is referred to this study for details of the dependent variable calculations for REALRANK and ADJRANK discussed in this paper.

[4]The original data file allocated a rank score for each nation for each event. In the event of a non-entry this value was the last place plus one. To generate the REALRANK scores and to count the number of events not entered (Z), a program was run which designated the total number of entries or last place finish for each event. The nations' rankings were then analyzed and those with values less than the last place finish were added to form the REALRANK score; if the value was greater than the last place finish their Z value was increased by one. Z is therefore a computed measure based on the last place finishes for each event which calculates the total number of events not entered by each nation.

REFERENCES

Ball, D. W.
  1972 "Olympic games competition: structural correlates of success." International Journal of Comparative Sociology 13:186-200.
Colwell, J.
  1981a "Sociocultural determinants of international sporting success." Pp. 242-261 in J. Segrave and D. Chu, (eds.), Olympism. Champaign, IL: Human Kinetics Publishers, Inc.
Colwell, J.
  1981b Sociocultural Determinants of International Sporting Success. Doctoral Dissertation, Kinesiology, University of Waterloo.
Gillis, J.
  1980 "Olympic success and religious orientation," Review of Sport and Leisure 5:2-20.
Grimes, A. R., W. Kelly and A. Rubin
  1974 "A socioeconomic model of national Olympic performance." Social Science Quarterly 55:777-783.

Ibrahim, H.
    "Olympic achievement and social differentiation." Whittier College. Unpublished paper in the files of the author.
Jokl, E.
    1964 "Health, wealth and athletics." In E. Jokl & E. Simon (eds.), International research in physical education. Springfield, IL: Thomas.
Kiviaho, P. and P. Makela
    1978 "Olympic success: A sum of non-material and material factors." International Review of Sport Sociology 2:5-17.
Lenk, H.
    1976 "Towards a social philosophy of the Olympics: values, aims, reality of the modern Olympic movement." Pp. 107-67 in P. Graham and H. Veberhorst (eds.), The Modern Olympics. Cornwall, N.Y.: Leisure Press.
Levine, N.
    1974 "Why do countries win Olympic gold medals? some structural correlates of Olympic games success: 1972." Sociology and Social Research 28:353-360.
Pooley, J., S. Shaw, J. Pare, and F. Promoli
    1975 "Winning at the Olympics: a quantitative analysis." Paper presented at the Association of Professional Health and Physical Education Research Assistants Annual Conference, Charlottetown.
Seppanen, P.
    1970 "The role of competitive sports in different societies." Proceedings of the 7th World Congress of Sociology. Varna.
Seppanen, P.
    1981 "Olympic success: a cross national perspective." Pp. 93-116 in G. Luschen and G. Sage (eds.). Handbook of Social Science of Sport. Champaign, IL: Stipes Publishing.
Shaw, S., and J. Pooley
    1976 "National success at the Olympics: an explanation." Proceedings 6th International Seminar: History of Physical Education and Sport. Trois Rivieres, Quebec.
Snyder, C.
    1936 "The real winners in the 1936 Olympic games." The Scientific Monthly 43:372-374.
Sutphen, R.
    1973 National Power and Olympic Success. Masters thesis. Memphis State University.

INVOLVEMENT IN SPORT: PROCESS AND OUTCOME

Section III

INVOLVEMENT IN SPORT: PROCESS AND OUTCOME

Socialization into and through sport has been and still is a salient area of research for sociologists interested in the study of sport. The four chapters in this section reflect this interest. The authors deal with how we become and remain involved in sport and what we learn through our involvement. The chapters reflect different approaches common in our field — theoretical (Brown), empirical (Hasbrook; Allison) and dialectic (Duquin).

Brown develops a conceptual model to analyze women's involvement in sport. In this model, involvement is defined as primary (e.g. athletic participation) and secondary (e.g., coaching and sports consumption). Brown also suggests that involvement can no longer be measured as a narrow unidimensional concept but should be analyzed as a process within the life cycle.

In a paper dealing with socialization into sport Hasbrook echoes the call for conceptual development sounded by Brown. She suggests that the unidirectional causal approach common in the literature does not adequately explain the process of socialization. Instead of the socializer exerting a one-way influence on the socializee, the process is really one of interaction between the parties involved. The reciprocal interaction between parents and children is examined in the socialization into sport of a sample of high school students.

Allison presents an analysis and discussion of "the nature of sportsmanship and fair play in sport." The author first provides some college student data to show that there are "distinct normative systems operating within sport which vary according to the sex and institutionalized competitive experience of the sub-

jects." Second, the author discusses several methodological problems which, she feels, detract from a meaningful assessment of the
nature of sportsmanship and fair play. The author concludes by
suggesting that we presently do *"not* really know what the term
sportsmanship means within the sport context," and by advancing
the contention that in order to achieve an understanding of sportsmanship, fair play, and ethical behavior in sport, we must *first*
come to understand the "norms" which guide behavior.

In the final chapter, Duquin focuses on values and structures
which have resulted in males holding onto superordinate status in
the professional world of physical education and sports. She states
that this continuing male domination is in part a result of the
socialization process. Combining socialist and radical feminist
theory, Duquin concludes that the growth of feminism in the
professional arena is dependent upon women correctly perceiving
their current status and uniting to change it.

Chapter 8

FEMALE SPORT INVOLVEMENT:
A PRELIMINARY CONCEPTUALIZATION

Barbara K. Brown, University of Waterloo

The recent past has witnessed, within the sociology and social psychology of sport, a tremendous increase in scholarly work related to the study of female involvement in sport. The accumulating body of literature has been described, however, as polemical, characterized by rhetoric (Loy *et al.*, 1978) and lacking in theoretical or paradigmatic grounding (Hall, 1978). More important, however, is the fact that the body of literature appears to lack any degree of conceptual coherence.

Traditional approaches to the study of women's involvement in sport have produced a vast array of facts — bricks for the sociology of sport brickyard (cf. McPherson, 1977) — with various contributions being linked only by virtue of their relationship to the nebulous notion of "female sport involvement." Although both the social commentary and data-based approaches have contributed to the growing body of literature, there is little evidence to suggest that the work has been in any sense cumulative. What is lacking is a framework within which the various contributions can be tied together.

The literature, with only a few exceptions (see Hall 1977, 1978, 1979, 1980), has been virtually devoid of critical evaluation. Hall's (1978) attempt to organize the literature according to major themes represents a singular attempt to introduce coherence to an otherwise chaotic collection of information. Although her effort succeeded in providing a general descriptive overview of the state of the art, it failed to accomplish her aim of integrating the existing literature into a meaningful whole. By concentrating on themes, she maintained the discrete, piecemeal character of the literature.

This paper argues the need for, and proposes a schema to, serve as an integrative framework within which the existing body of literature from sport sociology and social psychology, as well as related information from mainstream sociology and psychology, can be incorporated. Given that our ultimate purpose is to understand and explain female sport involvement, the framework suggested in this paper approaches the problem by viewing sport involvement as a process occurring within an historical, cultural and structural context. Such an approach allows us to identify the degree to which the body of literature has been cumulative, to identify those areas which have received research attention, to evaluate the adequacy of the information accumulated in terms of facilitating understanding of female sport involvement, and to identify those areas which remain to be explored.

THE DEVELOPMENT OF THE CONCEPTUAL SCHEMA

The Sport Involvement Process

The examination of female sport involvement demands a clear articulation of the phenomenon under consideration — that is, a clear and comprehensive delineation of what is to be included within the rubric of sport involvement. Like any other career, sport involvement can be conceived of most simplistically as a process extending through three broad phases from 1) initial exposure, through 2) participation to 3) retirement.

Yet, such a conceptualization is much too simplistic. The three broad categories ignore the inherent complexity of sport involvement which, from both a theoretical and empirical point of view, comprises the texture of what we, as sport sociologists, find interesting. There is a need, therefore, to focus attention on the complexity inherent in each of the three phases of the sport involvement process through consideration of options available at each stage.

Before such consideration can be given, however, there is a need to artciulate an acceptable definition of the focus of our attention, a definition which incorporates the full range of phenomena associated with female sport involvement. Let us turn first to a consideration of the term "sport." Although there have been numerous attempts at formulating a single acceptable definition for sport, these are concerned primarily, and most often exclusively, with delimiting the boundaries of sport itself, with defining the required characteristics necessary for a phenomenon to be labelled as sport. While somewhat useful for our purposes, such efforts fail to provide us with a comprehensive view of the total territory with which we are concerned.

A second course of action is to look to the literature in the area itself for some guidance as to what should be included. A cursory review of the literature to date would suggest that our definition of sport involvement has been somewhat narrow, confined almost exclusively to consideration of female involvement in sport in a competitive context.

Hall (1978:1) called for a broadening of the base of inquiry. She advocated that consideration be extended to include the "spectrum of physical activities which range from more recreational, unorganized pursuits of uncommitted individuals through competition at the highest levels requiring a high degree of intense commitment and arduous training." It must be recognized, however, that this definition, too, is inadequate for our purposes. It is unnecessarily restrictive, failing to acknowledge the full range of participation options available and the full constellation of sport roles in which females can become involved. It continues to focus only on those who are involved on the primary level *per se*, that is the active participants, ignoring involvement on the secondary level, those who are involved as coaches, managers, officials, administrators or consumers. In addition, the non-participant is ignored, as is the process of disengagement from involvement.

Sport involvement, in terms of our interests, then, can range from the purely recreational to the highly competitive as Hall (1978) pointed out. However, it can also take place on both amateur and professional levels; it can range from direct participation to involvement in a secondary role; and, in addition, may even concern non-involvement. Our conceptualization of sport involvement must thus encompass this full range of complexity inherent in the involvement process.

Initial exposure can result in either sport involvement or non-involvement. The non-involved may become involved at some later stage or may remain non-participants. Participation, too, is complex. Involvement can take place on either a secondary level as in the role of administrator, coach, manager, official or consumer or can occur at the primary level, that is, as an actual sport participant. Primary participation can be either recreational or competitive in nature and at the competitive level can be either amateur or professional. Retirement or disengagement from sport can involve a process of complete disassociation or may involve the maintenance of sport ties within a different role.

This representation is simplistic. It is not meant to imply that each of the options articulated in the schema is appropriate to every consideration of sport involvement nor that the sport involvement process proceeds necessarily through all of the possible options described. The involvement process is unquestionably far more complex than such a treatment suggests, no doubt involving numerous feedback loops and varying according to the population and particular sport situation under consideration. The schema has been formulated as a heuristic to assist in our conceptualization of and approach to the study of female sport involvement. It attempts to articulate the complexity inherent in the phenomenon we study and to provide a framework within which our ongoing research efforts can be integrated and interpreted.

At this point, it is appropriate to consider the existing body of literature relating to female sport involvement within the context of the schema proposed. The major themes of our work have changed little from those identified and examined by Hall (1978). Studies relating to female sport socialization encompassing both early childhood and continuing socialization, sport and femininity, role conflict, demographic and psychological profiles of participants and gender role socialization continue to dominate the literature.

Table 1 presents a preliminary (and far from complete) categorization of existing research according to the structure of the sport involvement schema. If we consider the focus of our attention to date, it becomes very clear that scholars purporting to have an interest in the sociology and social-psychology of female sport involvement have been concerned with only a very narrow definition of the phenomenon. Table 1 clearly indicates where that focus of attention has been directed. Competitive amateur sport has received the overwhelming majority of research attention.

The antecedents of sport involvement, those phenomena conceptualized to be of interest in the *exposure phase* of the sport involvement schema proposed, have received minimal attention in the literature. Barriers to involvement, the dispelling of biological and physiological myths and gender role socialization have received some limited degree of attention. These treatments have been located primarily within the body of literature labelled as social commentaries and the discussions presented have rarely received empirical verification. Although they represent one place in our literature in which we have drawn on information from disciplines outside our own (e.g., sociology and social psychology of gender roles, socialization), there remains to be tapped a continually expanding wealth of literature available from a number of disciplines.

Empirical attention directed towards the *exposure phase* has been limited. It has tended to be in the form of *ex post facto* surveys of competitive athletes examining socialization influences on their sport involvement patterns early in their lives. Thus, despite the fact that there has been some research attention directed to the *exposure phase* of the sport involvement process, there has been a tendency for it to be limited primarily to a narrow range of sport

Table 1

Categorization of the Literature Within the Schema

EXPOSURE PHASE

1. Involved

Brown, 1981; Harris, 1975; Lewko & Ewing, 1980; Smith, 1979.

PARTICIPATION PHASE

1a. Direct Involvement - Competitive - Amateur

Armitage, 1976; Eird & Williams, 1980; Brown, 1981; Butt,
1980; Butt & Schroeder, 1980; Coffey, 1973; Colker & Widom,
1980; Croxton & Klonsky, 1980; Davenport, 1978; Drancff,
1980; Duda & Roberts, 1980; Duquin, 1978a; Felshin, 1973,
1974a,b; Feltz, 1979; Fitness & Amateur Sport, 1980; Greendorfer, 1977a,b, 1978a,b; Hackman, 1978; Harris, 1975; Hasbrook & Greendorfer, 1980; Hawkes et al., 1975; Hogan, 1976;
Holland & Oglesby, 1979; Kingsley et al., 1977; Knoppers &
Weiss, 1980; Koehler, 1973; Kuscsik, 1976; Lewko & Ewing,1980; McElroy & Willis, 1979; McHugh et al., 1978;
McPherson et al., 1977; Myers & Lips, 1978; Ogilvie &
McGuire, 1980; Rohrbaugh, 1979; Sage & Loudermilk, 1979;
Scanlon & Passer, 1979; Smith, 1979; Snyder et al., 1976;
Soutar, 1979; Statistics Canada, 1977; Stone, 1979; Sutton-
Smith, 1979; Uguccioni & Ballantyne, 1980; Wark & Wittig,
1979; Westkott & Coakley, 1981.

1b. Direct Involvement -Competitive - Professional

Theberge 1977, 1980.

1c. Direct Involvement - Recreational

Harris, 1974; Heit & Malpass, 1974; Statistics Canada, 1977;
Unkel, 1981.

2. Secondary Involvement

Fitness and Amateur Sport, 1980; Theberge, 1981.

RETIREMENT PHASE

Butt, 1970; McPherson et al., 1977; Ogilvie & McGuire, 1980;
Westkott & Coakley, 1981.

involvement—sport participants involved directly in an amateur competitive context.

Our primary concern, as is clear from Table 1, has been with the *participation phase* of the sport involvement process and our focus has been the examination of direct sport involvement in an amateur, competitive context. Even within this narrow definition of sport involvement, our attention has been severely restrictive. Efforts have often been sport-specific with little indication of the generalizability of findings to other sport situations. In addition, such efforts have primarily provided snapshot views of the sport world. There has been little attention paid to the pattern of the sport career nor to the identification of relevant influences at various stages of the sport career.

Direct participation at either the recreational or professional levels has been virtually ignored. It might be argued that sport involvement at the recreational level falls outside of the legitimate jurisdiction of the sport sociologist, that it is the concern of sociologists whose focus is leisure behaviour. However, it should be recognized that recreational involvement by females in sport and physical activity represents only one category in a vast array of recreational pursuits ranging from participation in cultural activities to tourism. Thus, sport and physical activity participation is rarely the sole focus of inquiry for researchers interested in the sociology of leisure. Furthermore, within the context of the sport involvement schema proposed here, it is important that, as sport sociologists, we give consideration to the full range of sport involvement which necessarily includes this category of participation.

We have similarly all but ignored sport involvement on the non-direct level. We have given scant attention to involvement in such secondary roles as coach, manager, administrator, official or sport consumer.

There has been a dearth of attention to what could be classified within the *retirement phase* of the sport involvement schema. We have yet to examine the female sport drop-out with any intensity, nor have we examined to any great extent the retirement and adjustment patterns of those who retire after the termination of their sport career. What limited attention there has been to the retirement of females from sport has once again been concerned with athletes participating in the competitive context. Disengagement from sport involvement at other levels has been ignored.

What is of perhaps most significance in regard to the focus of our concern, is the fact that research attention, to date, has tended to concentrate on the most specialized levels of participation — those levels which have the fewest participants when one considers sport in its broadest context. The bulk of the population are non-participants[1] or participants in a recreational context. Yet a minority of research attention has focused on participation at these levels. It should be emphasized, however, that what is theoretically interesting is not the involvement level *per se* nor the role within which the participant is involved, but rather the pattern of sport involvement and the relevant influences which are operant at various stages in the sport involvement process.

Methodologically, we have relied, for the most part, on cross-sectional, one-time, *ex post facto* surveys, to the virtual exclusion of longitudinal studies.[2] Our research has been dominated by quantitative analysis and has been devoid of more qualitative approaches to the subject matter. Qualitative approaches to data collection and analysis, however, would serve to complement the more traditional quantitative approaches providing an enriched source of information. Such an approach is especially important if we are to understand the meaning attached to sport and physical activity in the lives of females.

If we continue with our narrow perspective of sport involvement and our equally restricted methodological approach to its study, we cannot hope to achieve an adequate understanding of the female sport experience in its full complexity. To do this, we must not only broaden our definition of sport involvement to encompass what is conceptualized in a schema such as the one presented in this paper, but we must also enrich our research through the adoption of alternative research strategies and methodologies, integrating both qualitative and quantitative approaches from a multidisciplinary perspective.

When one considers the full spectrum which sport involvement entails, it becomes evident that restricting our attention to a single dimension (e.g., primary involvement in the competitive context) is narrow indeed and misrepresents our claim to be studying female sport involvement. Our comprehension of female involvement in sport can only be as broad as the framework we adopt to examine it. It is both naive and inappropriate to continue to consider sport involvement as a unidimensional phenomenon referring only to a single involvement level. Nor is it appropriate to infer that what is determined about sport in a specific context applies to other levels of involvement or in other sport environments. Similarly, it is inadvisable to consider sport involvement in isolation from the societal context within which it takes place, a problem which is considered in the following section.

The Schema in Context — An Example

Consideration to this point has focused exclusively on the sport involvement process itself. We have been concerned with the development of an adequate schema for conceptualizing the spectrum of phenomena included under its rubric. In addition, we have attempted a preliminary integration of the existing literature concerning females in sport into the schema with the intention of identifying those areas on which our attention has been focused and those which have been ignored. Up to this point, no attention has been paid to the place of sport involvement within the social structure. Yet it must be acknowledged that it is totally inappropriate to examine sport involvement in isolation and out of the societal context within which it occurs. It is vitally important that as sociologists we attend to the historical, cultural and social structural elements which influence sport opportunities made available and females' involvement and experience in sport.

The life cycle provides one important example of the contextual background within which sport involvement should most appropriately be examined. The literature concerning socialization suggests that the salience of various types of factors varies according to stages in the life cycle. For instance, it appears intuitively reasonable to expect that concerns about childbearing or childrearing are unlikely to influence the sport involvement patterns of a young girl, but might well exert a strong influence on the female during her childbearing years, as might her role constellation of wife, mother, homemaker and employee.

Yet, life cycle considerations have received minimal attention in the sport literature. Rather, we have tended to approach the study of female sport involvement patterns as if life cycle and other societal factors could be held in suspension, thus eliminating any need for their consideration.

So far, the major focus of our attention has been directed towards the identification of sport patterns. Life cycle influences have been of secondary importance, if they have been afforded any consideration at all. Most of the attention paid to such factors has been located within the social commentary literature. Within the empirical literature, the consideration given to life cycle factors appears primarily within the discussion sections of reported studies where researchers attempt to use such information to explain their findings. There is only limited evidence that such influences have been given more than cursory consideration within the design and theoretical rationale of empirical studies.

The empirical approach to identifying life cycle influences has been restricted primarily to the examination of perceptions of early childhood socializing influences (e.g., the role of parents, peers, siblings, and the education system in the socialization of female athletes into sport roles). Little consideration has been given to socialization as a life-long process. Some minimal attention has focused on the identification of constraints on and barriers to participation but these tend to be at a very superficial level. Empirical considerations, consistent with most of our research efforts, have concentrated almost exclusively on competitive athletes.

The complexity of life cycle influences, the role constellations assumed by females at various stages and their influence on female involvement in sport across the full involvement spectrum have been virtually disregarded. Concentration has focused on elite, competitive athletes within a narrow age range. Very few studies have gone beyond the identification of the sport involvement patterns of females at various ages. Few attempts have been made to examine the influence that stage in the life cycle has on sport involvement. As sport involvement opportunities for females across a wider age range continue to expand, such an approach becomes increasingly inadequate. Consideration must be directed towards examining those factors which potentially influence female sport and physical activity involvement at all ages and at all involvement levels.

Hall (1977:49) argued that we need to examine "the role that sport and physical activity plays in the lives of 'ordinary' women." She suggested that we should study "the institutions of marriage and the family, the assumptions upon which they are based, and the restricting roles that women play within them" (Hall, 1977:29). She argued further that it is most important to take into consideration a woman's present situation and life cycle stage and her constellation of roles when examining her sport involvement (Hall, 1978).

Although made in reference to woman's involvement in occupational careers, some observations made by Laws (1976) serve to emphasize the importance of the inclusion of life cycle considerations in our conceptualization and treatment of women's sport involvement. She stated that existing research suggests some critical decision or transition points in the female life cycle regarding life planning, and she argued that various questions concerning how alternatives come to be viewed as options, how options are eliminated from consideration, how options become imbued with attractiveness and unattractiveness, and how perceptions change must be asked repeatedly at different points in the life cycle when options and priorities change.

It is at this level of consideration that the contributions to be made by disciplines outside of our own can best be appreciated. A significant degree of attention has focused on life cycle considerations within both the sociological and social psychological bodies of literature pertaining to women. Life cycle considerations have been incorporated into the literature dealing with such topics as socialization, sex and gender roles, the analysis of social structural elements which support and maintain gender inequalities in society and females in non-traditional occupations. Such information represents an invaluable resource for scholars concerned with female sport involvement. The potential applicability of such information to both our conceptualization of female sport involvement and our approach to its examination is readily apparent and it behooves researchers in our area to acquaint themselves with its content.

SUMMARY AND CONCLUSIONS

The sociological study of female sport involvement is a relatively new and rapidly expanding area of scholarly endeavour. To date, the focus of work in the area has been narrow and repetitive; the contributions, independent, disjointed and non-cumulative. Furthermore, research efforts have been unlinked to scholarly work examining women in other societal contexts. For the most part, the involvement of females in sport has been examined in isolation from the societal context within which it occurs. We have accumulated a significant amount of highly specific information as a consequence of a program of problem-specific research endeavours focused on females' sport participation in a very narrow context, that of competitive sport. We have failed to attend to the full range of sport involvement.

On the basis of this inadequate treatment of female sport involvement, this paper has argued for and suggested a conceptual schema designed to function as a heuristic in guiding our theoretical and empirical approaches to the study of women in sport. By providing a cohesive framework within which the existing and future body of literature can be integrated, this schema provides some potential degree of coherence to the otherwise scattered research efforts which typify the field. The schema enables the identification of those research areas which have received attention and those which remain to be explored; it documents both our strengths and weaknesses in terms of research strategies, methodologies and foci of attention.

Through a preliminary integration of the body of existing literature, it becomes evident that we have only begun to address the complexity of female involvement in physical activity and sport. We have paid little attention to the range of sport involvement and we are missing vital information on how females move through the sport involvement process, through the life cycle, and the interrelationships between the two processes. It is evident that our methodological approaches to the study of female sport involvement have been equally limited. Some of the questions we have asked and the ways we have elected to answer them have focused our attention on a social psychological, rather than sociological, level of inquiry as Hall (1980) pointed out. There is a need for more in-depth consideration of the social structural elements which influence the involvement of females in sport than has heretofore been provided. In addition, there is a need to incorporate social, historical and cultural considerations into our conceptualization of female sport involvement.

Subsequent stages in the application of the schema to the field will involve a detailed analysis of the literature with the intent of documenting the state of the art through the integration and synthesis of literature from both sport sociology and other relevant fields of study. Although this represents a monumental task, it is an essential step, if we are to be able to identify what we do know about the female sport experience and those areas in which we need to focus future attention.

If our overall aim is merely to answer specific research questions focused on a limited range of sport involvement, then perhaps the research strategies and foci adopted in the past are adequate. However, I would argue that our ultimate interest lies beyond this simplistic level. We are interested in describing and ultimately explaining female involvement in sport. From this perspective, then, it is of the utmost importance that we recognize how individual contributions, whether empirical or theoretical, contribute to our overall understanding of the female sport experience. On this basis, I suggest the need for an overall conceptual schema, such as the one proposed in this paper, within which a comprehensive representation of female sport involvement in a societal context can be constructed.

NOTES

[1]According to the 1976 Survey of Fitness, Physical Recreation and Sport (Statistics Canada, 1978) over 54% of the female Canadian population over the age of 14 years had not participated in any sport or physical recreation activity in the year preceding the survey.

[2]Longitudinal research would contribute a great deal more to our understanding of the complexity of the sport involvement process and the movement of females through their sport involvement career. However, it must be acknowledged that longitudinal research is both time and resource consuming and often its explanatory value is overshadowed by issues of practicality. The integration of research findings into the schema proposed in this paper would serve to some degree to circumvent the necessity for longitudinal research. Research efforts dealing with a variety of involvement patterns at different stages in the sport involvement career could theoretically be integrated within one overriding conceptual framework, thus providing a more coherent and comprehensive picture of the female sport involvement experience.

REFERENCES

Armitage, S.
    1976 "The lady as jock: A popular culture perspective of the woman athlete." Journal
        of Popular Culture 10:122-132.
Bird, A. M. and Williams, J. M.
    1980 "A developmental-attributional analysis of sex role stereotypes for sport perfor-
        mance." Developmental Psychology, 16:319-322.
Brown, B.
    1981 "Sport socialization of females: A study in discouragement." Unpublished
        manuscript in the files of the author.
Butt, D. S.
    1980 "Perspectives from women on sport and leisure." Pp. 70-88 in C. Stark-
        Adamec (ed.), Sex Roles: Origins, Influences and Implications for Women.
        Montreal: Eden Press Women's Publishers.
Butt, D. S. and Schroeder, M. L.
    1980 "Sex-role adaptation, socialization and sport participation in women." Interna-
        tional Review of Sport Sociology. 15:91-99.
Coffey, M. A.
    1973 "The modern sportswoman." Pp. 277-285 in J. Talamini and C. H. Page
        (eds.), Sport and Society. Boston: Little-Brown and Company.

Colker, R. and Widom, C. S.
1980 "Correlates of female athletic participation: masculinity, femininity, self-esteem, and attitudes toward women." Sex Roles 6:47-58.
Croxton, J. S. and Klonsky, B. G.
1980 "Causal attributions as a function of sports participation, performance outcome and sex of participant." Paper presented at the First Annual Meeting of the North American Society for the Sociology of Sport, Denver, October.
Davenport, J.
1978 "The women's movement into the olympic games." Journal of Physical Education and Recreation 49:58-60.
Dranoff, L.
1980 "Ask a lawyer." Chatelaine 53:25-26.
Duda, J. L. and Roberts, G. C.
1980 "Sex biases in general and causal attributions of outcome in co-ed sport competition." Pp. 27-36 in C. M. Nadeau, G. C. Roberts, K. M. Newell and W. Halliwell (eds.), Psychology of Motor Behavior and Sport — 1979. Champaign: Human Kinetics Publishers.
Duguin, M.
1978 "The androgynous advantage." Pp. 89-106 in C. A. Oglesby (ed.), Women and Sport — From Myth to Reality. Philadelphia: Lea and Febiger.
Felshin, J.
1973 "The social anomaly of women in sports." Physical Educator 30:122-124.
1974a "The triple option — for women in sport." Quest Monograph 21:36-40.
1974b "The social view." Pp. 179-279 in E. Gerber, J. Fleshin, F. Ferlin and W. Wyrick (eds.), The American Woman In Sport. Reading, Mass.: Addison-Wesley Publishing Company.
Feltz, D. L.
1979 "Athletics in the status system of female adolescents." A Review of Sport and Leisure 4:110-118.
Fitness and Amateur Sport.
1980 "Women in sport in Canada: Leaders and participants from a national perspective." Ottawa: Minister of State for Fitness and Amateur Sport.
Greendorfer, S.
1977a "Role of socializing agents in female sport involvement." Research Quarterly 48:304-310.
1977b "Female sport participation patterns." Pp. 30-36 in M. Adrian and J. Brame (eds.), NAGWS Research Reports, Volume 3. Washington D.C.: AAHPER Publications.
1978a "Social class influence on female sport involvement." Sex Roles 4:619-625.
1978b "Socialization into sport." Pp. 115-140 in C. A. Oglesby (ed.), Women and Sport: From Myth to Reality. Philadelphia: Lea and Febiger.
Hackman, C.
1978 "Influential factors in the development of sport for women." Physical Education Review 1:41-52.
Hall, M. A.
1977 "The sociological perspective of females in sport." Pp. 37-50 in M. Adriane and J. Brame (eds.), NAGWS Research Reports. Volume 3. Washington D.C.: AAHPER.
1978 "Sport and gender: A feminist perspective on the sociology of sport." CAHPER: CAHPER Sociology of Sport Monograph Series.

1979 "Intellectual sexism in physical education." Quest 31:172-186.
1980 "Sport, sex roles and sex identities." Paper presented at the First Annual Conference of the North American Society for the Sociology of Sport, Denver, October.
Harris, D. V.
1974 "Sexism in recreation programming." Pp. 119-127 in Indicators of Change in the Recreation Environment. National Research Symposium Proceedings. Pennsylvania State University, July 8-11.
1975 "Towards a better understanding of the female in sport." New Zealand Journal of Health, Physical Education and Recreation. 8:91-96.
Hasbrook, C. and Greendorfer, S.
1980 "Implications of social class background on female adolescent athletes and nonathletes." Paper presented at the First Annual Conference of the North American Society for the Sociology of Sport. Denver, Co. October 16-19.
Hawkes, P.; Dryen, R.; Torsh, D.; and Hannan, L.
1975 "Sex roles in school sport and physical education: the state of play." The Australian Journal for Health, Physical Education and Recreation. March: 8-17.
Heit, M. and Malpass, D.
1975 Do women have equal play? Toronto: Ministry of Culture and Recreation.
Hogan, C. I.
1976 "Fair shake or shakedown? Title IX progress report." Women Sports 3:50-54.
Holland, J. R. and Oglesby, C.
1979 "Women in sport: The synthesis begins." Annals September: 80-90.
Kaplan, J.
      Women and Sports. New York: The Viking Press.
Kingsley, J. L.; Brown, F. L.; and Seibert, M. E.
1977 "Social acceptance of female athletes by college women." Research Quarterly. 48:727-733.
Knoppers, A. and Weiss, M.
1980 "Sport socialization patterns of female collegiate volleyball players." Paper presented at the First Annual Conference of the North American Society for the Sociology of Sport. Denver, October 16-19.
Koehler, G.
1973 Agents who have Influenced Women to Participate in Intercollegiate Sport. M.Sc. Thesis, Brigham Young University.
Kuscsik, N.
1976 "The history of women's participation in the marathon." Annals of the New York Academy of Sciences 301:862-876.
Laws, J. L.
1976 "Work aspiration of women: False leads and new starts." Signs 1:33-49.
Lewko, J. H. and Ewing, M. E.
1980 "Sex differences and parental influence in sport involvement of children." Journal of Sport Psychology 2:62-68.
Loy, J. W.; McPherson, B. D.; and Kenyon, G. S.
1978 Sport and Social Systems. Reading, Mass.: Addison-Wesley Publishing Company.
McElroy, M. A. and Willis, J. D.
1979 "Women and the achievement conflict in sport: A preliminary study." Journal of Sport Psychology 1:241-247.
McHugh, M.; Duguin, M. E. and Frieze, I. H.
1978 "Beliefs about success and failure: Attribution and the female athlete." Pp. 173-

191 in C. A. Oglesby (ed.), Women and Sport: From Myth to Reality. Philadelphia: Lea and Febiger.

McPherson, B. D.; Marteniuk, R.; Tihanyi, J.; and Clark, W.
   1977 The Age Group Study of Ontario Swimmers. Toronto: Ontario Ministry of Culture and Recreation.

Myers, A. M. and Lips, H. M.
   1978 "Participation in competitive sports as a function of psychological androgyny." Sex Roles 4:571-578.

Ogilvie, B. and McGuire, L. G.
   1980 "How competition affects elite women swimmers." The Physician and Sportsmedicine 8:113-116.

Rohrbaugh, J. B.
   1979 "Femininity on the line." Psychology Today, 13:30-42.

Sage, G. H. and Loudermilk, S.
   1979 "The female athlete and role conflict." Research Quarterly 50:88-96.

Scanlon, T. K. and Passer, M. W.
   1979 "Sources of competitive stress in young female athletes." Journal of Sport Psychology 1:151-159.

Smith, M. D.
   1979 "Getting involved in sport: Sex differences." International Review of Sport Sociology 14:93-101.

Snyder, E. E.; Kivlin, J. E.; and Spreitzer, E. E.
   1976 "The female athlete: An analysis of objective and subjective role conflict." Pp. 204-210 in A. Yiannakis; T. D. McIntyre; M. J. Melnick; and D. P. Hunt (eds.), Sport Sociology: Contemporary Themes. Dubuque: Kendall/Hunt Publishing Company.

Soutar, A. J.
   1979 "Women in society and sport: Towards a closer understanding of the dilemma facing the female athlete." Momentum 4:16-27.

Statistics Canada. Education Science and Culture Division.
   1978 Culture Statistics — Recreational Activities, 1976. Ottawa: Statistics Canada.

Stone, G.
   1979 "On women and sport." Pp. 41-51 in The Dimensions of Sport Sociology. Proceedings of CIC Physical Education Body of Knowledge Symposia (Tenth). West Point, N.Y.: Leisure Press.

Sutton-Smith, B.
   1979 "The play of girls." Pp. 229-257 in C. B. Kopp (ed.), Becoming Female: Perspectives on Development. New York: Plenum.

Theberge, N.
   1977 An Occupational Analysis of Women's Professional Golf. Ph.D. Dissertation, University of Massachusetts.
   1980 "The system of rewards in women's professional golf." International Review of Sport Sociology 2:27-41.

Uguccioni, S. M. and Eallantyne, R. H.
   1980 "Comparison of attitude and sex roles for female athletic participants and nonparticipants." International Journal of Sport Psychology 11:42-48.

Unkel, M. B.
   1981 "Physical recreation participation of females and males during the adult life cycle." Leisure Sciences 4:1-27.

Wark, K. A. and Wittig, A. F.
    1979 "Sex role and sport competition anxiety." Journal of Sport Psychology 1:248-
        250.
Westkott, M. and Coakley, J.
    1981 "Women in sport: Modalities of feminist social change." Journal of Sport and
        Social Issues 5:32-45.

Chapter 9

THE THEORETICAL NOTION OF RECIPROCITY AND CHILDHOOD SOCIALIZATION INTO SPORT

Cynthia A. Hasbrook, University of Illinois

As early as 1969, Bandura clearly indicated that the process of socialization included both the notion of the socializing agent influencing the socializee and conversely the notion of the socializee influencing the socializing agent. He viewed this two-way process of socialization as reciprocal (Bandura, 1969). Within the theoretical framework of social learning theory, Bandura (1977) summarized the process of "reciprocal determinism":

> Thus, behavior partly determines which of the many potential environmental influences will come into play and what forms they will take; environmental influences, in turn, partly determine which behavioral repertoires are developed and activated. In this two-way influence process, the environment is influenceable, as is the behavior it regulates. (p. 195).

Intuitively one may agree with the notion that the greater a child's "natural" ability and interest in physical activity such as running, jumping, throwing and catching, the greater may be the likelihood of parental encouragement of that physical activity. For example, a father who observes that his four-year-old daughter is interested in throwing and catching a ball and appears to have a "natural" ability to do so may encourage her to play ball much more than he would had she not demonstrated that interest and ability. Conversely, it is quite feasible to suggest and it is supported by the childhood socialization into sport literature (Snyder & Spreitzer, 1976, 1978; Hasbrook et al., 1981) that the greater a parent's encouragement of a child's participation in physical activity, the higher the participation level of the child. Further, it is not unreasonable to propose that a child's interest and ability in physical activity may elicit encouragement and interest from peers and teachers, and conversely as the socialization into sport literature again supports, that peers' and teachers' encouragement of a child's participation in physical activity facilitates such childhood participation (Greendorfer, 1977; Greendorfer & Lewko, 1978). If we consider the aforementioned child-parent/peer/teacher interactions with the context of socialization into sport, we discover an interesting phenomenon. Bandura's (1969, 1977) notion of reciprocity has not been explored.

As Buss (1981) has pointed out: "Theories and research on socialization have long focused on the myriad ways in which parental behavior affects children (p. 59)." With the exception of a few studies which have investigated the notion of reciprocal interaction between child and parent in the general socialization process (Bell, 1968, 1971, 1974, 1977; Buss, 1981), the role that the socializee may play in eliciting behavior from significant others or socializing agents has not been explored (Buss, 1981). Such would appear to be the case of the socialization into sport research.

Traditionally, much of the research examining the socialization into sport process has been based on Sewell's (1963) social role-social system theoretical model. Briefly, this model portrays the socializee who possesses a distinct set of physical, sociological and psychological characteristics or "personal attributes" as being socialized by "significant others" found within several "social systems." Within the literature, these systems have typically been the home, school and/or community. Parents, siblings, peers and teachers have been considered to be the significant others within these social systems. Personal attribute variables have included age, sex, birth order, sibling status, social class, ethnic and religious background, and perceived sport ability. Socialization into sport research has been descriptive of such personal attributes and has examined the influence of various significant others on the sport participation level of children and adolescents (Greendorfer, 1977; Greendorfer & Lewko, 1978; Hasbrook et al., 1981; Spreitzer & Snyder, 1976). Sociologists of sport have examined if and how much significant others may influence/encourage children's participation in sport but have not explored if and how much children may elicit that influence/encouragement from their parents, peers and/or teachers by way of their own behavior.

It is not difficult to understand this unidirectional, causal approach to the study of socialization into sport. A few prominent sport sociologists have suggested and been successful in using recursive path analysis, a statistical method for studying unidirectional, cause/effect relationships as a means to understanding and explaining how and why people become sport spectators and participants (Kenyon, 1970; Kenyon & Knoop, 1978; Kenyon & McPherson, 1974; McPherson, 1972; Spreitzer & Snyder, 1976). For the most part, the variables "predictive" of sport involvement in these recursive systems have been time-sequential or "time-ordered" (Hage, 1972, 56). For example, Kenyon and Knoop (1978) used "adolescent" and "post adolescent" sport involvement variables to predict adult sport involvement. Incorporation of such time-sequential or ordered variables allows for the use of recursive models but eliminates the possibility of reciprocity among variables. This is not to suggest, however, that the use of time-ordered variables has no theoretical support. To the contrary, continuity theory would conceptually support the incorporation of time-sequential variables in the description of a behavior that may occur throughout an individual's life span (Atchley, 1977).

Additionally, when significant other influence has been conceptualized and operationalized in terms of role model behavior (Kenyon & Knoop, 1978), by definition, reciprocity is eliminated as a possibility. If it is assumed that significant others merely serve as role models for the socializee to imitate, significant other influence becomes static, set and cannot be altered or stimulated by the behavior of the socializee. However, if such influence is conceptualized as a more dynamic, interactional phenomenon between the socializee and socializing agent then indeed reciprocity is possible and the use of a unidirectional, cause/effect path model may be inappropriate.

It is when non-time-sequential variables are conceptualized as being predictive of childhood sport involvement and when significant other influence is conceived as being more than just static, one-way, role model behavior that the use of recursive path analysis may present problems. For example, Spreitzer and Snyder (1976) presented a recursive path model of adult socialization into sport. They utilized three non-time-sequential variables: "parental encouragement," "childhood sport participation," and "perceived ability" but portrayed them as time-sequential. Their recursive system depicted parental encouragement as leading to childhood sport participation and to perceived ability thus suggesting that parental encouragement precedes childhood sport participation and/or perceived ability in the socialization process. They also conceptualized significant other influence-parental encouragement, as being more than just role model behavior. Yet they depicted parental encouragement as a one-way influence on childhood sport participation and perceived ability. They could not portray the process as being reciprocal given their use of recursive path analysis.

Within the general socialization literature a small amount of research has been conducted into the effects of children's behavior on socializing agents (Bell, 1968, 1971, 1974, 1977; Buss, 1981). These studies although limited in number have produced results that have been unequivocal and indicate that children's behavior appears to influence the socializing behavior of parents and peers (Buss, 1981). For example, Buss (1981) hypothesized that: ". . . parent-child interactions involving highly active children would be marked by more strife and conflict than parent-child interactions involving more quiescent, less active children (p. 59)."

Within a standardized experimental situation, parents were given a battery of four cognitive tasks to teach their children. Activity level was measured by an actometer, a self-winding device that when strapped to a child's limb(s) or back registers movement. The results supported the experimental hypothesis in the case of father-daughter, mother-daughter and mother-son interaction but did not in the case of father-son interaction. Father-son inter-action was marked by considerably less strife and conflict. Buss cautioned against interpretation of these results until replication can be demonstrated.

Thus, one is led to wonder about the effect of a child's inter-est and ability in physical activity on the sport specific socializing behavior of significant others. Is childhood socialization into sport of a reciprocal nature between the socializee and socializing agents? Although this paper is predominately of a theoretical nature, results from an empirical study investigating childhood socialization into sport will now be discussed as supportive of the notion of reciprocity.

THE STUDY

A fixed-alternative questionnaire originally developed by Greendorfer (1977) to tap female childhood socialization into sport was administered to a total of 463 California high school students in June, 1981. The sample included 171 female athletes, 81 female nonathletes, 148 male athletes, and 63 male nonath-letes. Athletes were defined as those individuals who had or were presently participants on one or more varsity or junior varsity level high school teams. Nonathletes were defined as those indi-viduals who had never participated on an interscholastic varsity or junior varsity sport team.

Of the data generated by the questionnaire, three variables were selected to examine in relation to childhood sport participa-tion (variable 1). The selection of these particular variables with regard to sport participation was based on their noted predictive power as demonstrated within the socialization into sport literature (Greendorfer, 1977; Greendorfer & Lewko, 1978; Spreitzer & Snyder, 1976). The three variables were: (1) the socializee's interest in sport (variable 2); (2) the socializee's perceived sport ability (variable 3); and (3) the socializee's perception of parental encouragement (variable 4). A five point scale ranging from "not at all" to "very much" was utilized in measuring the first two variables. Parental encouragement was a constructed variable consisting of a combination of four separate questions. These questions asked subjects to recall how much their parents played with them, hinted that they should participate in sport, spent time teaching them sport skills, and gave them sport equipment. Each of these separate questions also utilized a five point scale ranging from "not at all" to "very much." Values for parental encouragement were derived by adding together the responses to these four questions and dividing by four.

RESULTS AND DISCUSSION

Table 1 presents an intercorrelation matrix of the dependent and three independent variables for each of the four groups: female athletes, female nonathletes, male athletes, and male nonathletes.

A stepwise multiple regression analysis was performed to determine the predictive importance of these three variables with regard to childhood sport participation for each of the four groups. The results indicated that these variables significantly predicted childhood sport participation for all four groups. Specifically, approximately 40% of the variance in the dependent variable (childhood sport participation) was accounted for within the female athlete group, 39% within the male athlete group, 33% with the female nonathlete group, and 17% within the male nonathlete group. Parental encouragement accounted for a significant amount of the variance in childhood sport participation only among the female athletes (1.7%, $p = .029$) (see Table 2).

To examine the notion of reciprocity, the investigator considered the extent to which children's perceived ability may have

Table 1. Correlation Matrix of Independent and Dependent Variables

	Female Athletes and Nonathletes*			
	V1	V2	V3	V4
V1	0	.6055**	.4488**	.1824**
	0	.5185**	.4740**	-.0306
V2		0	.5710**	
		0	.5401**	.0825
				.0878
V3			0	.2380**
			0	.1964
V4				0
				0

	Male Athletes and Nonathletes*			
	V1	V2	V3	V4
V1	0	.5965**	.4205**	.1155
	0	.5030**	.3688**	.1462
V2		0	.3726**	.0414
		0	.5642**	.0751
V3			0	.1836***
			0	.2435
V4				0
				0

* = nonathletes bottom figures of matrices
** = $p < .01$
*** = $p < .05$

Table 2.   Stepwise Multiple Regressions of Childhood Sport Participation
           on Interest, Ability and Parental Encouragement Among Male and
           Female Athletes and Nonathletes

	Female Athletes			Female Nonathletes		
	N = 171				N = 81	
Variable	Change in R^2	p		Variable	Change in R^2	p
Interest	.36668	0		Interest	.26888	.000
Parental Encouragement	.01767	.029		Ability	.05311	.016
Ability	.00943	.109		Parental Encouragement	.01424	.203
Total Variance Accounted for = 39.37%				Total Variance Accounted for = 33.62%		

	Male Athletes			Male Nonathletes		
	N = 148				N = 63	
Variable	Change in R^2	p		Variable	Change in R^2	p
Interest	.35309	0		Ability	.12248	.005
Ability	.02779	.012		Interest	.03216	.136
Parental Encouragement	.00681	.208		Parental Encouragement	.01971	.240
Total Variance Accounted for = 38.76%				Total Variance Accounted for = 17.43%		

elicited parental encouragement with regard to sport involvement. Given the non-significance of parental encouragement as a predictor of childhood sport participation for the two male groups, analyses were limited to females.

An initial examination of the zero-order correlation between perceived ability and parental encouragement among the female athletes (see Table 1) indicated a moderate, positive, and significant relationship between the two variables ($r = .2380$, $p < .01$). Among the female nonathletes the relationship was also moderate and positive although not significant ($r = .1954$, $p = .079$).

Partial correlation, a statistical technique employed to determine the relationship between two variables while controlling for the influence of a third variable, was then utilized (Kenny, 1979; Kerlinger & Pedhazur, 1973). Controlling for ability, the relationship between parental encouragement and childhood sport participation was compared with the zero-order correlation between parental encouragement and ability within each of the two groups. The partial correlations presented in Table 3 indicated that controlling for ability diminished the strength of the relationship between childhood sport participation and parental encouragement for the female athletes and strengthened the relationship among the female nonathletes.

Thus, given these results and the additional information that perceived ability was significantly greater among the athletes (mean $= 3.9$) than among the nonathletes (mean $= 3.2$) ($t = 3.802$, $df = 250$, $p < .01$) conceptually it could be suggested that controlling for the higher ability of female athletes diminished the parental encouragement/childhood sport participation relationship because the athletes' high ability elicited parental encouragement. When ability was controlled for or eliminated, so to speak, parental encouragement dropped and consequently the relationship between parental encouragement and childhood sport participation was lowered. Conversely, controlling for the lower ability of female nonathletes increased the parental encouragement/childhood sport participation relationship perhaps because the nonathletes' lack of ability subdued parental encour-

Table 3. Zero-Order and Partial Correlations Between Childhood Sport
          Participation and Parental Encouragement Controlling for
          Ability Among Female Athletes and Nonathletes

	Zero-Order $(r_{1,4})$	Partial $(r_{1,4 \cdot 3})$
Female Athletes	.1824	.0871
	p = .017	p = .259
Female Nonathletes	-.0306	-.1433
	p = .786	p = .205

agement. When ability was controlled parental encouragement increased and consequently the relationship between parental encouragement and childhood sport participation was strengthened.

It should be noted that the above "reciprocal" interpretation of results is based upon ". . . one's conception of the 'underlying reality' behind the data" (Blalock, 1979, p. 467). This interpretation tends to be supported by three sources of information: (1) Bandura's (1969, 1977) theoretical framework of "reciprocal determinism," (2) recent empirical findings with regard to the socialization process which have demonstrated a reciprocal interaction between parent and child (Buss, 1981); and (3) a statistical technique (partial correlation) which in and of itself cannot directly establish any kind of causal relationship, be it one-way or reciprocal in nature.

It must also be noted that "unidirectional" interpretations of these data are possible. Parental encouragement may simply lead to childhood sport involvement, and any apparent pattern arising from statistical analyses of the data — in this case the diminishing/strengthening pattern found in the correlation between childhood sport involvement and parent encouragement when ability was controlled — could be interpreted as a purely mathematical phenomenon, in this case resulting simply from the elimination of the shared variance between the variables.

It might also be argued that what appears to be a reciprocal interaction between parent and child may merely be an interaction between the child's perceptions of his/her ability and the child's perceptions of parental encouragement of that ability. Conceivably, the higher a child's perceptions of his/her ability the more likely he/she will interpret or perceive others as encouraging of that ability. In other words, it could be argued that parents whose children have high self-ability perceptions do not actually encourage such ability in their children to any greater extent than do parents whose children possess low self-ability perceptions. Children who perceive their ability as higher simply may interpret or perceive their parents as more encouraging of that ability than do children who perceive their ability as lower.

Thus, although the data tend to suggest the possibility of a reciprocal interaction between female children and their parents with regard to socialization into sport, the data do not negate the possibility of a unidirectional interpretation of the process. Actual parental behavior and parent-child interactions in addition to children's perceptions of parental behavior must be examined in future studies if the process of childhood socialization into sport is to be more fully understood.

REFERENCES

Atchley, R.
    1977 The Social Forces in Later Life, 2nd ed. Belmont, Calif.: Wadsworth.
Bandura, A.
    1969 "Social learning theory of identificatory process." Pp. 213-262 in D. Goslin
          (ed.), Handbook of Socialization Theory and Research. Chicago: Rand
          McNally.
Bandura, A.
    1977 Social Learning Theory. Englewood Cliffs, New Jersey: Prentice-Hall.
Bell, R. Q.
    1968 "A reinterpretation of the direction of effects in studies of socialization." Psy-
          chological Review 25:81-95.
Bell, R. Q.
    1971 "Stimulus control of parent or caretaker by offspring." Developmental Psychol-
          ogy 4:63-72.
Bell, R. Q.
    1974 "Contributions of human infants to caregiving and social interaction." In
          M. Lewis and L. H. Rosenbaum (eds.), The Effect of the Infant on its Care-
          giver. New York: Wiley.
Bell, R. Q. and L. V. Harper
    1977 Child Effects on Adults. Hillsdale, New Jersey: Erlbaum.
Blalock, H. M.
    1979 Social Statistics. Revised Second Edition. New York: McGraw-Hill.
Buss, D. M.
    1981 "Predicting parent-child interactions from children's activity level." Develop-
          mental Psychology 17:59-65.
Greendorfer, S. L.
    1977 "Role of socializing agents in female sport involvement." Research Quarterly
          48:304-310.
Greendorfer, S. L. and J. H. Lewko
    1978 "Role of family members in sport socialization of children." Research Quarterly
          49:146-152.
Hage, J.
    1972 Techniques and Problems of Theory Construction in Sociology. New York: John
          Wiley & Sons.

Hasbrook, C. A., S. L. Greendorfer, and J. A. McMullen
1981 "Implications of social class background on female adolescent athletes and non-athletes." Pp. 95-107 in S. Greendorfer and A. Yiannakis (eds.), Sociology of Sport: Diverse Perspectives. West Point, New York: Leisure Press, 1981.
Heise, D. R.
1975 Causal Analysis. New York: Wiley-Interscience.
Kenny, D. A.
1979 Correlation and causality. New York: Wiley.
Kenyon, G. S.
1970 "The use of path analysis in sport sociology with special reference to involvement socialization." International Review of Sport Sociology 5:191-203.
Kenyon, G. S. and J. C. Knoop
1978 "The viability and cross-cultural invariance of a reduced social role-social system model of sport socialization." Paper presented at the IX World Congress of the International Sociological Association, Uppsala, Sweden (August).
Kenyon, G. S. and B. D. McPherson
1974 "An approach to the study of socialization." International Review of Sport Sociology 9:127-138.
Kerlinger, F. N. and E. J. Pedhazur
1973 Multiple Regression in Behavioral Research. New York: Holt, Rinehart and Winston.
McPherson, B. D.
1972 "Socialization into the role of sport consumer: the construction and testing of a theory and causal model." Unpublished Ph.D. dissertation, University of Wisconsin.
Sewell, W. H.
1963 "Some recent developments in socialization theory and research." The Annals of the American Academy of Political Science 349 (September): 163-181.
Snyder, E. E. and E. Spreitzer.
1976 "Correlates of sport participation among adolescent girls." Research Quarterly 47:804-809.
Snyder, E. E. and E. Spreitzer
1978 "Socialization comparisons of adolescent athletes and musicians." Research Quarterly 49:342-350.
Spreitzer, E. and E. E. Snyder
1976 "Socialization into sport: an exploratory path analysis. Research Quarterly 47:238-245.

Chapter 10

SPORTSMANSHIP: VARIATIONS BASED ON SEX AND DEGREE OF COMPETITIVE EXPERIENCE

Maria T. Allison, Purdue University

As Elias and Dunning (1966) indicate, the structure of a game is, by definition, one of balance, equity, and equilibrium. For example, the game structure matches player to player, offense to defense, and task to task in order to insure that neither team has, at least initially, a one-sided advantage over the opposition. Rules act to insure that outcome is based on skill and mastery rather than on deceit and unfair manipulation. Although the outcome is to be one of disequilibrium — one winner — the initial idea of the game is one of equity and equilibrium.

But in addition to the ïdeational structure of the game, consider works by Lueschen (1976), McIntosh (1979), Webb (1969) and others (Chissom, 1978; Heinila, 1974; Kleiber, 1978; Martens, 1976) who suggest that the cultural goals of sport in contemporary society have come to emphasize victory over fairness; a win-at-all cost ethic over moral behavior. Consider, too, the studies by Bovyer (1963), Kistler (1957), Kroll and Peterson (1965), and Lakie (1964), which suggest that athletes are not as sportsmanlike as non-athletes, and the picture of what sport *is* and *does* becomes increasingly clouded.

One reason the picture is so clouded is that terms such as ethical/moral behavior, sportsmanship, fair play, and professionalization of attitudes are all concepts somewhat interrelated, value-loaded, and frequently used interchangeably to describe concepts or principles which guide decision-making in sport. Each concept is quite complex and multifaceted and each assumes that there is a fine line, perhaps a boundary, between what might be considered fair play and what might be considered deceit, cheating, or deviant behavior. The question becomes, "What is that boundary?" What is the boundary between sportsmanlike and unsportsmanlike behavior; what is the boundary between fair play and deceit? And beyond the principles which may guide an individual's behavior in a contest, is there a system-level normative structure which is accepted by the sport order as a whole? Thus, what is the fine line which distinguishes between what the sport order accepts as "part of the game or strategy" and that which is labelled as unfair and unethical behavior?

The purpose of this paper is twofold. First, the investigator presents data which suggest that there are distinct normative systems operating within sport which vary according to the sex and institutionalized competitive experience of the subjects. Secondly, the paper discusses several of the methodological problems which exist in trying to assess the nature of sportsmanship and fair play in sport.

METHODS

A questionnaire was constructed which described two sport-related ethical dilemmas. Each situation described was reflective of cases which had actually been discussed in the media, or were relayed to the investigator in personal communications with athletes.

The first situation is one where a coach, due to an inadvertent mistake on his/her part and the oversight of the officials and scorers, wins a game which he/she might not have won had the error been caught.

Subjects were asked to assume the role of the coach and respond to the four courses of action suggested.

Situation One
Figure 1

Situation 1: You are a coach of a basketball team. With 15 seconds left to play you
are losing by a score of 58-59. You quickly send in a substitute who
takes a desperation shot with three seconds to go. Just as the shot is
made you realize that the substitute had fouled out of the game earlier.
The scorers, officials and the other coach had missed the mistake. Your
team wins by one point. What would you do?

As a coach I would:

Forfeit the game to the other team; we really didn't win fairly.

5	4	3	2	1
strongly agree	agree	neutral	disagree	strongly disagree

Tell the official as soon as the game ends.

5	4	3	2	1
strongly agree	agree	neutral	disagree	strongly disagree

Forget it; it was the scorer's fault, not mine.

5	4	3	2	1
strongly agree	agree	neutral	disagree	strongly disagree

Forget it, it's part of the breaks of the game.

5	4	3	2	1
strongly agree	agree	neutral	disagree	strongly disagree

The second situation presented to the subjects was one which
clearly reflected blatant cheating within a game by several players
on a team. Again subjects were asked to take the role of the coach
and respond to each item as he/she felt he/she would most likely
act.

The initial population for this study included male and
female college varsity athletes ($N = 67$) and non-athletes ($N = 38$)
enrolled in a major university. Demographic information collected on non-athletes revealed quite a variation in participation
patterns in high school; therefore subjects were further subdi-
vided and data analyzed incorporating three subgroups based on
the degree of competitive experience: 1) *college athletes* (i.e., those

Situation 2

Figure 2

Situation 2: In a high school sectional baseball game your team is ahead one
             run in the bottom of the ninth inning.. The opposing team has the
             tying run on third base. After the first pitch to the batter, the
             catcher makes a pick-off throw down to third base in an attempt to
             get the runner. The ball sails out into left field bouncing down
             the foul line. The runner trots in toward home plate with the sure
             tying run. As he gets to home plate the catcher tags the runner out
             at the plate. After much confusion, it was discovered that the cat-
             cher had thrown a pealed potato into the outfield and had held on
             to the ball. (This is a true story).

If, as a coach I knew there was no explicit rule against such a play, I would
instruct my team to do it:

5	4	3	2	1
strongly agree	agree	neutral	disagree	strongly disagree

If I were the coach and did not have previous knowledge of the play by the catcher,
I would:

. . . forfeit the game

5	4	3	2	1
strongly agree	agree	neutral	disagree	strongly disagree

. . . kick the involved players off the team

5	4	3	2	1
strongly agree	agree	neutral	disagree	strongly disagree

. . . do nothing

5	4	3	2	1
strongly agree	agree	neutral	disagree	strongly disagree

who had participated in high school and were currently varsity college athletes; 2) *high school athletes only* (i.e., those who had participated on one or more varsity interscholastic teams); and 3) *non-athletes* (i.e., those who had never participated on an interscholastic team). All data were further analyzed to determine whether or not sex differences existed in the response pattern of each group.

RESULTS

Despite the limitations of the questionnaire, some very interesting tendencies were revealed in the data. In general the data indicate that in Situation 1 (i.e., the basketball example) there was a wide variability in response by group. In Situation 2 (i.e., the baseball example), the variability was not as marked yet ANOVA analyses revealed significant differences between groups. Turning first to Situation 1, an ANOVA of Group x Response indicated significant differences $p \leqslant .001$ between means of each group on each response (i.e., forfeit; tell the official; forget it, it was the scorer's fault; and forget it, it's the breaks of the game). A discriminant analysis revealed that the response variables were significant discriminator variables between groups $p \leqslant .003$. Perhaps the most intriguing pattern revealed in Situation 1 was that the relative mean ranking between groups was similar on each item. The response of male/female non-athletes and the female high school athletes tended to cluster together, whereas the responses of male high school and college athletes tended to cluster on the other end of the scale. For example, male/female non-athletes and female high school athletes tended to agree with the item "Forfeit the game"; male athletes, both college and high school, tended to disagree. This same pattern held true on the item, "Tell the official." On the items "Forget it, it was the scorer's fault," and "Forget it, it's the breaks of the game," male athletes tended to agree with those statements, while non-athletes tended to disagree. The female athletes tended to cluster somewhere between these extremes.

In addition to the finding that each of these groups reveal a very different response pattern, within each item, a comparison of mean scores between items also reveals an interesting pattern. Specifically the means of male athletes, both high school and college, reveal the following order: 1) Forget it, it's the breaks of the game, 2) Forget it, it's the scorer's fault, 3) Tell the official, and 4) Forfeit the game. A look at the means of the male and female non-athletes and female athletes reveals a different ranking: 1) Tell the official, Forfeit, Forget it — it was the scorer's fault, and forget it — it's the breaks of the game. These data indicate that these groups seem to base their decision-making on very different sources of rationalization. The male athletes seemed to have

Situation 1

ANOVA Group x Response

Figure 3

Situation 1	Forfeit	Tell Official	Scorer	Breaks
	$\overline{X}$	$\overline{X}$	$\overline{X}$	$\overline{X}$
Male college (N=11)	2.55	2.91	3.27	3.45
Male high school (N=13)	2.46	2.46	3.46	3.46
Female college (N=18)	3.22	3.53	2.42	2.42
Female high school (N=25)	3.84	3.96	1.92	2.16
Male non-athletes (N=11)	3.73	3.82	2.09	2.00
Female non-athletes (N=27)	3.85	4.22	1.78	1.81
	$F_{5, 104}=4.879$	$F_{5, 105}=5.74$	$F_{5, 105}=7.66$	$F_{5, 105}=7.15$
	$p \leq .001$	$p \leq .001$	$p \leq .001$	$p \leq .001$

incorporated the error as part of the game and felt no need to rectify the situation. Further questioning of subjects revealed statements such as: "As a coach, there's nothing you can do; the officials should have caught it." Another official, "As a coach it's not within your rights to change the rules — it was the scorer's fault, you can't change that." Finally, another offered, "Forget it, you win some, you lose some; it never shoulda happened but it did, so forget it."

Whereas male athletes indicated that this situation was internal to the game and not much could, or should, be done about it, the other groups (i.e., non-athletes, and female athletes) indicated that direct action should be taken. Either the official

Situation 1

Relative Mean Ranking

Figure 4

Forfeit		$\bar{X}$
Female	Non-athlete	3.85
Female	High school	3.84
Male	Non-athlete	3.73
Female	College	3.22
Male	College	2.55
Male	High school	2.46

Tell Official		$\bar{X}$
Female	Non-athlete	4.22
Female	High school	3.96
Male	Non-athlete	3.82
Female	College	3.53
Male	College	2.91
Male	High school	2.46

Forget it; scorer's fault		$\bar{X}$
Male	High school	3.46
Male	College	3.27
Female	College	2.42
Male	Non-athlete	2.09
Female	High school	1.92
Female	Non-athlete	1.78

Forget it; breaks of the game		$\bar{X}$
Male	High school	3.46
Male	College	3.45
Female	College	2.42
Female	High school	2.16
Male	Non-athlete	2.00
Female	Non-athlete	1.81

Range 5 = strongly agree/1 = strongly disagree

should be told and/or the game should be forfeited. The female athletes and non-athletes (both male and female) seemed to indicate that individual action should be taken to rectify the situation, while the male athletes rationalized the outcome as part of the game. Clearly, each group had quite different notions as to the source of the inequity and therefore would respond quite differently to such a situation.

An analysis of Situation 2 indicates the same pattern of response styles between groups. All groups indicated that they disagreed with the item "I would coach it." However, significant mean differences ($F_{5,104} = 3.94$, p;$\leqslant$.003) were found between the groups. Again, male athletes, both high-school only and college, had a higher mean ranking on this item than non-athletes (i.e., male and female). Whereas most groups tended to rank forfeiture highest, the male college athletes gave "I would coach it" the highest mean rating. This finding is consistent with data presented by Heinila (1974) which indicate that highly professionalized athletes tend to approve of any strategy which insures vic-

Within Group Rankings

Figure 5

Male high school and	Male, female non-athletes;
male college athletes	female high school and college athletes
Forget it, breaks	Tell the official
Forget it, scorer's fault	Forfeit
Tell official	Forget it; scorer's fault
Forfeit	Forget it; breaks of the game

Situation 2

ANOVA Group x Response

Figure 6

Situation 2	Coach it	Forfeit	Kickoff	Nothing
	$\bar{X}$	$\bar{X}$	$\bar{X}$	$\bar{X}$
Male college	2.91	2.18	2.64	2.64
Male high school	1.85	3.15	2.31	2.36
Female college	1.56	3.06	2.67	2.06
Female high school	1.44	3.80	2.64	1.56
Male non-athletes	1.91	3.18	2.55	2.36
Female non-athletes	1.52	3.22	3.11	1.63

$F_{5, 104}=3.94$ $F_{5, 104}=3.87$ $F_{5, 104}=1.34$ $F_{5, 104}=5.07$
$p \leq .003$ $p \leq .003$ $p \geq .25$ $p \leq .001$

tory. As in Situation 1, these data indicate that quite different definitions of acceptable behavior seem to exist among the groups.

DISCUSSION

What do these data indicate? Do they indicate that athletes for the most part are less sportsmanlike than non-athletes? There does appear to be a tendency for those who have been involved in competitive programs longest to have less sportsmanlike attitudes. However, some discussion of the questionnaire must precede such a conclusion.

A brief analysis of the items on the questionnaire and past methods utilized to assess sportsmanship reveals one basic dilemma. We do not really know what the term sportsmanship means within the sport context. For example, one could look at Situation 1 and suggest that the only ethical thing to do would be to forfeit the game. However, many could suggest several game-related, rule-oriented reasons why that would not be an appropriate response.

The methodological difficulty of trying to assess sportsmanship is revealed in a study by Haskins (1960) who developed an instrument to measure sportsmanlike attitudes. The study validated a series of items through the use of objective, external raters to insure that they were indeed measuring sportsmanship. Again, some would accept such behavior as intelligent, strategical manipulation of an opponent, while others might consider it deviant, unfair behavior. The point is that we are not clear as to what sportsmanship, fair play, and other such terms mean within sport. Is there some fixed definition of fair play? Is an attempt to

Sportsmanship Item
(Haskins, 1960)

Figure 7

Player A is playing Player B in a tennis match. Player A beats B in the first set, 6 games to 1. Player B continually stops to tie his shoes, wipes his face every few minutes, and moves slowly into position for each play. Player B discovers that these actions upset Player A. He continues these maneuvers and beats Player A in the second and third sets, winning the match.

a. Player B is clever to use these tactics since they helped him win.

b. Player A should use the same tactics against Player B.

c. Player B should not take unfair advantage of Player A.

d. Since Player A could use the same tactics as Player B, Player B was right to use them.

e. Player A, if he were a good player, would not let Player B's tactics bother him.

"take out" the quarterback with a hard tackle unethical or part of
the accepted norms of behavior. Or is it both? What is that fine
line, the boundary which separates the right from the wrong in
sport? And methodologically speaking, is there some objective,
external criteria which we can impose on a questionnaire to assess
fair play and sportsmanship or do we have to go to those in the
sport system and try to get at their interpretations of reality. It
could well be, for example, that the definitions and dimensions of
fair play and sportsmanship "carried in the minds" of athletes,
coaches, and the sport order in general are quite different indeed
from those imposed from the outside world. The data presented
do indicate that there are distinct normative systems which appear
to operate within each group. It seems, however, that we cannot
label such discrete patterns as sportsmanlike or unsportsmanlike,
as ethical or deviant until we understand the nature and structure
of sport itself, the changing norms and expectations which sur-
round the game world, and finally the interpretation of that world
as seen through the eyes of the participants (both players and
coaches). To impose external, seemingly objective criteria on
behavior and label it as "more or less sportsmanlike" may be missing the realities of the structure of the game. As Lueschen (1977)
has indicated, the game by its very nature strategically demands
the *pressing* of boundaries between rule following and rule break-
ing. The strategical reality of the contest may in fact be quite separate from the ethical parameters which guide behavior in the
larger society. In fact, McIntosh (1979: 101) presents a careful
philosophical analysis of ways in which the "rules of games and
sports supercede the rules and indeed the moral code of life outside the game." Such analyses can only help clarify the complex
demands placed on participants in the game world and suggest
important considerations which should be incorporated in future
sociological research.

The data presented do not clarify or answer the moral question about what behaviors should or should not be considered
sportsmanlike or fair play. Consistent with past research (c.f.
Heinila, 1974; Webb, 1969) the data do indicate, however, that

very different norms are operating among participants within the sport system.

Perhaps what we have here is not the question of sportsmanship but rather a phenomenon similar to Webb's (1969) professionalization of attitudes. However, whereas Webb referred to a reprioritizing of values from an emphasis on fairness to skill, here I refer to an expansion of the boundaries of what is considered appropriate behavior within a game system. Specifically, the data indicate that the response patterns for each situation varied to quite an extent based on the degree of experience in institutionalized competitive programs. Those in highly competitive sport experiences, such as male varsity college and high school athletes and female college athletes, had different definitions of appropriate behavior from those who had not participated. Those in highly institutionalized programs seemed to have more professionalized orientations in that they defined much behavior as "part of the game" and in the name of the game whereas non-athletes had a more narrow definition of appropriate behavior. Perhaps as the system becomes increasingly institutionalized, competitive, and win-oriented, there is a concommitant change in what behaviors are accepted and rewarded as appropriate. What is initially considered inappropriate may in fact over time come to be defined by the sport system as totally acceptable. Thus, the normative boundary of sport seems to be fluid and flexible rather than rigid and fixed.

To conclude, it is suggested that before we try to understand the nature of sportsmanship, fair play, and ethical behavior in sport, we must first come to understand the norms which guide behavior. What is the boundary between what those in the sport system define as appropriate behavior and those they define as inappropriate? What behaviors are athletes and coaches rewarded for and what behaviors and attitudes receive negative sanction? What forces act on the coach and athlete to engage in fair play and what forces act on the participants to engage in deviant behavior?

The concepts of sportsmanship, fair play, and ethical/moral behavior are quite complex. Some behaviors may in fact be blatant violations of some conception of fair play, others may simply be viewed as strategical manipulation of the opponent. Before we can begin to impose external criteria or conceptions of what ethical/ moral system permeates the sport order, we need first to define norms which define the contest: This is not to say that there is no absolute or clear cut system of ethical behavior in sport, but rather that before understanding such a system we must understand the nature of sport itself. One obvious methodological strategy which would allow us to understand the normative structure of sport is to turn to those involved in sport and attempt to capture their reality, their conception of morality, and allow them to define for us the code of sportsmanship and fair play which guides behavior in the sport world.

REFERENCES

Bovyer, G.
  1963 "Children's concepts of sportsmanship in 4th, 5th, and 6th grade." Research Quarterly 34:282-87.
Chissom, B.
  1978 "Moral behavior of children participating in competitive sport." Pp. 193-199 in R. Magill, M. Ash, and F. Smoll (eds.), Children in Sport: A Contemporary Anthology. Champaign, IL Human Kinetics.
Elias, N. and E. Dunning
  1966 "Dynamics of sport groups with special reference to football." British Journal of Sociology 4: 388-402.
Haskins, M. J.
  1960 "Problem solving test of sportsmanship." Research Quarterly 31:601-6.
Heinila, K.
  1974 Ethics of Sport. Jyvaskyla, Finland: University of Jyvaskyla.
Kistler, H. W.
  1957 "Attitudes expressed about behavior demonstrated in certain specific situations." College Physical Education Association Proceedings 60:55-58.
Kleiber, D.
  1978 "Games or sports for children: what difference does it make?" Paper presented at AAHPER meetings, Kansas City, April.
Kroll, W., and K. Peterson
  1965 "Study of values test and collegiate football teams." Research Quarterly 36:441-47.
Lakie, W.
  1964 "Expressed attitudes in various groups of athletes toward athletic competition." Research Quarterly 35:479-503.
Lueschen, G.
  1977 "Cheating." IN D. Landers (ed.), Social Problems in Athletics. Champaign, IL.: University of Illinois Press.

Martens, R.
  1976 "Kids sports: a den of inequity or land of promise." NCPEAM Proceedings: 102-
        12.
McIntosh, P.
  1979 Fair Play. London: Heinemann.
Webb, H.
  1969 "Professionalization of attitudes toward play among adolescents." IN G. Kenyon
        (ed.), Aspects of Contemporary Sport Sociology. Chicago: The Athletic
        Institute.

Chapter 11

FEMINISM AND PATRIARCHY IN PHYSICAL EDUCATION

Mary E. Duquin, University of Pittsburgh

In sport and physical education a patriarchal system maintains and perpetuates the subservient position of women through economic, physical, and psychological control mechanisms which discourage deviancy and place a premium on conformity (Chafe, 1977).

Patriarchy is defined ". . . as a set of social relations between men, which have a material base, and which, though hierarchical, establish or create interdependence and solidarity among men that enable them to dominate women" (Hartmann, 1981:14). Patriarchal practice has varied in form and intensity across societies and throughout recorded history. Additionally, the degree to which women have been and continue to be subjected to patriarchal power is influenced by such factors as age, race, class, marital status, nationality, and sexual orientation. According to Hartmann (1981) and Ehrilich (1981) the major components of patriarchy as we currently experience them include (a) male control of female labor by controlling access to economic resources, thereby making women dependent upon a male controlled system and/or upon a particular male; (b) male control of institutions and decision making; (c) control of female sexuality; (d) homophobia, i.e. the fear and aversion of homosexuality; (e) male power expressed in violence or the threat of violence against women; (f) differential sex socialization accompanied by the ideology of male superiority, resulting in women's feelings of low self worth, self deprecation, passivity, isolation, and conformity.

In this paper, I conduct an analysis of the structural and ideological sources of patriarchal practice within our profession. The theoretical framework developed in this paper draws upon both socialist and radical feminist theory.

Male domination in sport and physical education is first explored by examining men's economic and physical hegemony, the most overt forms of male power in our profession. Next I discuss the ways our profession impacts on beliefs pertaining to sexuality and sexual function including the role of homophobia in influencing both the material and psychological reality of women's lives. Finally, I identify and explain how particular professional belief patterns serve as internal controls which inhibit interpreting the status of women in the profession as a breach of social justice.

ECONOMIC AND PHYSICAL POWER

Money symbolizes power. Women's economic dependence on men has long been perceived as the root of women's subservient and inferior status. As Chafe (1977:67-68) notes:

> If a group is assigned a "place," there are few more effective ways of keeping it there than economic dependency . . . Even those in the most prestigious positions illustrated how money could be used as an instrument of social control. If they were to succeed in raising funds, college administrators in black and women's schools frequently found that they had to shape their programs in conformity to social values that buttressed the status quo.

The history of women's dependence on male prerogative in decisions affecting the implementation and quality of women's physical education programs is well documented by Lee (1978). As the primary administrators in sport and academia today, men continue to control the institutions and decision making processes which regulate female access to economic resources (Mathews, 1982). Men hold both reward and coercive power over women through decisions concerning women's salaries, tenure, job position and responsibilities. As gate keepers, men control access to publications, presentations, and selection for status positions such as keynote speakers, decisions which influence women's career advancement.

In a recent survey of women physical educators between 29 and 42% of the respondents reported that they had experienced sex discrimination in salaries, job positions, work responsibilities, career advancement and administrative support (Duquin et al., 1981). As in society at large, control of women's labor and competition in sport and physical education through a predominately male administrative system results in economic advantages for those in power (Beck, 1980; Parkhouse and Lapin, 1980).

In addition to economic domination, the threat of physical force acts as a metaphor for power. The physical strength of men, the image of the potentially violent man, the fear of being struck or raped — these are important instruments in controlling women's freedom of action (Brownmiller, 1975; Chafe, 1977).

In sport and physical education, physical intimidation takes on a blatant aspect not found in many other spheres. The profession has implicitly and explicitly endorsed sport as a means of developing male aggression and dominance (Blanchi, 1980; Komisar, 1980). Sports have also traditionally served as a focus for male bonding. This bonding represents the political relation of gender dominance, especially among working class men, where natural masculinity is related to physical strength, ascribed authority, male solidarity, and skill in traditional male roles (Ehrlich, 1981; Stewart, 1981). Thus it is not surprising for females to feel threatened by the use of brute male force in sport or by mandatory coeducational physical education where males may try to assert their sexual dominance by physical intimidation and aggression against females, all in the name of the game (Beck, 1980). As long as sport is used as an expression of male solidarity and dominance over females, the physical threat to females is real.

This threat of violence creates fear and passivity in women which serves to keep male supremacy unchallenged.

SEXUALITY AND HOMOPHOBIA

Institutionalized power over women's sexuality serves primarily as a means of controlling the production and reproduction of labor power and providing sexual service to men (Brown, 1981; Harris, 1977; Tavis and Offir, 1977). Patriarchal religious beliefs, class and race discrimination and poor mass public health education limit women's control over their bodies, their sexuality and their reproductive functions. Despite rising teenage pregnancy and sexual violence statistics, sex and family education, including information on contraception, pregnancy, marriage contracts, sex preference, wife battering, self defense and rape, are often left out of the health curriculum in schools (Rosen and Weinstein, 1982). Where sex education is included, it is often taught by physical educators who are given little, if any, adequate preparation. The low priority of women's health issues in our profession is evidenced by our failure to prepare educators to deal adequately with these issues and by our political reticence to lobby vigorously for the inclusion of such topics in the health curriculum. As the primary source of mass public health education, our profession has failed in its responsibility to provide females with information necessary to promote their health, well-being, and control over their reproductive lives.

An aversion and fear of homosexuality is part of the history of sport and this profession (Bouton, 1979; Friedenberg, 1980; Kennard, 1977). According to Marmor (1980:137) "fear of sexuality combines, in homophobia, with fear of those who violate established sex role conventions in appearance and activity." In a national survey of 479 physical educators, Duquin et al., (1981) found that 19% of women and 42% of men physical educators opposed "gay rights." The more negative response of the men, in comparison to the women, can, in part, be attributed to the relationship between sports participation and the development of the traditional male sex role (Klassen and Levitt, 1974; Sabo and Runfola, 1980). The highly sex-typed nature of sport and physical education promotes fear and ridicule of inappropriate sexual looks and behaviors (Lee, 1978; Marlowe et al., 1978). As Kopay and Young (1980:93) state, "Homosexuality in (sport) is considered such a taboo the coaches and players not only feel free but obligated to joke about it. To be homosexual is to be effeminate, like a girl . . . If you don't run fast enough or block or tackle hard enough, you're a pussy, a cunt, a sissy." In sports, the relationship between homosexuality and sex role status is made clear. As Ehrlich (1981:121) states, ". . . the most negative stereotype of male homosexuals is that they act like women; by descending from their superior position and copying the behaviors of the inferior sex they have done the unforgiveable. They have given up patriarchal power . . ."

The negative stereotype of women in sport, including questions of sexual orientation, has long been an agenda of concern among professionals (Felshin, 1974; Kennard, 1977; Twin, 1979). Although rarely discussed openly, most professional advice regarding this stereotype has been limited to encouraging female physical education majors toward proper carriage, good grooming, and feminine dress (Halsey, 1961; Helmker, 1970). There are, however, some professionals who are wont to admit that homosexuality in physical education amounts to an occupational hazzard. As Althoff (1970: 69-71) writes in her article "A gay world in physical education?":

> Looking . . . at the college . . . woman; one finds a very apt candidate for homosexuality among the physical education majors and minors. Many of these women are the exact replicas of the public image of a lesbian whether they actually are or are not . . . Magee notes that teaching is one of the preferred professions of lesbians as they are able to gain some maternal-like satisfaction from instructing the students and at the same time provide themselves with a rich environment for homosexual activity . . . Physical education offers the

lesbian all of these advantages, and as a result probably draws a proportioned share of these people into its ranks. Thus, many a girl in physical education displays masculine characteristics, is heterosexually starved, is prone to develop crushes on her favorite heroine, is continually surrounded by other girls, and is likely to have at least one or two very "experienced" teachers. She is seemingly a very apt candidate for lesbianism . . . Health and physical educators must open their eyes to the lesbianism in their field and work toward the prevention of its growth . . . We can . . . help to initiate an educational chain reaction which will not only face homosexuality, but meet it with the force of prevention.

Rare though this clarion call for professional witch hunting may be, it demonstrates that among other things lesbianism is a political issue and a threat to a patriarchal system.

Lesbian is the word, the label, the condition that holds women in line. When a woman hears this word tossed her way, she knows she is stepping out of line. She knows that she has crossed the terrible boundary of her sex role . . . For in this sexist society, for a woman to be independent means she can't be a woman — she must be a dyke . . . As long as the label "dyke" can be used to frighten a woman into a less militant stand, keep her separate from her sisters . . . then to that extent she is controlled by the male culture (Koedt, Levine and Rapone, 1973: 241-243).

Homophobia alienates women physical educators from one another, making it difficult to build a sense of solidarity with other women. Given the teaching nature of our profession, many women who are not lesbians dread the label, and those who are have a justifiable right to fear the consequences of a substantiated accusation. Homophobia not only controls women's sexuality and diminishes women's potential for combining with other women, but, in a substantial way controls women's pursuit of an economic livelihood in our profession.

Relative Deprivation

Dominance is "not merely technological or economic or military, it is also emotional, cultural, and psychological, producing in the dominated a pervasive sense of inferiority and insecurity" (Boals, 1974:322). Psychological messages defining and limiting women's aspirations continue to be effective social control mechanisms used by the patriarchal system to keep women in their place. The results of this socialization affect women's perceptions of their relative deprivation in many ways. Without feelings of deprivation women will not move to unite against oppression and exploitation. In order for a group to feel deprived they must (a) see something others have that they have not, (b) want it, (c) feel they deserve it, (d) believe that it's possible to get, and (e) feel that it's not their fault for not having it (Crosby, 1976).

Seeing what others have has been and still is a problem in our profession. Segregation, secret budgets, limited information exchange between men and women and even between women and women, the "old boy" network, and the lack of women's control over institutions all contribute to a blindness toward the discrepancies existing in our profession.

In order to sense deprivation, women must want what men have. A pattern of complex inter-relationships emerges when one explores this criterion in relation to our profession. Logic dictates that the benefits, structure, and values of the dominant male group be admired and desired by those at the bottom of the hierarchical system. But when woman's *telos* is disjoined from man's and separate spheres are constructed, complete with sex specific roles, characteristics and virtues, both sexes come to believe that women do not, or at least should not, want what belongs to or is associated with men's sphere. The ideology of sexual romanticism requires that women be concerned with preserving the human need for love, caring and intimacy against the individualistic, "dog eat dog" market place world of men which rewards only the victorious and strong. The liberal feminist focus on equal rights denies a separate *telos* for women and puts forth the sexual rationalist's goal of women's assimilation into the public sphere on an equal status with men. As attractive as this concept of equality might be for some women, others legitimately question the desirability of the kind of sport world women are buying into. Within the male model, social justice is determined by women's ability to compete like men and, often, against men for operational dollars. Some women physical educators question whether equal rights for women in sport must necessarily entail accepting the male model of sport with its history of hypocrisy, corruption and athlete exploitation. Many women see no way out of this romanticist/rationalistic dialectic, and so, confusion and contradiction exist among professionals on these issues (Alperstein, 1981; Heide, 1978). Ironically, there exist striking philosophic similarities between many of the old guard women, perceived as conservative by liberals, and the most radical social feminists who call for a revolution of, and not an assimilation into, the male system of sport (Beck, 1980; Lee, 1978; Oglesby, 1978).

Another deterrent to "wanting" what men have is the belief among many women that the desire for what men have and the fight for equal rights have a negative effect on women's feminity. This fear of identification with the oppressor is expressed in the negative image of the feminist as an overaggressive, overbearing, obnoxious, masculine woman who wants to be like a man (Duquin et al., 1981). Freire (1970:32-33) captures this conflict when he states:

> The oppressed suffer from the duality which has established itself in their innermost being . . . They are at one and the same time themselves and the oppressor whose consciousness they have internalized. The conflict lies in the choice between being wholly themselves or being divided; between ejecting the oppressor within or not ejecting him; . . . between following prescriptions or having choices; between being spectators or actors; between acting or having the illusion of acting through the action of the oppressors; between speaking out or being silent . . .

The fear of becoming like the oppressor by laboring for one's freedom and self determination continues to inhibit the growth of a feminist movement within the profession. "As long as (women) live in the duality in which *to be* is *to be like*, and *to be like* is *to be like the oppressor* . . .'-' patriarchal practice survives intact (Freire, 1979:33).

The question of women's deservedness is decided on many bases. The ideology of patriarchy assumes women's inferiority and thus women's lack of deservedness in comparison to men. However, women may also feel that they are not deserving because under the competitive notion of social justice they very often lose out to men in the capitalistic marketplace. For example, if you can't draw the crowds, you don't deserve the money. Using the social justice notion of equity, women are told that they don't give enough, aren't good enough, aren't serious enough, haven't fought long enough, and don't sacrifice the way men do, and thus, aren't as deserving as males (Duquin et al., 1981). The capitalistic requirement of labor, that it be free in terms of time and energy from familial responsibilities, is a structural and ideological constraint which places many women in a "Catch 22" position as regards their ability to fulfill successfully both their salaried professional duties and their unsalaried work as homemakers. This dual responsibility, which the patriarchal system does not impose on men, affects the perceptions of woman's deservedness in the realm of professional work.

Patriarchy and biological determinism encourage the belief that change is not possible. When women feel a change in their status is not likely, when they aren't informed of other women's successfully won conflicts, when they feel they are alone in trying to alter too large a system, many women, socialized to conform to the status quo, become apathetic to changing their situation (Parkhouse and Lapin, 1980). As Freire (1979:32) notes, ". . . the oppressed, who have adapted to the structure of domination in which they are immersed, and have become resigned to it, are inhibited from waging the struggle for freedom so long as they feel incapable of running the risks it requires."

Feeding into this system of inaction is the criterion that women must believe that it is not their fault for not having the benefits men have. This criterion is especially hard for women physical educators to meet, for many are prone to believe that women's problems, if they see any, exist within women themselves, not the system. This belief is accompanied by the belief that if women want to be treated equally, all they have to do is achieve it, each within her own situation (Duquin et al., 1981). This idealistic perspective suggests that change need only take place in the mind of each individual. Sources of oppression and inequality exist not in the material and ideological aspects of male controlled institutions but in one's own poor attitude toward the rules, standards, goals and means of evaluation established by men. Such a perspective leads women into self reproachment or self help strategies but rarely into concerted action with other women to change the structural and ideological realities which shape their professional lives.

CONCLUSIONS

The most effective instrument of continued control of women is socialization which produces, within the group itself, an internal pressure to conform. Women keep each other in line and act to perpetuate the status quo in order to avoid alienating the dominant group, as a means of group self defense, as a strategy for advancement and as a means of maintaining self respect in choosing to play a role in which familiar patterns provide security (Chafe, 1979). Patriarchy, both structurally and ideologically is thus perpetuated and maintains its control. "Only as (women) discover themselves to be "hosts" of the oppressor can they contribute to the midwifery of their liberating pedagogy . . . Liberation is thus a childbirth and a painful one (Freire, 1979:33). The growth of feminism in the profession of physical education and sport is dependent upon women perceiving the social injustice of their status and working together for change.

REFERENCES

Alperstein, Ellen
1981 "Ruth doesn't live here anymore." Women's Sport 3:16-19.
Althoff, Sally
1970 "A 'gay world' in physical education?" Your Challenge V: 1:59-71. Division of PEHR, University of Toledo.
Beck, Bonnie
1980 "The future of women's sport: issues, insights, and struggles." Pp. 299-314 in D. Sabo and R. Runfola (eds.), Jock: Sports and Male Identity. New Jersey: Prentice-Hall.
Bianchi, Eugene
1980 "The super-bowl culture of male violence." Pp. 117-130 in D. Sabo and R. Runfola (eds.), Jock: Sports and Male Identity. New Jersey: Prentice-Hall, Inc.
Boals, Kay
1974 "The politics of cultural liberation." Pp. 322-42 in J. Jaquette (ed.), Women in Politics. New York: Wiley.
Bouton, James
1970 Ball Four. New York: World.
Brown, Carol
1981 "Mothers, fathers and children: from private to public patriarchy." Pp. 239-268 in L. Sargent (ed.), Women and Revolution. Boston: South End Press.
Brownmiller, Susan
1975 Against our Will. New York: Bantam Books.
Chafe, William
1977 Women and Equality. New York:; Oxford University Press.
Crosby, Faye
1976 "A model of egotistical relative deprivation." Psychological Review 83:85-113.
Duquin, Mary, Brenda Bredemier, Carole Oglesby and Susan Greendorfer
1981 "Social, political and feminist attitudes of physical educators." Unpublished manuscript. University of Pittsburgh.
Ehrenreich, Barbara and Deidre English
1978 For Her Own Good: 150 Years of the Experts' Advice to Women. New York: Anchor Press.
Felshin, Jan
1974 "The Social View." In E. Gerber, J. Felshin, P. Berlin and W. Wyrick (eds.), The American Woman in Sport. Massachusetts: Addison-Wesley.
Freire, Paulo
1970 Pedagogy of the Oppressed. New York: Seabury Press.
Friedenberg, Edgar
1980 "The changing role of hormoerotic fantasy in spectator sports." Pp. 177-192 in D. Sabo and R. Runfola (eds.), Jock: Sports and Male Identity. New Jersey: Prentice-Hall.
Hackensmith, C.
1966 History of Physical Education. New York: Harper and Row.
Halsey, Elizabeth
1961 Women in Physical Education. New York: Putnam's Sons.
Harris, Marvin
1977 Cannibals and Kings: The Origins of Culture. New York: Random House.

Hartmann, Heidi
  1981 "The unhappy marriage of marxism and feminism: towards a more progressive
        union." Pp. 1-41 in L. Sargent (ed.), Women and Revolution. Boston: South
        End Press.
Heide, Wilma Scott
  1978 "Feminism for a sporting future." Pp. 195-204 in C. Oglesby (ed.), Women
        and Sport; From Myth to Reality. Philadelphia: Lea and Febiger.
Helmker, Judith
  1970 High School Girls' Athletic Associations: Their Organization and Administra-
        tion. New Jersey: A. S. Barnes.
Holt, Joan and Roberta Park
  1981 "The role of women in sports." Pp. 115-128 in W. Baker and J. Carroll (eds.),
        Sports in Modern America. Missouri: River City Publishers.
Kennard, June
  1977 "The history of physical education." Signs 2:835-842.
Klassen, Albert and Eugene Levitt
  1974 "A search for the structure of public attitudes and perceptions of homosexual-
        ity." Paper presented at the meeting of the American Anthropological Associa-
        tion, Mexico City.
Koedt, Anne, Ellen Levine, and Anita Rapone
  1973 Radical Feminism. New York: Quadrangle.
Komisar, Lucy
  1980 "Violence and the masculine mystique." Pp. 131-142 in D. Sabo and
        R. Runfola (eds.), Jock: Sports and Male Identity. New Jersey: Prentice-Hall.
Kopay, David and Perry Deane Young
  1980 "Homosexuality and marchismo sport: a gay jock speaks out." Pp. 89-94 in
        D. Sabo and R. Runfola (eds.), Jock: Sports and Male Identity. New Jersey:
        Prentice-Hall, Inc.
Lee, Mabel
  1978 Memories Beyond Bloomers. Washington, D.C.: American Alliance for Health
        Physical Education and Recreation.
Marlowe, Mike, Bob Algozzine, Harold Lerch and Paula Welch
  1978 "The games analysis intervention as a method of decreasing feminine play pat-
        terns of emotionally disturbed boys." Research Quarterly 49:484-490.
Marmor, Judd
  1980 Homosexual Behavior. New York: Basic Books, Inc.
Mathews, Jane
  1982 "The new feminism and the dynamics of social change." In L. Kerber and
        J. Mathews (eds.), Women's America" Refocusing the Past. New York: Oxford
        University Press.
Oglesby, Carole
  1978 Women and Sport: From Myth to Reality. Philadelphia: Lea and Febiger.
Parkhouse, Bonnie and Jackie Lapin
  1980 Women Who Win. New Jersey: Prentice-Hall.
Rosen, Efrem and Stellye Weinstein
  1982 "Sex education outreach." Health Education 13:13-15.
Sabo, Donald F. and Ross Runfola
  1980 Jock: Sport and Male Identity. New Jersey: Prentice-Hall.
Sefton, Alice Allene
  1941 The Women's Division National Amateur Athletic Federation California: Stan-
        ford University Press.

Stewart, Katie
    1981 "The marriage of capitalist and patriarchal ideologies: meanings of male bond-
        ing and male ranking in U.S. culture." Pp. 269-312 in L. Sargent (ed.), Women
        and Revolution. Boston: South End Press.
Tavris, Carol and Carole Offir
    1977 The Longest War. New York: Harcourt Brace Jovanovich.
Twin, Stephanie
    1979 Out of the Bleachers. New York: McGraw Hill.

PERCEPTIONS OF SPORTS INVOLVEMENT

Section IV

PERCEPTIONS OF SPORTS INVOLVEMENT

Howard Becker in *Outsiders: Studies in the Sociology of Deviance* showed us how in-group and out-group membership affected the perception of deviance. Although he studied jazz musicians and marijuana users, he could just as well have used athletes. The three chapters in this section deal with views of sport from the outside. Two of the three compare the outside view to the inside view.

In the first paper Vanreusel and Renson examine the concept of social stigma in the high risk sports of mountain climbing, scuba diving and spelunking. Based upon data collected through participant observation methods, the authors suggest that outsiders stigmatize members of risky-sports groups. At the same time stigma develops within the group and is used by members to support the sub-cultural value system.

Woodford and Scott survey the attitudes of metropolitan residents towards the participation of women in intercollegiate athletics. Their analysis shows that respondents had generally positive attitudes toward participation, but that these attitudes were affected by age and level of education but not by the sex of the respondent. Younger and more educated male and female respondents had a more positive attitude towards women participating in intercollegiate athletics than did older, less educated respondents.

Finally, Lerch applies the concept of relative deprivation to the perception of the salaries of professional athletes by other professional athletes (in-group comparison), and by non-athletes (out-group comparison). Finding dissatisfaction within both groups, he proposes a model to explain how this dissatisfaction is translated into action. This action involves strikes and holdouts by the players, and non-attendance or violence by the fans.

Chapter 12

THE SOCIAL STIGMA OF HIGH-RISK SPORT SUBCULTURES

B. Vanreusel and R. Renson,
Institute of Physical Education, K. U. Leuven, Belgium

Days before the British royal wedding between Lady Diana Spencer and Prince Charles, newspapers reported the British police had caught two young men stealing explosives. Later on, the two assumed terrorists were exposed as spelunkers, illegally gathering some equipment for their hobby (De Standaard, 1981). True or false, the press report reflects the social stigma associated with several sport settings because of deviant or perceived deviant behavior shown by participants. Studies have repeatedly indicated that certain types of behavior, commonly perceived as deviant, may be totally or partially accepted within some segments of society (Becker, 1963; Goffman, 1961; Cloward & Ohlin, 1966). Involvement in risky sports activities may be included as an example of this type of behavior. Klein (1976) has argued that all members of society learn to regard risk-taking as desirable and that hazardous recreation attracts those individuals who are unable to satisfy their need for risk-taking in educational, occupational or other socially productive activities. In this study, an opposite position is taken. Participation in hazardous sport activities may be a means to dissociate from the mainstream of society and to associate with a subculture. Social stigma constitutes the basic concept of this paper which is based on an empirical study of the subculture of three non-spectator high-risk sports: spelunking, rock climbing and scuba diving. The proposition that perceptions of social stigma by the participants contribute to the formation and maintenance of high risk sport subcultures will be examined.

In an extensive analysis of the literature on the concept of subculture, Jansegers (1980) discovered four constants in the definition of a subculture, leading to the following synthesis:

A subculture is an identifiable collectivity
1) with a specific cultural pattern of values, norms, sanctions, beliefs, rituals and symbols
2) with a specific social structure
3) with an identifiable impact on the behavior and the lifestyle of its members
4) which operates as an entity but not totally independent from the dominant culture.

While the need to study sport in natural groups has been emphasized (Loy, 1973), the subculture of sports characterized by risky activities such as rock climbing, mountaineering, scuba diving, spelunking and skydiving has received relatively little attention. The fact that the subculture of high-risk sports has, until now, escaped the extensive attention of sport sociologists may be attributed to several reasons. First, risky sports are often characterized by a rather informal organization and a volatile structure. This makes it more difficult for the sociologist to penetrate the social milieu than if he were observing a more formally organized sport environment. Second, non-spectator risky sport subcultures tend to hold a marginal position outside the mainstream of the sport interest, physically distant from arenas, courts and stadiums. Sport sociologists, like the overall public, seem to be attracted to more visible and accessible sports when determining their focus of attention. Third, during their years as researchers and participants in some sports, commonly labelled hazardous activities, the authors shared the unproven feeling that members of the risky-sport milieu have developed subtle defense mechanisms to protect their territory against penetration by undesired intruders such as sociologists.

However, it would be incorrect to assert that the realm of risky-sport subcultures is still situated on the dark side of the moon. Journalistic literature sometimes offers a revealing description of the subculture of risky-sport milieus. Editing a collection of press articles on mountaineering and rock climbing Wilson (1978) contributed to the understanding of the 'Games Climbers Play' from a subcultural perspective. Insight into the subculture of high-risk sports can also be obtained through reports on expeditions or explorations or other narrative descriptions by participants. Abundant literature is available on mountaineering, written by heroes of the past such as Hillary, Herzog or Terray, as well as by current masters of the art like Messner and Bonington. Although written for other purposes than social research, these writings often reflect subcultural values, norms and symbols. In the seventies, a number of more stringent studies considerably enriched the literature. In most of these studies direct observation was utilized as a methodological approach. Arnold (1972, 1976) reported on the subculture of skydiving. Csikszentmihalyi (1975) and Donnelly (1980) participated and conducted research in the milieu of climbers. Status hierarchies among spelunkers were experienced and analyzed by Edwards (1976). Also, Pearson (1977, 1979) investigated the surfing scene on the beaches of New Zealand and Australia during what he called his 'surfari.'

A large number of researchers have focused on risk-seeking in sport. It is not an aim of this study to reopen the discussion on the delimitation of the concept of risk nor to propose another model to pinpoint the definition. Let it simply be said that the risk factor in sport may be determined by the degree of control over at least three elements: the environment, the action, and the self (FIG. 1).

Sport activities labelled as high risk sports usually demand a high degree of control of each element. At the same time, chances for a failure of control are enhanced by engaging in this type of activity, which may result in physical injury with death as an ultimate sanction. Among participants, a distinction is often made between the subjective risk, which depends on the individual

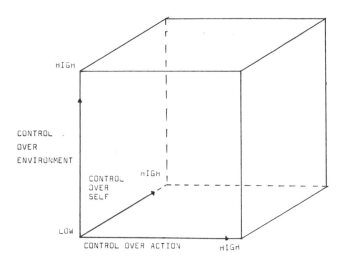

FIGURE 1:   Some Components Determining The Degree of Risk In Sport

(e.g., the risk taken by a climber trying to conquer a cliff on or beyond the limits of his competence) and the objective risk proceeding from the environment (e.g., the risk for a climber of being caught by rocks toppling down).

Generally, high-risk sports can be described by at least two common characteristics:

1) risk constitutes an essential part of the activity
2) participants engage in risky situations on a voluntary basis.

In the literature, risk-seeking has traditionally been related to characteristics of the individual. Therefore, risk takers have often been studied from a psychological point of view. Gray (1968) and Lester (1969) have studied relationships between participation in climbing and personality. Nichols (1969) has investigated the personality of scuba divers. Motivations of mountaineers have been explored by Bratton, et al. (1979), Houston (1967) and Boedts (1980). Griffiths, et al. (1979) and Splichal (1977) conducted research on anxiety as an intervening factor on the performance of scuba divers. Zuckerman (1977) approached sensation-seeking behavior, such as participation in dangerous sports, from a theory of arousal. Rock climbing, as a potential flow activity, has been studied and utilized by Csikszentmihalyi (1977) to explain the concept of 'deep play.'

The centrality of the concept 'risk' in sport is the common characteristic of these studies. However, a study of risk-seekers, not only as individuals but also as members of a subculture where risk-taking prevails as a social value, even as a shared norm, might be fruitful in order to understand participation in risky sports. It is important to realize that risk-taking sport activities are interpreted in different ways. What may be perceived as a dangerous act by many outsiders may constitute an essential part of the routine or behavior that falls within the boundaries of a subcultural norm and value pattern. The premises of the symbolic interactionist perspective as developed by Blumer (1969) were applied in the realm of sport by Fine (1981), among others.

One of these premises suggests that meanings are modified through an interpretive process. This process obviously is taking place with regard to hazardous behavior in sport. For example, intense discussions on the sense or the nonsense of solo climbing, a booming subdiscipline among rock climbers, are mostly defeated by disparate interpretations of risk taking. The symbolic interactionist viewpoint may be an important value in the analysis of the subculture of high risk sports. Split perceptions of risk in sport by the in-group versus the out-group may contribute to the origin of the stigma that is resting upon risk sports.

HIGH-RISK SPORTS AND SOCIAL STIGMA

In his study on stigma, Goffman (1963) outlined the origin and evolution of the concept: "The Greeks originated the term stigma to refer to bodily signs designed to expose something unusual and bad about the moral status of the signifier. Today the term is widely used in something like the original sense, but is applied more to the disgrace itself than to the bodily evidence of it." As an extension of Goffman's interpretation, a social stigma can be described as a discrediting typification that rests upon the members of an identifiable group. This typification contributes to the process of the stigmatized persons being seen as a group by outsiders and consequently perceiving themselves as a group.

Although Philips and Schafer (1976) generalize that sportsmen usually share approved or desirable characteristics rather than a stigma such as drug addiction or homosexuality, an exception could be made for conspicuous risk takers in sport. Exposing themselves voluntarily to consciously enhanced risk, skydivers, rock climbers, spelunkers, scuba divers and other sport participants can be seen as stigmatized because they share norms and values which are in conflict with the mainline values of the dominant culture. Hazardous sport activities are often perceived and labelled as a kind of deviant behavior. The process of negative labelling may lead to the ascription of social stigma to the participants in dangerous sports. Two different sources of social stigma among high risk sports can be distinguished:

1) social stigma as a result of stereotyping

Although enhanced danger is a substantial part of several sport settings, it is obviously not the only feature. Nevertheless the connection between high risk sports and the negative results of risk such as accidents and precarious situations is continuously being made by outsiders. This association of risky sports and disaster, often emphasized by the media, creates stereotypes. Jokes, cartoons and comic strips as crosscultural expressions of social stereotypes mostly outline the risk taker in sport in a critical situation which usually comes to a bad end. Themes such as 'the scuba diver and the shark', 'the climber on the snapping rope' or 'the spelunker above the invisible abyss', offer an unfailing variety of cynical jokes and create the stereotype of the nut constantly acting at death's door or the fanatic with a suicidal drive. Whereas participants in traditional sports are commonly described as athletes, those involved in risky sports are usually labeled as addicts.

Still more colorful is the term 'the adrenaline junkie,' used to refer to the thrill seeker in sport.

2) social stigma as result of role identification

As a response to the ascription of social stigma by outsiders, a second source of social stigma is assumed to be found among the participants themselves. Although their behavior is often labeled by outsiders as partially deviant, participants in risky sports frequently appear to identify with and even enhance their image as outlaws. With regard to climbers, Donnelly (1976) advances the thesis that climbers may be considered as outsiders and often are perceived as crazies, nuts or fanatics. But he adds: "I also have a sneaking suspicion that many climbers enjoy their roles as outsiders." Bumper stickers indicating that "climbers do it on the rocks," "Spelunkers do it in the dark," "divers do it deeper," and "skydivers do it in the air" not only raise sexual connotations but also seem to approve the risk taker in his role of the marginal athlete.

More support for the assumption that individuals or groups might affirm themselves in their role as stigmatized persons is given by Goffman (1963). He distinguished a specific kind of deviance ". . . presented by individuals who are seen as voluntarily declining and accepting openly the social place accorded them and who act irregularly and somewhat rebelliously in connection with our basic institutions . . ." Goffman calls them disaffiliates. Skydivers, rock climbers, scuba divers, spelunkers and other risky sport participants who reinforce their social stigma by voluntarily participating in dangerous activities willingly make themselves seen as disaffiliates. This process of acquisition and cultivation of social stigma by members of high-risk sport milieus may lead to perceptions of isolation on the part of the participants. An alternative set of values and normative expectations focused on risk-taking behavior might develop in specific high-risk sport settings and consequently contribute to the formation of risky sport subcultures.

In summary, the proposed thesis states that the acquisition and cultivation of social stigma by participants in high-risk sports, due to voluntary exposure to risk, contributes to the creatin of high-risk subcultures. As an attempt to test this proposition, a field study has been carried out within the natural setting of three risky sports: 1) scuba diving 2) spelunking 3) rock climbing.

METHODS

The data for this study were extracted from three research reports on the subculture of scuba divers (Wellens, 1981), spelunkers (Kooreman, 1981) and rock climbers (Viveys, 1981). These reports are part of a global research project on sport as subculture.[1] A methodological option was made for data gathering by complete participation and covert observation. This choice was inspired by authors such as Talamini and Page (1973) who pointed out that ". . . the study of the culture of any group . . . calls for an understanding of the meaning of the particular culture or subculture for those who share it. To gain such understanding requires field research, study which involves close observation, participation and not least a measure of empathy with members of it . . ." The writings on field research by Douglas (1976) were extremely helpful in developing the strategy and techniques of the field study.

Three independent observers, one for each sport activity, carried out the field work in their roles of club members.[2] Each of the observers was already involved in the particular sport before the observation period at a knowledgeable (scuba diver and spelunker) or expert (climber) level. The observers were trained in the theory of sport subcultures and the methodology of covert participant observation, but were unaware of the proposition of social stigma attached to risky sport subcultures. The observation period covered one to two years. The observers were involved in all club activities: weekly meetings, training sessions, weekend excursions and expeditions or camps abroad.

The data were recorded by observation schedules, field notes and informal interviews. The observers were trained to record verbal communication, behavior, events and material circumstances in a non-interpretive manner. A qualitative anlaysis of the data was made by the observers, referring to cultural aspects (values, norms, sanctions, symbols, rituals, beliefs) and structural aspects (roles, positions, status, subgroups). In the light of the 'stigma thesis,' a comparative analysis across the three studies was made by another independent researcher (FIG. 2). Only those aspects which appeared in all three studies were taken into account. Utilizing this design helps to maintain the reliability of the participant observation method (Friedrichs and Luedtke, 1975; McCall and Simmons, 1969; Thomson, 1977). The influence of the unplanned fact that the three observers were female could not be measured.

RESULTS

Although the nature of the observed activities differed, in many aspects, from more traditional sports, each of the observers reported a set of values which could be ascribed to the general sport environment. The requirement of a high degree of skill on the part of the group members can be seen as a typical value in

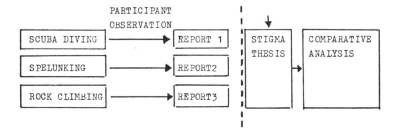

FIGURE 2: Rationale For The Study On Three High-Risk Sport Subcultures

sport subcultures. Since spelunkers, rock climbers and scuba divers essentially depend on technically complex equipment, the members of the subculture had to demonstrate their knowledge of the technology as well as technical skill. At the same time the mastering of an extended set of physical skills was highly esteemed. Scuba divers and spelunkers showed a pronounced respect for the ecosystem. Topics such as fauna, flora and geological conditions were discussed and studied intensively. Scuba divers and spelunkers appeared to wrap their activities in scientism. Among the observed group of climbers the knowledge of the environment was, instead, aimed toward the difficulties to be surmounted.

Nature, as the 'common ground' for each of the three observed sport settings was obviously perceived in different ways. The environment, approached as a subject of curiosity by the diver and the spelunker, was seen as a challenging obstacle by the climber. Where scuba divers and spelunkers appeared to identify with the role of the explorer, the climbers adopted the image of the conqueror as a role model.

The observation reports pinpointed a varying degree of nonconformity. Acting in a close relationship with a challenging and often hostile environment, most participants consciously ignored a number of cultural values relating to comfort. The orientation toward nonconformity was less obvious in the milieu of scuba divers who tended to be more rigorous in their activities and demonstrated highly disciplined, almost military-like drills in their training program. Among the climbers and spelunkers, nonconformity claimed a central position. The observed group of spelunkers could be described as cultural outlaws as far as their behavior is concerned. During their trips and expeditions spelunkers tended to disregard all the basic rules of hygiene, planning, organization and time scheduling. Furthermore, they showed obvious dislike for neatness, politeness, sociability and other mainstream values. Obscenities constituted a substantial part of their conversation. Changing the wetsuit for dry clothes after a caving trip has become a collective striptease, publicly performed in winter and summer.

Nonconformist behavior was reported several times to continue outside the sport context. In a certain area, well known for its caves, spelunkers added to their reputation by entering the local bars and restaurants while still wearing their sludgy wetsuits. The results also revealed that the trend toward nonconformity often dominated the entire lifestyle of the members. Some climbers used to camp in tents during winter ski vacations to steel themselves against a hostile climate. Others were reported to practice their skills on a wall of their home they had converted into an artificial climbing wall. One of the observers recorded a group of spelunkers who celebrated New Year's Eve in their favorite cave.

From the standpoint of the overall culture one would expect safety and survival to be supreme value orientations among high-risk sport participants. Yet each of the three research reports revealed a highly ambiguous attitude toward safety and survival. On the one hand, safety was constantly promoted via an elaborate set of both formal and informal prescriptions and prohibitions in each of the observed sport settings. The emphasis on safety skills, the training in emergency procedures and a rigorous check of the equipment before each activity appeared to indicate the central position of values related to safety and survival in the subcultural value system. Especially among scuba divers, an extensive set of safety-related signs is part of their formalized non-verbal communication. On the other hand, a number of reported events, conversations and ways of behavior demonstrated that both formal and informal norms on safety were permanently and consciously broken, sometimes leading to extremely risky situations. As long as it was an individual act, not putting other persons in danger, neither formal or informal sanctions on risky behavior were reported among climbers or spelunkers. A penalty system for infringing safety rules was in force among some groups of scuba divers, but only in the context of organized club sessions. Thus, safety and survival, esteemed values at first glance, apparently were disregarded as subcultural values, whereas boldness and risk-seeking attitude were often informally appreciated.

This ambiguity was less obvious in the milieu of scuba divers than it was among the spelunkers and rock climbers. The existence of a hierarchical status system was unanimously reported by the observers. The components of status in the subculture can be reduced to a constellation of three values:

1) a high degree of exposure to risk

Some high status activities are solo climbing without safety devices or siphon diving (diving into a water-filled cave with an outlet into another, often unexplored cave)

2) a high degree of involvement in the subculture

Rookies do not gain any status by exhibiting risky behavior. On the contrary, risk-taking rookies are perceived as violating the subcultural norms and they may be expelled from the subculture. Risk-taking is accorded status only for experienced members who have been part of the subculture for a while.

3) a high level of performance

In scuba diving and rock climbing international standards of performance have been developed based upon the degree of difficulty of braving the environment. This trend to objectify performances is a rather recent evolution in the changing subcultural scene of hazardous sports and has created a new means for status achievement. The former components of status are intertwined and status seekers have to fulfil the requirements of each component. For example, the highest status may be achieved by an experienced climber surmounting an extremely difficult cliff alone and without the use of safety devices.

This trinity of values determining the subcultural status hierarchy was also detected in the content of many stories circulating in each of the settings. Together with the jargon of highly specialized "techno talk," adventurous stories accounted for the greatest part of communication among the members of the different subcultures. The content of the stories was consistently focused on risky situations (the ultimate rescue, the insurmountable difficulties, the unexpected blow) or on accidents often with a fatal end during the sport action. The following value orientations can be inferred from each story:

— a latent admiration of risk
— a cynical joking relationship toward the negative outcomes of risk such as accidents and death.
— an attitude of fatalism toward self-experienced accidents.
— a cult of heroes, functioning as trendsetters for new developments and styles in each sport.

The hero created in the stories was a hero of boldness, acting on the boundaries of survival. The fact that in many cases the hero was dead and buried as a result of his heroism did not reduce his status but even seemed to enhance it.

The ambiguous attitude toward survival and safety in the subcultural value system of high-risk sports and the tendency to perceive a risk-seeking attitude as a norm also showed up in the treatment of novices by climbers and spelunkers. On the one hand, the novices were initiated into the required technical and physical skills regarding safety, and as mentioned before, risk-increasing initiatives by novices were looked on with disfavor. On the other hand, experienced club members often took them on a trip which exceeded the competence of the novice. Through this kind of initiation rite, novices were confronted very soon with risk as a prevailing subcultural value.

DISCUSSION

Since a considerable differentiation of value orientations was found among the observed sport groups, it became obvious that the concept 'high-risk sport subculture' cannot be used as an overall label, even for sport activities which have an enhanced exposure to risk in common. The subcultures of rock climbers, spelunkers and scuba divers are different from each other in many

perspectives. It thus seems more legitimate to look at each particular sport setting as a specific subculture.

The field observations of climbers and spelunkers revealed a
fairly similar set of value orientations, norms and a status hierarchy partially based upon a risk-seeking attitude and noncon-
formism. Yet, the subcultural value pattern of scuba divers which
was rather oriented to 'law and order,' seemed more parallel to
dominant value orientations. With regard to the thesis about the
origin of social stigma in the subculture of risky sports, a distinction has to be made among three types of subcultural values.

The following pattern relates primarily to the observed settings of climbers and spelunkers and only in a minor degree to the
scuba divers.

1. Concordant values (FIG. 3,a)

A demonstrated knowledge of technology and environment,
physical and technical skill, respect for the ecosystem, exploring
and conquering are all highly esteemed values in the observed
subcultures. These values can be seen as harmonious with the
expectations of the dominant culture. They do not imply disfa-
vorable labeling on the part of the overall culture, nor do they
suggest a process of disaffiliation by the members of the subculture. Therefore, no support for the thesis that a social stigma orig-
inates among the members of risky sport subcultures can be
deduced from these type of values. On the contrary, they seem
rather to generate the acceptance of risky sport activities within
the prevailing norms and values.

2. Discordant values (FIG. 3,b)

As opposed to the concordant values, nonconformity, voluntary exposure to risk, the appreciation of a risk-seeking attitude, fatalism and boldness can be seen as conflicting with the
mainstream cultural values. Whereas participants in high-risk
sport activities may be labelled as 'nuts' or fanatics by outsiders,
they obviously contribute to this image through the adoption of
a value set which can be considered a self-induced source of social

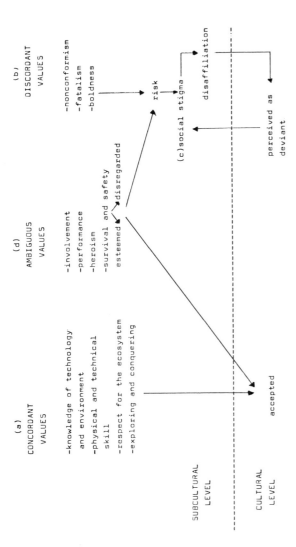

FIGURE 3: Value Orientations And Social Stigma In The Subculture Of Spelunkers
And Climbers. An Empirical Model

stigma. It was assumed that a discordant value orientation might cause perceptions of deviance on the part of the dominant culture and, therefore, a degree of disaffiliation on the part of the members of the subculture. This value constellation seems to provide empirical support for the proposition. Since the process of disaffiliation from the dominant culture enhances the social stigma of risky sport settings, a vicious cycle emerges (FIG. 3,c) which causes the social stigma of spelunkers and climbers to accumulate.

3. Ambiguous values (FIG. 3,d)

The degree of involvement, the level of performance, heroism, survival and safety obviously hold a split position in the value system of climbers and spelunkers. Because they are generally acknowledged and esteemed, these values contribute directly to the acceptance of the observed risky sport activities into the ruling value system. Otherwise, survival and safety appear to depreciate informally in the subculture of climbers and spelunkers in favor of the appreciation or risk. Involvement, performance and heroism only became esteemed subcultural values through their association with the acceptance of a high level of risk. Thus, this set of values may place risk taking activities in harmony with the overall culture. In their subcultural meaning though, the same value orientation may initiate perceptions of social stigma.

CONCLUSION

The study of three high-risk sport subcultures provides at least partial empirical support for the thesis that a social stigma attached to risky sports can originate in, and be reinforced by, the subcultural value system. Yet it should be noted that these findings relate only to the observed groups of climbers and spelunkers and, only in minor degree, to the scuba divers.

Although we share the opinion that a 'natural' methodological approach, such as participant observation, should be utilized in the study of sport subcultures, methodological weaknesses and limitations with regard to the observed sample prevent more gen-

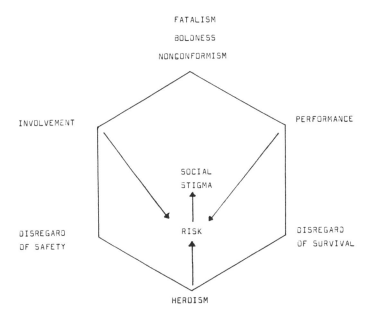

FIGURE 4:   Values Contributing To Social Stigma Among Spelunkers And Climbers

eral conclusions. A comparative analysis of data gained by both qualitative and quantitative methods would undoubtedly provide a more solid base to test the proposition.

A final observation can be made, namely, that those already involved in high-risk subcultures view this "massification" process with regret. Perhaps self-induced social stigma among risky sport participants may be a social reflex to protect the subculture against being invaded by the masses. Risk seekers in sport may still prefer to be seen as "fools on the hill" rather than to be "just another brick in the wall."

NOTES

[1]'Sport as a subculture' is a research project run since 1978 by the research unit 'Social and Cultural Kinantropology' under the supervision of Professor R. Renson, Institute of Physical Education, K. U. Leuven, Belgium.

[2]The authors are indebted to Annelise Kooreman, Lutgarde Viveys and Rita Wellens, students at the Institute of Physical Education, K. U. Leuven, Belgium, for the collection of the data.

REFERENCES

Arnold, D. O.
    1972 "The social organization of sky diving: a study in vertical mobility." Presented at the Pacific Sociological Association Meeting, Session on Leisure, Sport and Recreation. Portland.
    1976 "A sociologist looks at sport parachuting." Pp. 143-145 in A. Yiannakis, et al. (eds.), Sport Sociology: Contemporary Themes. Dubuque, Iowa: Kendall Hunt.
Becker, H. S.
    1963 Outsiders: Studies in the Sociology of Deviance. New York: Free Press.
Blumer, H.
    1969 Symbolic Interactionism; Perspective and Method. New York: Prentice-Hall.
Bratton, R. D., G. Kinnaer and G. Koroluk
    1979 "Why man climbs mountains." International Review of Sport Sociology 14:23-35.
Cloward, R. and L. E. Ohlin
    1966 "Norms of delinquent subcultures." Pp. 144-148 in B. J. Biddle and E. J. Thomas (eds.), Role Theory: Concepts and Research, New York: Wiley.
Csikszentmihalyi, M.
    1975 "The Americanization of rock climbing." Pp. 484-488 in A. Yolly and K. Sylva (eds.), Play. Penguin.
    1977 Beyond Boredom and Anxiety. San Francisco: Jossey-Bass.
De Standaard
    1981 "Britten met explosieven waren speleologen." (British with explosives were spelunkers.) August 8.
Donnelly, P.
    1976 "Outsiders — The climber as a deviant: a reply to Greitsbauer and Kingsley." Climbing 1:31-33.
    1980 The Subculture and the Public Image of Climbers. Doctoral Dissertation, University of Massachusetts, Dept. of Sport Studies. Amherst.
Douglas, J. D.
    1975 Investigative Social Research. Beverly Hills, London: Sage.
Edwards, D. D.
    1976 The Development and Mechanism of Sub-group Status Hierarchies. Unpublished dissertation, University of Lancaster, Lancaster.
Fine, G. A.
    1981 "Small groups and sports: a symbolic interactionist perspective. Presented at the Conference of the North American Society for the Sociology of Sport. Fort Worth, November 12-15.
Friedrichs, J. and H. Luedtke
    1975 Participant Observation. Theory and Practice. Lexington: Saxon.
Fritschner, L. M.

1978 "The making and maintenance of the underdog class." Journal of Sport Behavior. 1:3-13.

Goffman, E.
1961 Asylums. Garden City, New York: Anchor.
1963 Stigma, New York: Prentice Hall. 1-2; 140-147.

Gray, D.
1968 "Personality and climbing." The Alpine Journal. November:167-172.

Griffiths, T. J., D. H. Steel and P. Vaccaro
1979 "Relationship between anxiety and performance in scuba diving." Perceptual and Motor Skills. 48, 1009-1010.

Houston, C. S.
1967 "Mountaineering" Pp. 616-636 in R. Slovenko and J. A. Knight (eds.), Motivations in Play, Games and Sport. Springfield: Thomas.

Jansegers, L.
1981 Sport als Subcultuur, Conceptueel kader en literotuuroverzicht. (Sport as subculture, conceptual framework and review of literature) unpublished licentiate thesis, Catholic University of Leuven, Institute of Physical Education, Leuven.

Klein, D.
1976 "The relationship of risk-taking to recreational injury." Pp. 90-93 in T. T. Craig (ed.), The Humanistic and Mental Health Aspects of Sports, Exercise and Recreation. Chicago: American Medical Association.

Kooreman, Annelise
1981 Sport als subkultuur, speleologie. (Sport as subculture, Spelunking) unpublished licentiate thesis, Catholic University of Leuven, Institute of Physical Education, Leuven.

Lester, J. T.
1969 "Personality and Everest." The Alpine Journal 74:101-107.

Loy, J. W.
1973 "Reaction to Luschen paper" Pp. 78-79 in Marie Hart (ed.), Sport in the Sociocultural Process. Dubuque: Brown.

McCall, G. J. and J. L. Simmons (eds.)
1969 Issues in Participant Observation. Mass.: Addison Wesley.

Nichols, A. K.
1969 "The personality of sub-aqua divers." Research Papers in Physical Education, 8:3-9.

Pearson, K.
1979a "Surfing subcultures of Australia and New Zealand." Queensland: University of Queensland Press.

Pearson, K.
1979b "Outgroups: clubbies and surfies." Momentum 2:53-70.

Philips, J. C. and W. E. Schafer
1976 "Subcultures in sport: a conceptual and methodological approach." Pp. 131 in A. Yiannakis et al. (eds.) Sport Sociology: contemporary themes. Dubuque, Iowa, Kendall Hunt.

Splichal, P.
1977 "Test psychologique d'anxiete et plongee sportive" Medecine du sport 5:59-62.

Talamini, J. T. and C. H. Page
1973 Sport and Society. An Anthology. Boston, Toronto: Little Brown:36.

Thompson, R. W.
1977 "Participant observation in the sociological analysis of sport." International Review of Sport Sociology 4:99-109.

Viveys, Lutgarde

1981 Sport als subkultuur, Alpinisme (Sport as subculture, mountaineering.)
       Unpublished licentiate thesis, Catholic University of Leuven, Institute of Phys-
       ical Education.
Wellens, Rita
1981 Sport als subkultuur, Diepzeeduiken (Sport as subculture, Scuba diving.)
       Unpublished licentiate thesis, Catholic University of Leuven, Institute of Phys-
       ical Education.
Wilson, K. (ed.)
1978 Games Climbers Play. San Francisco: Sierra.
Zuckerman, M.
1979 Sensation Seeking, Beyond the Optimal Level of Arousal. Hillsdale: Erlbaum.

Chapter 13

ATTITUDES TOWARD THE PARTICIPATION OF WOMEN IN INTERCOLLEGIATE SPORTS: EVIDENCE FROM A METROPOLITAN AREA SURVEY

Robert C. Woodford and Wilbur J. Scott,
University of Oklahoma

There has been a long-held belief in our culture that women who engage in vigorous physical activity or exercise run the risk of physically harming themselves. For many years this belief served as a rationale for the negative social sanctions accorded females who became involved in sport. Physiological research, in the meantime, has proven that women are quite capable of participating safely in vigorous activity. Further, with the passage of Title IX of the Education Amendments Act of 1972, and with the women's movement of the 1970's, women are participating more now in intercollegiate sports than at any other time in American history.

Yet, the jury still seems to be out on what is regarded as female role-appropriate behavior in sport. Fairly recent literature reports that female athletes are still stigmatized as being in some way unfeminine (cf. Eitzen & Sage, 1978). These findings persist despite the fact that most previous research related to participation in sport by women utilizes samples drawn from university or high school settings where attitudes are expected to be more supportive than in the general population. The present study attempts to tap this broader population by surveying an adult metropolitan area sample. This investigation gauges the attitudes of the general public in three broad areas: (1) the general appropriateness of female students participating in intercollegiate sports; (2) the relative appropriateness of participating in specific intercollegiate sports by female students; and (3) the perception that women's intercollegiate sports programs detract from, and conflict with, men's programs.

REVIEW

The majority of studies focusing on attitudes concerning the participation of females in sport have compared the views of students in public school and college settings. The work of Selby and Lewko (1976), who gauged grade school children's attitudes toward female involvement in sports, is typical. Their findings indicate that girls at grade levels 3 through 9 have significantly more favorable attitudes toward female participation in sports than the boys, and that there is a tendency for older children to view women in sports more favorably than children in the earlier grades. In addition, grade school girls, who themselves are participants, are reported to have more favorable attitudes than non-participants, while the opposite is found for the two groups of grade school boys. The investigators speculate that the more negative orientation of participant than non-participant boys might stem from the feeling by the former that they are competing with participant girls for sport facilities and attention of the coaches.

Similarly, Griffin (1973) examined college students' perceptions of several roles for women, including that of housewife, woman athlete, girlfriend, woman professor, mother, and "ideal woman." The female athlete and woman professor were the least valued roles. In examining the semantic space between concepts, she found the most distance between female athlete and ideal woman. Griffin concluded that there is a continuing existence of the traditional sex roles for women and that a conflict continues to exist for a woman who chooses to pursue a nontraditional profession.

Finally, Fisher and his colleagues (1978) reported the results of two concurrent investigations. In a departure from the questionnaire format, the two studies utilized slides of sportswomen in action to tap the perceptions of women in sport. In the first study, college male and female athletes and nonathletes were shown 15 slides and asked to rate each slide on a scale of 1-10 indicating their perceptions of the female depicted as the "ideal female." The study revealed that males and nonathletes perceived the female sportswoman as significantly less ideal than did females and athletes. In the second study, high school male and female urban and rural athletes were asked to view and rate the same slides. The investigators found that male and urban athletes perceive the female sportswoman as significantly less ideal than female and rural subjects. Though these two studies reveal gender differences in the perception of women in sport, they also report moderate acceptance of the female athlete by both sexes.

There is considerable evidence that participation in certain sports has traditionally been considered more socially acceptable than others for women. The springboard for much of this research is the work of Metheney (1965) who classified "acceptable" sports for women on the basis of survey data from a sample of college women. Sports which require application of force to a heavy object, body contact or hard running and throwing are found to have low social approval (i.e., track and field, basketball and softball), while sports emphasizing skill and grace or having a spatial barrier or distance from an opponent have been more widely accepted for female participation (i.e., tennis, swimming, and gymnastics).

Snyder and Kivlin (1975) verified Metheney's conclusions by asking a sample of residents in the Toledo metropolitan area, "In your opinion, would participation in any of the following sports enhance a girl's/woman's feminine qualities?" Affirmative responses by sport were: swimming, 67%; tennis, 57%; gymnastics, 54%; softball, 14%; basketball, 1..4%; and track and field,

13%. These findings also suggest that individual sports are more socially acceptable than team sports. This has been a consistent finding in studies of female participation in sport (Debacy et al., 1970; Del Ray, 1977; Harres, 1968; Sage & Loudermilk, 1979).

In a later comparative study of college female athletes and nonathletes, Snyder and Kivlin (1977) found that over 50% of intercollegiate female basketball and track and field athletes felt that social stigma is accorded to women participating in those sports, while only 40% of the female swimmers and divers, and 31% of the female gymnasts perceive a stigma associated with their specialities. By comparision, 65% of the control group of women nonathletes feel there is a stigma attached to women's participation in sports.

Several investigators have suggested that a slight change in the social acceptability of female participation in sport is evident, and that the conflict between the roles of woman and athlete seems to be fading (Snyder et al., 1979; Sage & Loudermilk, 1979). These observations concur with the research findings of Kingsley et al. (1977), who asked college women athletes and nonathletes to rate the degree of social acceptability of high- and low-success aspirations of softball players and dancers. Their study contains no evidence to support the belief that a woman who aspires to, or engages in, a traditionally masculine sport is viewed more negatively than a woman who is less aspiring or engaged in a more traditionally feminine sport.

These latter findings and observations are also supportive of studies which have surveyed female athletes' perceptions of their own self concept, feminine image and other areas of personal feelings. A longitudinal study by Mulumphy (1970), of National Intercollegiate Women's Golf and Tennis Tournament participants, reports that these female athletes view their participation as contributing to their feminine image and making them more attractive to males and more interesting to be with. Similarly, Vincent (1976) administered the Tennessee self-concept scale to college women athletes and nonathletes. Her findings reveal that women physical education majors and participants in high school competitive athletic programs have significantly higher self-concept scores than all other groups. Likewise, Snyder and Kivlin (1975) find that women sports participants in the 1972 National Intercollegiate Championships and Olympic Gymnastics tryouts have higher scores on measures of psychological well-being and body image than female nonathletes in university level sociology classes. Similar results are found by Snyder and Speitzer (1976) at the high school level where female athletes indicated a more positive attitude about their body image than their nonathlete peers. More recently, Nicholson (1979) sampled attitudes associated with sport participation among junior high school females. She reports no significant differences between participants and non-participants with regard to self-perception of happiness, affection, feminity, sensitivity, gentleness, and attractiveness.

STATEMENT OF THE PROBLEM

With the exception of the Snyder and Kivlin (1975) study, previous research related to female participation in sport is based exclusively on samples of athletes and/or nonathletes drawn from populations within universities, high schools or grade schools. The major problem with these restricted samples is that age and education are held constant and thus are removed as explanations of attitudes toward women's participation in sports. Furthermore, no previous studies have raised the issue of opposition to women's sports because it is seen as a threat to men's sports at the institutional level. Selby and Lewko (1976) raise the possibility of this conflict by noting that grade school boys who participate in sports have more negative attitudes toward sports involvement by females than boys who do not participate in sports.

This study attempts to address both of these shortcomings by utilizing a metropolitan sample and by assessing the attitudes of the "general public" concerning: (1) the desirability of female students participating in intercollegiate sports in general; (2) the participation of women in specific intercollegiate sports; and

(3) the extent to which women's intercollegiate sports programs conflict with men's programs.

DATA COLLECTION AND ANALYSIS

Data were collected during the Spring of 1981 as part of an annual survey of Oklahoma City and its surrounding suburbs. Three hundred fifty-three respondents were interviewed in their homes by trained interviewers. The sample was drawn randomly from the Polk Directory; persons in the initial sampling frame who refused to participate were replaced by resampling. The respondents range from 18 to 84 years of age and should be representative of adults in the Oklahoma City metropolitan area. Subjects were asked to use a four point format ranging from "strongly agree" to "strongly disagree" to register their response to each item. Responses are crosstabulated by gender, education, and age, and chi-square statistics are presented as an indication of statistical significance. Since this is a preliminary investigation, the .10 probability level is used as the significance level.

FINDINGS

Table 1 contains the crosstabulations of items measuring general attitudes toward participation of women in intercollegiate sports by gender, education and age. Agreement with the items reflects a more negative view of participation by females in intercollegiate sports. Basically, sample respondents view the participation of women in intercollegiate sports very favorably. Although more than half of the sample (53.6%) agree that men seem "naturally" to know more about sports than women, less than a third of them agree with any of the other items. Only 27.2% and 21.9% agree that "women are likely to develop unsightly muscles if they exercise regularly" and that "to excel in organized sports, a woman must be more like a man than a woman"; only 11.6%, 11.7%, and 10.8% think that "women ought to stick to cheerleading . . . ;" that "participation in organized sports takes time away from the other important things a

TABLE 1

GENERAL ATTITUDES TOWARD PARTICIPATION OF WOMEN IN INTERCOLLEGIATE SPORTS, BY GENDER, BY EDUCATION, BY AGE

Items	Total (n=353)	Gender			Education			Age			
		Males (n=147)	Females (n=206)	P of χ^2	No College (n=181)	College (n=172)	P of χ^2	18-30 (n=100)	31-50 (n=123)	50+ (n=130)	P of χ^2
Women are likely to develop unsightly muscles if they exercise regularly.	27.2[a]	23.1	30.1	.15[b]	37.0	16.9	.00	19.0	22.0	38.5	.00
Women ought to stick to cheerleading and leave participation in organized sports to men.	11.6	10.2	12.6	.48	17.7	5.2	.00	7.0	9.8	16.9	.05
Participation in organized sports only takes time away from the other important things a woman ought to be doing.	11.7	10.9	12.1	.72	17.1	5.8	.00	8.0	6.5	19.2	.00
A woman cannot be both a good athlete and a truly feminine person.	10.8	12.9	7.8	.21	11.0	8.7	.46	9.0	5.7	14.6	.06
Men seem naturally to know more about sports than women.	53.9	59.2	51.0	.13	53.6	55.2	.75	46.0	51.2	63.8	.02
To excel in organized sports, a woman has to be more like a man than a woman.	21.9	21.8	21.9	.99	26.0	17.4	.05	20.0	16.3	28.5	.06

[a] Percent who "strongly agree" or "agree somewhat."

[b] Probability that difference(s) between reported proportions is (are) due solely to chance. P < .01 listed as .00.

woman ought to be doing," and that "a woman cannot be both a good athlete and a truly feminine person."

The chi-square probabilities reveal no significant differences between the responses of males and females to the six items. However, when the sample is broken down by education into those respondents having college experience and those having no college experience, four of the six items differ significantly between groups. In each case, a larger percentage of subjects with no college experience express agreement with the item, thus reflecting a more traditional view of women's participation in intercollegiate sports. Finally, significant differences are found between the responses of three age groups— 18 to 30, 31 to 50, and older than 50 — for all six items. In each case, the largest percentage of agreement is found among subjects in the oldest age category (50+ years) and indicates that they hold more traditional views than their younger counterparts.

The data presented in Table 2 reflect the extent to which a woman is thought to lose some of her desirable qualities by participating in specific sports at the intercollegiate level. Again, sample respondents view the participation of women in specific intercollegiate sports quite favorably. Less than one in five of the respondents feels that a woman tends to lose some of the desirable qualities a woman should have by participating in intercollegiate basketball (15.7%), gymnastics (16.6%), softball (12.6%), swimming (9.6%), tennis (9.1%), track (16.2%), and volleyball (12.3%). Just under a third of them (30.0%) view participation in field events (e.g., shot put or discus) negatively. No significant differences are found between male and female respondents. In contrast, the chi-square probabilities reveal significant differences between groups across all sports by education and by age. For each sport, a larger percentage of people with no college experience than those who attended college indicate that a woman loses desirable qualities by participating. Likewise, subjects over 50 years of age are more likely to hold this view than subjects in the two younger categories.

TABLE 2

ATTITUDES TOWARD PARTICIPATION OF WOMEN IN SPECIFIC INTERCOLLEGIATE SPORTS,
BY GENDER, BY EDUCATION, AND BY AGE

Item: By participating in (   ) at the intercollegiate level, a woman tends to lose some of the desirable qualities I think a woman should have.

Sport	Total (n=353)	Gender			Education			Age			
		Males (n=147)	Females (n=206)	P of χ^2	No College (n=181)	College (n=172)	P of χ^2	18-30 (n=100)	31-50 (n=123)	50+ (n=130)	P of χ^2
Basketball	15.7[a]	15.0	16.0	.79[b]	21.5	9.3	.00	11.0	13.8	20.8	.10
Field Events	30.0	31.3	29.1	.66	38.1	21.5	.00	25.0	22.8	40.8	.00
Gymnastics	16.6	15.6	17.0	.74	25.4	7.0	.00	8.0	11.4	27.7	.00
Softball	12.6	14.3	11.2	.38	17.1	7.6	.00	6.0	10.6	19.2	.00
Swimming	9.6	8.8	10.2	.87	16.6	2.3	.00	6.0	4.1	17.8	.00
Tennis	9.1	8.8	9.2	.90	15.5	2.3	.00	3.0	4.1	18.5	.00
Track Events	16.2	15.0	17.0	.61	23.8	8.1	.00	9.0	12.2	25.4	.00
Volleyball	12.3	11.6	12.6	.76	19.3	4.7	.00	5.0	7.3	22.3	.00

[a] Percent who "strongly agree" or "agree somewhat."

[b] Probability that difference(s) between reported proportions is (are) due solely to chance. P < .01 listed as .00.

Table 3 contains items which measure the perception that women's intercollegiate sports conflict with men's sports programs. About one respondent in five — 19.6% and 19.5% — agree that "the addition of women's sports at the university level unfairly cuts into the place of men's sports" and that "the extra demand for funds created by the addition of women's sports programs makes them more trouble than it is worth." Further, only 39.9% think that it is not right ". . . for a university to cut back on men's sports in order to set up women's sports programs." About half (49.3%) feel that ". . . it is only fair that in the future less is spent on men's programs" and about two-thirds (64.6%) endorse the statement that "universities have an obligation to build up women's sports, even if they have to cut corners in men's sports programs."

No significant differences are found between male and female responses to the five items. Findings for education and age are consistent with the first two tables. Nine of the ten comparisons for the five items indicate significant differences. Respondents with no college experience and the oldest age group are much more likely to view women's intercollegiate sports as being in conflict with men's sports than are people who attended college and persons less than 50 years of age.

The final two tables present multivariate analyses of the same items reported in Tables 1 and 3. Gender was not found to be a significant factor in any of these earlier analyses and, therefore, is omitted from further consideration. However, the relationship among education, age, and attitudes toward the participation of women in intercollegiate sports requires additional clarification. The bivariate findings are potentially deceiving because education is confounded with age. Each age group contains a greater percentage of persons who never attended college than the younger age categories. Likewise, the no-college group contains a greater percentage of older people than the college group. Therefore, on the basis of bivariate presentations, we cannot tell whether the oldest age group is more traditional than the younger groups because they are older or, because they are less likely to have

TABLE 3

PERCEPTION THAT WOMEN'S INTERCOLLEGIATE SPORTS CONFLICT WITH MEN'S SPORTS, BY GENDER, BY EDUCATION, BY AGE

Items	Total (n=353)	Age			Education			Age			
		Males (n=147)	Females (n=206)	P of χ^2	No College (n=181)	College (n=172)	P of χ^2	18-30 (n=100)	31-50 (n=123)	50+ (n=130)	P of χ^2
It does not seem right to me for a university to cut back on men's sports in order to set up women's sports programs.	39.9[a]	42.2	37.9	.41[b]	44.2	34.9	.07	35.0	40.7	42.3	.51
The extra demand for funds created by the addition of women's sports programs makes them more trouble than it is worth.	19.5	19.7	19.5	.94	23.2	15.7	.08	11.0	17.9	27.7	.01
Since universities now spend a great deal more on men's than women's sports, it is only fair that in the future less is spent on men's programs.	49.3	47.6	51.0	.53	45.3	54.1	.10	50.0	40.7	57.7	.03
The addition of women's sports at the university level unfairly cuts into the place of men's sports.	19.6	18.4	20.9	.56	24.3	15.1	.03	13.0	20.3	24.6	.09
Universities have an obligation to build up women's sports, even if they have to cut corners in men's sports programs.	64.6	66.0	63.1	.58	55.8	73.8	.00	70.0	67.5	56.9	.08

[a] Percent who "strongly agree" or "agree somewhat."

[b] Probability that difference(s) between reported proportions is (are) due solely to chance. P < .01 listed as .00.

attended college. Nor can we tell if the no-college group is more traditional because they have not attended college or, because they are on the average older than the college group. A multivariate presentation may help solve these riddles.

Table 4 presents multivariate data concerning general attitudes toward the participation of women in intercollegiate sports. On four of the six items in the table, seven significant chi-square probabilities are found between the college and no-college groups while controlling for age. In six of these significant comparisons, a higher percentage of agreement with the items exists among subjects with no college experience. Hence, when controlling for differences in age, we find that subjects in the study with no college experience still tend to be more traditional in their attitudes than subjects with college experience. Four additional significant probabilities are noted for the comparisons between age groups which hold education constant. In three of the four cases, subjects over the age of 50 with no college experience exhibit a much higher percent of agreement with the items than do their younger counterparts. In other words, the tendency of the oldest subjects to project a more traditional view of women's participation in sports appears to be a function of both their older age and lower education.

The findings presented in Table 5 measure the perception that women's intercollegiate sports conflict with men's sports for finances, facilities, and the like (note items 1 through 4). People of all age groups without college experience are not consistently more likely than those who attended college to see a conflict betwen women's and men's programs. Only three of the twelve comparisons in columns 1, 2, and 3 are statistically significant. However, three of the four significant comparisons between age groups in columns 4 and 5 reveal that the oldest age category among those who never attended college think such conflict is present. To summarize the trend in Tables 4 and 5, those over fifty who never attended college stand out from the other age and education groups as being more traditional — in this case, more negative — about the participation of women in intercollegiate

TABLE 4

GENERAL ATTITUDES TOWARD PARTICIPATION OF WOMEN IN INTERCOLLEGIATE SPORTS, BY
EDUCATION CONTROLLING FOR AGE AND BY AGE CONTROLLING FOR EDUCATION

Age	18-30		31-50		50+		P of chi-square test [a]				
Item / Education	No College (n=41)	College (n=59)	No College (n=52)	College (n=71)	No College (n=88)	College (n=42)	1 [b]	2	3	4	5
Women are likely to develop unsightly muscles if they exercise regularly.	29.3 [c]	11.9	30.8	15.5	44.3	26.2	.03	.04	.05	.14	.15
Women ought to stick to cheerleading and leave participation in organized sports to men.	12.2	3.4	13.5	7.0	22.7	4.8	.09	.24	.01	.22	.64
Participation in organized sports only takes time away from the other important things a woman ought to be doing.	12.2	5.1	9.6	4.2	23.9	9.5	.20	.23	.05	.06	.49
A woman cannot be both a good athlete and a truly feminine person.	2.3	13.6	7.7	4.2	17.0	9.5	.06	.41	.26	.03	.17
Men seem naturally to know more about sports than women.	41.5	49.2	50.0	52.1	61.4	69.0	.45	.82	.39	.09	.10 [c]
To excel in organized sports, a woman has to be more like a man than a woman.	24.4	16.9	17.3	15.5	31.8	21.4	.36	.79	.22	.16	.72

[a] Probability that difference(s) between reported proportions is (are) due solely to chance. p<.01 listed as .00.

[b] 1. No College vs. College for those 18-30 years of age.
2. No College vs. College for those 31-50 years of age.
3. No College vs. College for those over 50 years of age.
4. 18-30 vs. 31-50 vs. 50+ for those with No College.
5. 18-30 vs. 31-50 vs. 50+ for those with College Experience.

[c] Percent who "strongly agree" or "agree somewhat".

TABLE 5

PERCEPTION THAT WOMEN'S INTERCOLLEGIATE SPORTS CONFLICT WITH MEN'S SPORTS, BY EDUCATION
CONTROLLING FOR AGE AND BY AGE CONTROLLING FOR EDUCATION

Age	18-30		31-50		50+		P of chi-square test[a]				
Education / Item	No College (n=41)	College (n=59)	No College (n=52)	College (n=71)	No College (n=88)	College (n=42)	1[b]	2	3	4	5
It does not seem right to me for a university to cut back on men's sports in order to set up women's sports programs.	43.9[c]	28.8	46.2	36.6	43.2	40.5	.12	.29	.77	.94	.44
The extra demand for funds created by the addition of women's sports programs makes it more trouble than it is worth.	9.8	11.9	21.2	15.5	30.7	21.4	.74	.42	.27	.03	.43
Since universities now spend a great deal more on men's than women's sports, it is only fair that in the future less is spent on men's programs.	39.0	57.6	36.5	43.7	53.4	66.7	.07	.43	.15	.10	.05
The addition of women's sports at the university level unfairly cuts into the place of men's sports.	7.3	16.9	28.8	14.1	29.5	14.3	.16	.04	.06	.02	.89
Universities have an obligation to build up women's sports, even if they have to cut corners in men's sports programs.	61.0	76.3	55.8	76.1	53.4	64.3	.10	.02	.24	.72	.32

[a] Probability that difference(s) between reported proportions is (are) due solely to chance. p<.01 listed as .00.

[b] 1. No College vs. College for those 18-30 years of age.
2. No College vs. College for those 31-50 years of age.
3. No College vs. College for those over 50 years of age.
4. 18-30 vs. 31-50 vs. 50+ for those with No College.
5. 18-30 vs. 31-50 vs. 50+ for those with College Experience.

[c] Percent who "strongly agree" or "agree somewhat".

sports and as being more likely to think that women's programs unfairly encroach upon men's programs.

Item 5 taps the belief that universities ought to spend more money on women's programs even if corners have to be cut in men's programs to do so. Regardless of age and education group considered, over half the respondents feel such expenditures ought to be made. The only significant differences occur in the two youngest age categories. In these two age categories, college educated respondents are more likely to favor additional expenditures for women's programs (even at the expense of men's programs) than are those younger respondents without college experience.

DISCUSSION AND CONCLUSION

This study gauges the attitudes of a metropolitan area sample toward the participation of women in intercollegiate sports. Attitudes toward both the participation issue in general and the participation in specific sports are examined. The study marks an advance over the previous literature in two respects. One, previous studies rely almost exclusively on samples drawn from student populations, thereby removing age and education as explanatory variables in accounting for variations in attitude. Two, no previous study addresses the possibility that some people oppose women's athletics at the intercollegiate level because they think women's programs undermine institutional support for men's programs.

Data from this investigation provide strong evidence that age and education are strong correlates of attitudes toward women's participation in sports. Generally, younger respondents, and those who have attended college, are more positively oriented toward the participation of women in intercollegiate sports than are older and less educated respondents. These younger and better educated respondents also are more likely to think that men's and women's sports are locked in a struggle for funds, facilities, and the like but that universities nevertheless have the obligation to proceed with the implementation of women's programs. When the age and education variables are considered simultaneously-, one group—persons over the age of 50 who did not attend college —stands out as the most traditional. In fact, relationships at the bivariate level between age, education, and attitude toward women in sports probably are detected because this group is so much more traditional than the other age/education groups.

The data also indicate that the orientation of the general public toward the participation of women in intercollegiate sports is basically positive. The percentage of persons in the sample who endorse negative stereotypes of women athletes is low, usually around one-fourth to one-third of the sample. With the exception of participation in field events, about one-tenth or so of the sample feels that participation in specific sports for women at the intercollegiate level is unfeminine. Only one-third of the sample feels that a woman does lose some desirable female qualities by participating in field events. Finally, though over half the sample perceives conflicts of interests between men's and women's intercollegiate programs, one-half to three-fourths of the sample think women's programs should receive even more institutional support. These figures all represent a high level of acceptance and support for women's intercollegiate sports in a metropolitan population otherwise known for its political conservatism. Future research would do well to consider the issue of sports participation by women within the context of other nontraditional modes of activity.

REFERENCES

Coakley, J.
   1978 Sport in Society: Issues and Controversies. St. Louis: C. V. Mosby Co.
Debacy, D., R. Spaeth, and R. Busch
   1970 "What do men really think about athletic competition for women?" Journal of
      Health, Physical Education and Recreation 41:28-29.
Del Rey, P.
   1977 "In support of apologetics for women in sport." In R. Christina and D. Landers
      (eds.), Psychology of Motor Behavior and Sport. Champaign, Illinois: Human
      Kinetics Publisher.
Eitzen, S., and G. Sage
   1978 Sociology of American Sport. Dubuque, Iowa: William C. Brown Publishers.

Fisher, A., P. Genovese, K. Morris, and H. Morris
  1978 Perceptions of women in sport." In R. Christina and D. Landers (eds.), Psychology of Motor Behavior and Sport. Champaign, Illinois: Human Kinetics Publisher.
Griffin, P.
  1973 "What's a nice girl like you doing in a profession like this?" Quest 19:96-101.
Harres, B.
  1968 "Attitudes of students toward women's athletic competition." Research Quarterly 39:278-284.
Kingsley, J., F. Brown, and M. Seibert
  1977 "Social acceptance of female athletes by college women." Research Quarterly 48:727-733.
Malumphy. T.
  1970 "The college woman athlete: questions and tentative answers." Quest, 14:18-27.
  1971 "Athletics and competition for girls and women." In. D. Harris (ed.), DGWS Research Reports: Women in Sports. Washington, D.C.: American Association for Health, Physical Education, and Recreation.
Metheny, E.
  1965 Connotations of Movement in Sport and Dance. Dubuque, Iowa: William C. Brown, Publishers.
Nicholson, C.
  1979 "Some attitudes associated with sport participation among junior high school females." Research Quarterly 50:661-667.
Sage, C., and S. Loudermilk
  1979 "The female athlete and role conflict." Research Quarterly 50: 88-96.
Selby, R., and J. Lewko
  1976 "Children's attitudes toward females in sports: their relationship with sex, grade, and sports participation." Research Quarterly 47:453-463.
Snyder, E., and J. Kivlin
  1975 "Women athletes and aspects of psychological well-being and body image." Research Quarterly 46:191-196.
  1977 "Perceptions of the sex role among female athletes and nonathletes." Adolescence 45:23-29.
Snyder, E., J. Kivlin, and E. Spreitzer
  1979 "The female athlete: analysis of objective and subjective role conflict." In F. Yiannakis (ed.), Sport Sociology: Contemporary Themes. Dubuque, Iowa: Kendal Hunt Publishing Company.
Snyder, E., and E. Spreitzer
  1976 "Correlates of sport participation among adolescent girls." Research Quarterly 47:804-809.
Vincent, M.
  1976 "Comparison of self-concepts of college women: athletes and physical education majors." Research Quarterly 47:218-225.

Chapter 14

REFERENCE GROUP THEORY AND THE ECONOMICS OF PROFESSIONAL SPORT

Steve Lerch, Radford University

The recent drastic escalation of salaries paid to upper-echelon (i.e., "major league") professional athletes has been decried by nearly all connected with sports. Owners of professional franchises are nearly unanimous in condemning athletes as "selfish," "greedy," unconcerned about the "good of the game," etc. They express fears that increased payrolls will have to be met through increasing ticket prices; such increases, they say, will drive fans from stadiums and arenas and will eventually "kill the sport." (Obviously, they are less likely to note that they are in large part responsible for the increases themselves — or that their ultimate desire is to minimize salaries in order to maximize team profits.) Sportswriters often question the necessity of rewarding so handsomely the athletes they watch perform — athletes who are sometimes viewed, after all, as "only playing a game." Fans hear and read the lamentations of owners and sportswriters that high salaries are pricing them out of the ticket-buying market and that "it isn't sport anymore, it's business." Even certain athletes are asking themselves whether they may (in conjunction with the owners) be "killing the goose that lays the golden egg."

Most observers of professional sports in the United States have a rudimentary understanding of and appreciation for the salaries paid to "star" athletes. The mid-1970s court decisions which provided athletes with new negotiating freedoms — especially the right of "free agency" (or the threat of same, to use as a bargaining lever with one's present team) — led to a near immediate salary windfall for many professional athletes. Top athletes — those proclaimed most "valuable" on and off the field — earn whatever the sports market will bear. Questions are asked, however, about the "non-star" athletes: how is it that many with only moderately successful careers have asked for (and been rewarded with) multi-year, multi-million dollar contracts? In baseball alone, for example, recent years have seen the Giants give a virtually-lame Rennie Stennett $3 million over five years, the Braves pay a no-longer-fierce Al Hrabosky $2.2 million over five years, and the Angels give nearly $2.5 million in a five year contract to a sore-armed Bruce Kison (Chass, 1980:52). What has driven the salaries of even mediocre athletes to such an astonishingly high level?

REFERENCE GROUP THEORY AND SPORT

Both the upward salary spiral (e.g., baseball's average salary up 511% since 1970, basketball's up 450% over the same period, according to *Inside Sports* July, 1980) and the reactions to the increase can be at least partially explained in terms of reference group theory. This theory, which is basically an extension of Mead's notion of the "generalized other," was given substance by Merton, who applied the theory to the data of *The American Soldier*. Merton summarizes reference group theory as follows (1967:234):

> In general, then, reference group theory aims to systematize the determinants and consequence of those processes of evaluation and self-appraisal in which the individual takes the values or standards of other individuals and groups as a comparative frame of reference.

Phrased more succinctly, reference groups are those against which we evaluate ourselves — groups which we utilize as standards to tell ourselves how well (or how poorly) we are doing. Reference groups may also serve a normative function through setting norms for behavior.

Although the authors of *The American Soldier* do not use the term "reference group," reference group concepts play an important part in the interpretative apparatus they utilize (Merton, 1967:225). Specifically, the authors found that the soldier's evaluation of his own situation depended in large part upon comparisons he made between himself and others. For example, compared with their unmarried friends, married men felt they were making a great sacrifice by becoming soldiers; compared with black civilians they saw in local towns, black soldiers in the South felt that they enjoyed wealth and dignity (Bassis, Gelles, and Levine, 1980:140). In effect, says Merton (1967:229-230), status attributes such as race, marital status, educational achievement and age are utilized as independent variables. The situation of the soldier (e.g., attitude toward induction or appraisal of chances for promotion) is the dependent variable, and the frame of reference becomes the intervening variable.

One finding from *The American Soldier* which is noteworthy for our analysis of the situation in professional sport is that there are at least three different frames of reference which can be utilized. In some cases, the attitudes of the soldiers with regard to their own situation depended upon comparison with other soldiers with whom they were in *actual association*. A second basis of comparison was with others of the *same status or same social category*; a third frame of reference was those of a *different status or social category*. In more general terms, our reference groups may be "in-groups," either narrowly (actual association) or more broadly (same status or social category) defined, or "out-groups," in which we compare ourselves to those to whom we are dissimilar.

In this paper, of course, we are concerned with explaining reactions toward increasing salaries in professional sports. (We shall deal below with the reasons for such increases.) The thrust of our contention is that the differing attitudes on the part of athletes, fans, sportswriters, and owners (i.e., the dependent variable) can be partially explained through status as an athlete or a non-athlete (the independent variable) with one's frame of reference as the intervening variable. Specifically, the argument is this: athletes tend to use in-groups as their frame of reference in judging whether or not their salaries are equitable. These in-groups are sometimes other athletes with whom they are in actual association; e.g., the athlete who compares himself to teammates who earn more/less than he. Other times athletes compare themselves to those of the same status or social category. These terms can be broadly or narrowly defined, ranging from those playing the same position on one's team to all other professional athletes in the same sport. Clearly, such in-group comparisons will yield very different attitudes toward salaries than non-athletes' frames of reference; these individuals utilize out-group comparisons. Those in disparate social positions are likely to take a negative view of the high salaries in professional sports — since they are comparing them to their own salaries which are almost inevitably less extravagent.

There is, of course, another way to analyze the attitudes athletes and non-athletes have toward salaries in professional sports. Non-athletes, it can be argued, have the tendency to view salaries in an *absolute* sense; i.e., by looking only at the monetary figures involved. A five year contract for $4.5 million seems outrageous because the numbers involved are staggering. The athlete himself, however, is more likely to evaluate his salary *relative* to other members of his reference group—other professional athletes making equally large (as objectively measured) salaries, especially those in the same sport, on the same team, with the same abilities, having the same amount of experience, playing the same position, etc. Comparing the income of the average professional athlete to that of the average assistant professor, for example — and coming to the conclusion that the former is over- and the latter underpaid— is as useless as comparing the assistant professor's salary to that of the average cook at a fast-food restaurant and reaching the same conclusion. Only within group salary comparisons are truly useful.

RELATIVE DEPRIVATION AND SPORT SALARIES

The use of these in-group comparisons, it is argued, is in large part responsible for the upward spiral of salaries in professional sports. Athletes expressing displeasure with their salaries do so not by utilizing absolute dollar figures involved in contracts, but rather by examining their salaries relative to other members of their reference groups. In sociological parlance, the athletes are experiencing relative deprivation.

According to Merton, relative deprivation can provisionally be regarded as a special concept in reference group theory (1967:235). Although Merton does not state a formal definition of the concept, it has been variously defined as "a sense of deprivation in relation to some standard" (Lauer, 1978:250), "actors' perception of discrepancy between their value expectations and their value capabilities" (Gurr, 1970:24), or "feeling you have gotten a bad deal in comparison with other people, especially in comparison with your reference group" (Babbie, 1977:526). Basically, then, the concept suggests that the important determinant of satisfaction or discontent is not the absolute or "objective" level of achievement or deprivation but is rather the level of achievement *relative* to some standard employed by the individual as a basis of comparison or self-evaluation (Crawford and Naditch, 1970:208).

For example, de Tocqueville (1955:175-77) noted that just prior to the French Revolution, the economic situation in France was actually improving (the objective situation). However, the French were apparently comparing their situation to some other standard than their past, and relative to this standard, there was widespread dissatisfaction. In more modern times, the concept of relative deprivation has frequently been utilized to explain the situation of poverty-stricken Americans, especially members of minority groups. Robertson (1980:182), for example, has noted that people are poor not only in relation to their needs but also in relation to those who are not poor. Thus, the poor in America can see the affluent all around them, and they evaluate their poverty not only in relation to their basic needs but also in relation to the surfeit of wealth in the surrounding society (Miller, 1968:182-83).

Professional athletes, of course, are by no means deprived in any objective sense. However, they may perceive deprivation as they compare themselves to other athletes. In Merton's terms, " 'deprivation' is the incidental and particularized component of the concept of relative deprivation, whereas the more significant nucleus of the concept is its stress upon social and psychological experience as 'relative' " (1967:235). Thus, although fans and sportswriters may be astounded that an athlete can claim he is underpaid at $100,000 or more per season, from the athlete's point of view, he may very well be experiencing relative deprivation.

Here, again, we see the importance of one's frame of reference in the explanation of variations in attitudes. Davis (1959:283) discusses in-group/out-group comparisons and their impact upon attitudes. His assumptions (made with reference to *The American Soldier* data), are no less valuable as applied to the situation of professional sports. First is an in-group comparison:

> If a person (ego) compares himself with a person (alter) when ego and alter differ in their deprivation, ego experiences a subjective feeling opposite in direction to the evaluation of alter's condition.
>
> a. When a deprived person compares himself with a non-deprived, the resulting state will be called "relative deprivation."
>
> b. When a non-deprived person compares himself with a deprived person, the resulting state will be called "relative gratification."

The first case, of course, is the one which most concerns us here. The shortstop who enters negotiations with the desire to become the "highest paid shortstop in baseball" or the defensive end who complains that his salary is lower than that of other ends of his ability and experience are both experiencing relative deprivation.

Importantly, for the present discussion, players are now privy to detailed and accurate information regarding what other players are making. This fact is responsible for a major part of the escalation in salaries. Kaplan (1981:36) explains how this occurs, using baseball as an example:

> Before salary figures were published, a player had to take an owner's word that his income measured up well with that of his teammates. In the mid-'60s Dodger player representative Ron Fairly was a satisfied customer. The Dodgers had assured him that among his teammates only Sandy Koufax and Don Drysdale made more than he. But when the Players Association asked Fairly to poll the players, he discovered he was in 12th place. Fairly had been had.
>
> Today all figures are known, and players can spot lesser performers who are making more. It's an irresistable argument for an increase. No wonder almost all major leaguers are well-paid.

It only takes one owner, therefore, desperate to fill a need on his team and willing to go to any expense to do so, to "raise the scale" for all athletes in the sport. One of the most obvious recent examples of this phenomenon occurred when owner Ted Turner of the Atlanta Braves signed free agent outfielder Claudell Washington, a career .279 hitter, to a five year, $3.5 million contract. Other ballplayers' frame of reference was changed before the ink dried on Washington's contract. Similarly, ever-increasing calls by athletes for contract renegotiation — words that are anathema to owners — are based upon athletes comparing their contracts (with which they were once evidently pleased) to those more recently signed by their counterparts.

Examples of "relative gratification" in sport are far more difficult to come by. Theoretically, this is because only the highest paid will ever feel "gratified"; all others have the potential to compare themselves to those better rewarded economically. Such expressions of "gratification" are most likely to emanate from player agents — sometimes, as they inflate the contracts of the athletes they represent in an effort to make themselves appear better negotiators.

Davis also postulates an assumption about out-group comparisons (1959:283):

> If a person (ego) compares himself with a person (alter) in an out-group when ego and alter differ in their deprivation, ego will experience a feeling toward alter's group opposite in direction to the evaluation of alter's condition.
>
> a. When a deprived person compares himself with a non-deprived out-group member, the resulting attitude toward the out-group will be called "relative subordination."
>
> b. When a non-deprived person compares himself with a deprived out-group member, the resulting attitude toward the out-group will be called "relative superiority."

Given the present nature of the economics of sport, the deprived person is almost invariably the non-athlete. Thus, the first case is one we have mentioned above — the non-athlete (fan, sportswriter, etc.) who compares his salary to the athlete's. He experiences "subordination" because he almost inevitably comes up on the short end of such a comparison. Furthermore, the feelings of subordination may be heightened by his evaluation of the importance of the task given the size of the remuneration: the social service performed by the $15,000 per year high school teacher is by most objective measures more vital than that performed by the $150,000 per year middle linebacker.

The latter case is the reverse — the non-deprived athlete comparing his situation to that of the deprived non-athlete. Although this may actually occur frequently, the public is alerted to it only occasionally, as when athletes remark "I realize how lucky I am" or "I really don't deserve this kind of money." Too many expressions of "relative superiority," of course, may have the consequence of alienating sports fans and diminishing their interest in the sport.

THE ECONOMIC FUTURE OF SPORT: IS REVOLUTION IN THE OFFING?

One of the more interesting applications of the concept of relative deprivation has been as an explanatory factor in revolutions; Davies (1962), among others, has discussed this phenomenon. First, he notes that Marx's most famous thesis — that progressive degradation of the industrial working class would finally reach the point of despair and inevitable revolt — is not the only one Marx fathered. Marx also described, as a precondition of widespread unrest, not progressive degradation of the proletariat but rather an improvement in workers' economic condition which did not keep pace with the growing welfare of capitalists and therefore produced social tension (Davies, 1962:5). Likewise, de Tocqueville utilizes this latter thesis in his study of the French Revolution:

> Revolutions are not always brought about by a gradual decline from bad to worse. Nations that have endured patiently and almost unconsciously the most overwhelming oppression often burst into rebellion against the yoke the moment it begins to grow lighter. The regime which is destroyed by a revolution is almost always an improvement on its immediate predecessor . . . Evils which are patiently endured when they seem inevitable become intolerable when once the idea of escape from them is suggested (de Tocqueville, 1955:176-77).

Davies, then, concludes that revolutions are more likely to occur when a prolonged period of objective economic and social development is followed by a short period of sharp reversal (1962:6). This situation is diagrammed in Figure 1. Davies explains Dorr's Rebellion of 1842, the Russian Revolution of 1917, and the Egyptian Revolution of 1952 with his "J-curve" theory of revolutions; others have utilized the theory to explain the urban riots in the United States in the 1960s.

Figure 1: Need Satisfaction and Revolution (Davies, 1962:6)

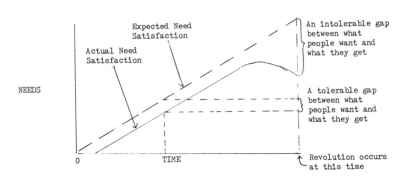

The J-curve theory is also applicable to the economics of professional sport. Actually, the theory may be implemented to speculate on the economic future of sport from the perspective of both athletes (individually and in groups) and non-athletes.

Individual athletes, for example, comparing their salaries to those of their peers, may come to the conclusion that their salaries (actual need satisfaction) are not keeping pace with those of their contemporaries of equal or lesser abilities, experience, etc. Thus, their actual needs satisfaction is falling short of their expected needs satisfaction. Although the actual need satisfaction may not resemble a "J" — since salaries in sport rarely decline — there is still the potential for an ever-widening gap between what the individual feels he deserves and what he actually receives. Typically, the "revolution" that occurs by individual athletes when an intolerable gap is reached is the walkout, holdout, or "retirement" until the gap is closed. (See Figure 2.)

From the group perspective, the theory can be utilized to explain recent "job actions" taken in various sports; e.g., the

Figure 2: Expectations and Actual Salaries, Individual Athletes

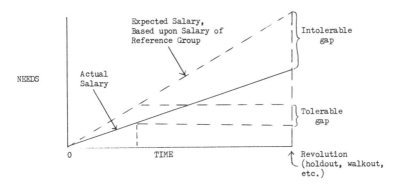

baseball strike of the summer of 1981. In the past 15 years, the players have grown accustomed to a series of successes both at the bargaining table and in the courtroom. In the most recent negotiations over baseball's "Basic Agreement," the owners apparently decided to take a hard line approach and refuse to make further concessions. Thus the previous successes had raised the expectations for continued victories; when the owners decided not to "give in" (and, indeed, actually attempted to recover from past "losses"), an intolerable gap between expectations and reality resulted, and the players went on strike. (See Figure 3.)

Far more vital to the future of professional sport is the potential for a revolution by non-athletes, especially fans. One of the by-products of increasing salaries paid to athletes is the expectation by fans of higher quality performances on the part of both individual athletes and the teams for which they participate. These expectations, of course, are heightened by owners and sportswriters; athletes receiving large salaries continually are asked to "prove" they are deserving of such huge monetary

Figure 3: Negotiation Expectations and Outcomes (Group)

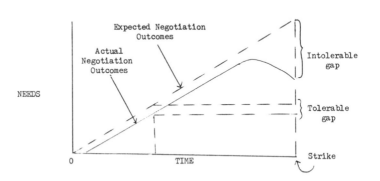

rewards. If the fans' expectations are not met — if an intolerable gap develops between what people want (in terms of winning percentage, championships, etc.) and what they get, the potential for a revolution is present. Furthermore, since salaries have more than outstripped performances, the potential for such a revolution is ever-increasing. (See Figure 4.)

We can speculate that the revolution may take one of two forms: first, dissatisfied fans may simply refuse to attend sports contests, causing severe financial problems for sports franchises. The most obvious recent example of this type of revolution may be the situation of the Philadelphia 76ers of the National Basketball Association. Since 1975, team management has acquired a variety of superstars; we can assume that they are being paid accordingly. (We know for a fact that the average NBA salary has risen from $93,000 in 1975 to $180,000 in 1980. The 76ers surely are among the highest-paid teams in the sport.) Over this period, the team has met some expectations: winning percentage for the regular season has increased steadily (with one season's

Figure 4: Fan Expectations and Rewards

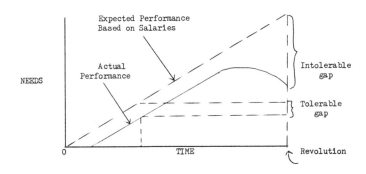

exception) from .110 in 1972-73 to .756 in 1980-81. However, the ultimate goal — an NBA championship — has eluded the 76ers. Meanwhile, attendance increased through the 1977-78 season; that year, the highly regarded 76ers finished first in their division but lost in the conference finals in post-season play. Apparently, this, combined with a small decline in winning percentage in 1978-79, produced the intolerable gap between expectations and performance: attendance has declined steadily since 1977-78, and the franchise changed ownership in 1980.

The second form of revolution is more serious: violence directed at individual athletes who fail to meet expectations. We must note, of course, that the violent fan may be no more than the intoxicated lout who indiscriminately directs violence at any player, or who sees violent acts (e.g., hurling objects at athletes) as a type of recreation (e.g., see how close to hitting him one can come). Thus, our theory by no means explains all sports violence. However, we can speculate that certain instances of violence are likely to be directed against those players deemed responsible for team failures — again, sportswriters and owners are at least partially responsible for determining culpability. At any rate, fans are most likely to vent their frustrations over losses at athletes they think should be able to do the most to prevent them — those receiving the highest salaries, of whom the most is expected. For example, Dave Parker, outfielder of the Pittsburgh Pirates, has been the target of batteries, bolts, and bullets thrown from the stands in Pittsburgh as a result of his failure to meet the expectations that attend to a $1 million annual salary.

IMPLICATIONS

Although reference group theory and relative deprivation have some utility in explaining increasing salaries in sports and the reaction to them, as many questions are raised by this discussion as are answered. For example, why does one choose a particular reference group? In the present context, which in-groups are chosen as reference groups by athletes — teammates, holders of the same position, those of similar ability, experience, etc.? Does the athlete always choose the reference group in which he appears to fare the worst — so he can plead "deprivation" and increase his salary? These and other questions remain to be answered.

Similarly, we may predict revolutions of fans and athletes based upon felt relative deprivation. However, we cannot pinpoint a time at which the gap becomes intolerable, nor predict with any accuracy the form of the revolution. Neither can we distinguish a quantifiable relationship between athletes' salaries and fans' performance expectations. Moreover, large-scale fan revolutions, though they may plague individual teams (e.g., attendance declines) or athletes (e.g., violence), may not be on the horizon for professional sports in general. On the other hand, declining attendance following the baseball strike may be an indication that some fans have reached an intolerable gap between their expectations of athletes and the realities delivered. At any rate, the sports establishment would be wise to pay heed to the widening gap between salaries and the expectations they engender — which are theoretically limitless — and the performances which are limited by man's athletic abilities.

REFERENCES

Babbie, E. G.
  1977 Society by Agreement. Belmont, California: Wadsworth.
Bassis, M. S., R. J. Gelles and A. Levine
  1980 Sociology, An Introduction. New York: Random House.
Chass, M.
  1980 "Baseball's consumer guide to free agents." Inside Sports 2 (November 30): 51-54.
Crawford, T. J. and M. Naditch
  1970 "Relative deprivation, powerlessness, and militancy: the psychology of social protest." Psychiatry 33: 208-223.
Davies, J. C.
  1962 "Toward a theory of revolution." American Sociological Review 27: 5-19.
Davis, J. A.
  1959 "A formal interpretation of the theory of relative deprivation." Sociometry 22: 282-298.
de Tocqueville, A.
  1955 The Old Regime and the French Revolution. New York: Anchor Books.
Gurr, T. R.
  1970 Why Men Rebel. Princeton: Princeton University Press.
Inside Sports Magazine
  1980 "What the average player makes." Inside Sports 2 (July 31): 19.
Kaplan, J.
  1981 "Is there a ceiling?" Sports Illustrated 54 (January 5): 35-38.
Lauer, R. H.
  1978 Social Problems and the Quality of Life. Dubuque: Wm. C. Brown.
Merton, R. K.
  1967 Social Theory and Social Structure. New York: The Free Press.
Miller, H.
  1968 "Changes in the number and composition of the poor." In E. C. Budd (ed.), Inequality and Poverty. New York: Norton.
Robertson, I.
  1980 Social Problems. New York: Random House.

.

EFFECTS OF PARTICIPATION IN SPORT

Section V

EFFECTS OF PARTICIPATION IN SPORT

The chapters in this section raise some significant questions about (a) the method by which we have previously examined some critical effects associated with participation in sport, and (b) the conclusions that have emerged from previous research and subsequently been widely accepted.

Nixon proposes four alternative explanations of the relationship between athletic involvement and a variety of aspects of academic orientation and performance. He provides an "exploratory test of these models" which, though not generating any obvious support for any one of the models, demonstrates the "inappropriateness of viewing athletically inclined college students in simple stereotypic terms as academically incompetent." Nixon does, however, present some evidence suggesting that there is conflict between the "athlete" and "student" roles among those included in his sample.

The next chapter, by Messner and Groisser, presents an interesting examination of the relationship between intercollegiate athletics and academic performance at a selected Ivy League school. This work is particularly intriguing when viewed in light of the concerted effort the Ivy League schools have made to "prevent athletics from subventing academic goals." Messner and Groisser's results show a modest, though statistically significant, negative association between participation in intercollegiate athletics and grade point average obtained in required (university core) courses.

In the final chapter of this section, Chu and Griffey provide data which, they argue, demonstrate the "over-simplicity" of the general contact-theory of racial integration as posited by Allport

(1954). Alternatively, this research "suggests that as the environments of sport vary, their effect on inter-racial behavior and attitudes may also vary." A particularly interesting finding is that athletes and non-athletes in the sample do not differ in their interracial "thoughts or behavior." Chu and Griffey also provide evidence in support of the need for multivariate approaches to the study of racial integration, an approach somewhat atypical of previous research.

Chapter 15

THE ATHLETE AS SCHOLAR IN COLLEGE: AN EXPLORATORY TEST OF FOUR MODELS[1]

Howard L. Nixon, University of Vermont

Much attention has been focused recently on the scandal concerning credits obtained by big-time college athletes for courses they did not attend or that did not demand any academic work from them. In fact, this scandal was the cover story of major sports magazines such as *Sports Illustrated* (May 19, 1980) and even major news weeklies such as *Newsweek* (September 22, 1980); the *Chronicle of Higher Education* reported in an issue in 1980 that the FBI had announced plans to investigate nearly twenty colleges allegedly involved in falsifying academic transcripts of athletes (cited in Figler, 1981: 130).

Despite the substantial publicity and righteous indignation prompted by this recent scandal, the issue of academic cheating in intercollegiate athletics is not new. The most recent manifestation of this issue once again raises the more fundamental issue of the integrity or credibility of the athlete as scholar or student in college. This more fundamental issue has existed at least as long as intercollegiate athletics has been commercialized. Scandals such as the falsifying of academic transcripts not only call into question the reputation of the colleges and athletes involved; they also cast doubt upon the academic commitment and competence of college athletes. Thus, in this latter regard, they may reinspire some unflattering stereotypes of the intellectual and academic interests and abilities of athletes. After all, if athletes need to have their grades "fixed," either they are not smart enough to earn good grades on their own or they do not have enough interest in their studies to try.

According to NCAA administrator Ted Tow, the results of a recent NCAA-commissioned study should "(put) to rest the perception some people have that athletes do not do as well in the classroom as nonathletes" (AP, 1981). The study, which was conducted by the American College Testing Program, surveyed male students who had entered college in the fall of 1975 at 46 predominantly Division I NCAA member schools. It reported that by Spring, 1980, 52% of the athletes had received their degrees, but only 41.5% of the nonathletes had graduated. The study also found that among the athletes, those least likely to graduate were in the major sports of football (42.9%) and basketball (41.9%).

Such departures from the graduation rate for athletes in general might raise some questions about Tow's assertion. In addition, it was not clear from the reported results whether the pressure on athletes to remain academically eligible for athletics translated into a more serious academic commitment, better classroom performance, and a better quality education than their nonathlete counterparts, conclusions that might be inferred from Tow's remark. It also was not clear whether the athletes who left the college they entered in 1975 were as likely as the nonathlete dropouts to continue their studies and earn their degree at another college. These questions, as well as questions about variations in the results across colleges, suggest possible qualifications of Tow's assertion. Further reservations are suggested by a review of recent studies by Figler (1981: 125-127).

Figler found no basis for definitive conclusions of any sort about college athletic participation and academic performance or attainment. Findings concerning grade point averages (Davis and Berger, 1973; Hanford, 1974; Ewing, 1975; Harrison, 1976) and reports of graduation rates (LeBar, 1973; Harrison, 1976; Rothenberg, 1977; College Athletics and Graduation, 1978) revealed to him no consistent patterns across colleges or time.

The cloudy and incomplete picture of the athlete as a student at the college level — and perhaps at the high school level as well — that has been painted by past research indicates a need for further empirical and theoretical efforts to try to understand better how and why athletic involvement by students is related to their academic values, aspirations, and performance. This paper is a modest effort in this vein. It proposes a set of four models to try to make systematic theoretical sense of how the athlete and scholar roles might be related for high school or college students. Then it offers a preliminary and limited test of these models by using data generated from a survey of students at the state university and at a small, prestigious, coed liberal arts college in Vermont. Of course, it is recognized that this research is only the first step in trying to refine our understanding of how the athletic and academic roles are related. A basic premise underlying the formulation and testing of the models proposed here is that different levels (e.g., from male to female and from Division I to Division III) and domains (e.g., from major varsity competition to intramurals and casual physical recreation) of athletic involvement may require different models to explain the relationship between the athlete and scholar roles. Significantly, both schools in the research reported in this paper competed largely outside the realm of big-time college athletics. In fact, the university had not had a football team since the early 1970s. Thus, it should be evident why this research is envisioned only as a first step in the testing of the theoretical models proposed here.

THEORETICAL MODELS

The set of four models presented in this section is not meant to exhaust the theoretical possibilities for understanding how the athlete and student or "scholar" roles might be related. However, these models represent at least a starting point in a systematic theoretical approach to understanding the nature of this relationship at various levels and in various domains of college and high school athletic involvement. A key concept in the formulation of each of these models is "role conflict," which refers to a relationship between roles in which the expectations, responsibilities, or demands of different roles in an individual's role set are, or are perceived to be, contradictory. The concept of role conflict used here refers to the relationship between the athlete and scholar roles. In two of the models to be presented — i.e., the "Academically Incompetent Jock" and the "Anti-Intellectual Jock" Models, it is assumed that the athlete and scholar roles are in some degree of conflict. In the other two models — i.e., the "Scholar-Athlete" and the "Athlete as Ordinary Student" Models, no significant role conflict is assumed.

Each of the four models presents a different picture of the athlete as scholar because each is based on different assumptions about how these two roles are related. It is assumed that we can test the relative validity or applicability of these models at particular levels and in particular domains of athletic involvement because a different set of predictions about student-athlete images, values, performance, and aspirations and about the overall school experience is generated from each model. The picture of the athlete as scholar built into each model will be described briefly before the predictions generated by these models are presented.

Academically Incompetent Jock Model.

This model assumes there is conflict between the athlete and scholar roles because attraction to sports or certain types of sports is greater among those with less academic skills and interests and less intelligence. The assumption of a mind-body dichotomy is strongest in this model, which presents the most unflattering stereotype of the athlete as academically incompetent and unmotivated.

Anti-Intellectual Jock Model.

This model assumes there is conflict between the athlete and scholar roles because attraction to the concrete and physical world of sport leads to some scorn for the world of abstract ideas, intellect, and scholarship. The anti-intellectual jock may have the intelligence to do well in academic studies and may even earn good grades, but this type of person tends to view school and grades from a narrow, concrete, and instrumental or practical perspective.

Scholar-Athlete Model.

This model assumes that there is no significant conflict between the athlete and scholar roles because accomplishment in sport encourages or is reinforced by a serious commitment to accomplishment in scholarship and other phases of school life. In this model, mind and body are assumed to be closely integrated rather than dichotomous. Students who pursue athletics are assumed to see, and be inspired by, the same general sort of challenge to learn and accomplish in both academics and athletics. The extra demands associated with being an athlete as well as student imply that individuals with academic commitment or intelligence are the most likely to be student-athletes.

Athlete as Ordinary Student Model.

This model assumes that there is no conflict between the athlete and scholar roles because athletic involvement is one of the numerous roles contained in the role set of the student and has no special meaning or poses no unusual demands. In effect, this model is a sort of residual one in assuming that the athlete and scholar roles have no significant bearing on each other.

The predictions from the models that were tested in this research are in five areas: student-athlete image, academic values, academic performance, (current and future) academic aspirations, and assessment of school experience. A summary of the predictions from the four models appears in Table 1.

Although the factors represented in the predictions do not cover the full range and depth of the experience of the athlete as student or scholar, they seem varied enough to provide a fairly complex picture of the relationship between the athlete and scholar roles. This picture, conveyed by the combination of pre-

Table 1. Predictions from Student-Athlete Models

	Model 1: Academically Incompetent Jock	Model 2: Anti-Intellectual Jock	Model 3: Scholar-Athlete	Model 4: Athlete as Ordinary Student
Student-Athlete Image	"Dumb jock" stereotype rejected more by athletes than by non-athletes.	"Dumb jock" stereotype rejected more by athletes than by non-athletes.	"Dumb jock" stereotype rejected more by athletes than by non-athletes.	No difference between athletes and nonathletes.
Value Work for Grades	Value accepted less by athletes than by nonathletes.	No difference between athletes and nonathletes.	Value accepted more by athletes than by nonathletes.	No difference between athletes and nonathletes.
Academic Performance	Athletes receive lower grades than nonathletes.	No difference between athletes and nonathletes.	Athletes receive higher grades than nonathletes.	No difference between athletes and nonathletes.
Student Aspirations	Goal of becoming the top student ranked lower by athletes than by non-athletes.	Goal of becoming the top student ranked lower by athletes than by non-athletes.	Goal of becoming the top student ranked higher by athletes than by non-athletes.	No difference between athletes and nonathletes.
Graduate Study Aspirations	Less interest in continuing studies after college among athletes than nonathletes.	Less interest in continuing studies after college among athletes than nonathletes.	More interest in continuing studies after college among athletes than nonathletes.	No difference between athletes and nonathletes.
Assessment of College Education	More positive assessment of quality of education among athletes than nonathletes.	Less positive assessment of quality of education among athletes than nonathletes.	More positive assessment of quality of education among athletes than nonathletes.	No difference between athletes and nonathletes.

dictions, is different for each of the four models. What is most common is the assumption that athletes will be sensitive to unflattering, "dumb jock" stereotypes and be more inclined than nonathletes to reject these stereotypes. The exception to this assumed pattern is in the case of the Athlete as Ordinary Student Model, in which it is assumed that the athlete's role and identity have no special salience.

In the case of the Academically Incompetent Jock Model, athletes are assumed to be more likely than nonathletes to reject the stereotype, which actually is somewhat valid, because the athletes so strongly identify with their athletic role. As a result of this strong identification, athletes are especially sensitive to criticism and at least for defensive reasons, they are likely to reject any unflattering public characterizations associated with their athletic involvement, whatever the validity of the characterizations. However, because in reality they are not especially smart nor serious about their studies, they are likely to express a weaker acceptance of academic values, perform worse in the classroom (particularly in demanding courses), and have lower aspirations as students and for continued study after college than nonathletes. Perhaps surprisingly, though, it is expected that their assessment of the quality of their college education, while they are students, will be more positive than the assessments made by nonathletes. This prediction is based on the assumption that the athletic experience will have a "halo effect" and inflate their general assessment of the quality of the school where their athletic involvement has taken place. In addition, it is assumed that relatively unintelligent or unintellectual athletes will have less inclination than their nonathlete classmates to make critical judgments or evaluations of the quality of their educational experience.

The Anti-Intellectual Model also assumes that athletes will be more inclined than nonathletes to reject the dumb jock stereotype. The athletes are sensitive to such stereotypes because they know athletes are not unintelligent nor academically incompetent. They see themselves as being just as smart as their nonathlete counterparts. Even though they may scorn or reject the "ivory

tower" world of intellect and abstract ideas, they still are assumed
to express the same amount of respect as nonathletes for classmates who work hard at their studies to get good grades because
they recognize as much as nonathletes that good grades can
enhance their career mobility after college. It is assumed that
anti-intellectual jocks perform about as well as nonathletes in the
classroom. However, because they are anti-intellectual and have
little regard for the value of serious scholarship, these athletes are
assumed to have relatively less interest in becoming a top student
and to have lower aspirations for continued study after college
than their classmates who are not athletes. Anti-intellectual jocks
also are expected to render less positive judgments about their college education than nonathletes because these athletes tend to be
critical of many of their instructors and courses, especially in liberal arts, for "wasting" their times with "useless" ideas, assignments, discussions, and lectures.

The Scholar-Athlete Model assumes that athletes are more
inclined than nonathletes to reject the "dumb jock" stereotype
because it conveys an image precisely the opposite from these athletes. These scholar/athletes are likely to be quite serious about
and committed to whatever activities they undertake on campus.
They are achievers. As a result of this fact, they are likely to value
more highly those who work hard to earn good grades, earn
higher grades themselves, have higher aspirations as students,
and have higher aspirations for study after college, than their non-
athlete classmates. Furthermore, because they are achievers and
perhaps even campus leaders, scholar-athletes are likely to have an
especially high regard for the college education that has provided
them with their opportunity to succeed.

The basic premise of the Athlete as Ordinary Student Model
is that athletic involvement does not distinguish athletes from
nonathletes in any significant academic respects. Thus, just as no
difference between athletes and nonathletes in their acceptance or
rejection of the "dumb jock" stereotype is predicted, it also is predicted that there will be no differences between athletes and non-
athletes in their academic values, academic performance, colle-

giate and post-collegiate academic aspirations, and assessment of the quality of their college education.

METHODS

The predictions in the prior section were the main focus of the research reported in this paper. The data were collected in a survey conducted during the fall 1976 at the state university and at a prestigious coed liberal arts college in Vermont. Questionnaires were distributed by campus mail or the U.S. Postal Service to randomly selected samples of 525 undergraduates (out of a population of approximately 7850) at the state university and 235 undergraduates (out of a population of approximately 1890) at the liberal arts college. Using a multi-stage follow-up procedure, response rates of 62.1% (326/525) for the state university and 71.5% (168/235) for the smaller college were achieved. The overall response rate was 65% (494/760). At least in terms of sex, state of residence, and year in school, the respondents appeared to be representative of undergraduates at their respective schools. Students at both schools were predominantly white and from relatively affluent families, which was a noteworthy limitation of the results of this study.

MEASURES

Two dimensions of athletic involvement were operationalized in this research: (a) past success in organized sports, or *Past Sports Success*, and (b) current enthusiasm for sports or physical recreation as a fan or an active participant, or *Sports Enthusiasm*. Past Sports Success was measured by a scale containing five items concerning the number of different organized sports in which one has competed, the number of high school varsity and junior varsity letters earned, membership on a championship team, special distinction earned as an individual in sports competition, and self-evaluation of general athletic ability. Sports Enthusiasm was measured by a scale of four items indicating frequency of active participation in organized or unorganized sports competition or physical recreation, interest in watching or participating in sports activities, enjoyment of sports participation, and importance of sport in one's life. For both scales, responses were trichotomized into "high," "medium," and "low" categories.

In formulating these scalar measures of athletic involvement, it was believed that they would provide a somewhat more complex picture of the relationship between athletic involvement and academic orientation and performance than a reliance only on measures of participation or nonparticipation in intercollegiate athletics. Unfortunately, the random sampling procedure employed in this research yielded a category of "college varsity athletes" that was too small for the purposes of this analysis.

Each of the aspects of academic orientation or performance studied in this research was measured by a single questionnaire item. The *Student-Athlete Image* factor was measured by an item asking for agreement or disagreement with the statement: "Athletes are generally not as intelligent or as serious about their studies as nonathletes." Response categories were collapsed into two: "strong disagreement" and "agreement to disagreement with reservations." The *Value Work for Grades* factor was measured by an item asking how much admiration one felt for others who worked at "studying hard to get good grades in school." The response categories were collapsed into two: "always admire" and "depends on the situation or always dislike." The *Academic Performance* factor was measured by a fixed-choice item asking for the respondent's college cumulative average. The categories used in the data analysis were "A" (3.5-4.0), "B" (2.8-3.49), and "≤C" (<2.8). Since the questionnaire was answered during a fall semester, first semester freshmen who did not yet have a college GPA were excluded from this aspect of the analysis. The *Student Aspirations* factor asked for a ranking of the relative importance (from first to fourth) of the goal "to be recognized as the student with the best academic record on campus" in relation to three other possible goals concerning recognition as the "top student leader," "best athlete on campus," and "best-liked student on campus." The rankings were collapsed into two categories: "1st or 2nd" and "3rd or 4th."

The *Graduate Study Aspirations* factor was measured by an item asking whether the respondent planned "to do graduate or professional degree work beyond college someday." The response categories used for this measure were "definitely yes," "probably yes," and "probably or definitely no." The *Assessment of College Education* factor asked the respondent to "rate the quality of your college education." The responses to this item were collapsed into two categories: "excellent" and "poor, fair, or good."

RESULTS

The results of the main data analysis are in Tables 2-7. They can be summarized briefly in the following way.

Student-Athlete Image.

(See Table 2.) For both Past Sports Success and Sports Enthusiasm, increasing athletic involvement is associated with a greater tendency to disagree strongly with the unflattering student-athlete (or "dumb jock") stereotype.

Value Work for Grades.

(See Table 3.) For both Past Sports Success and Sports Enthusiasm, there is no relationship between athletic involvement and admiration for people who work hard for good grades.

Academic Performance.

(See Table 4.) There is a tendency for those with higher levels of past sports success in organized sports to be somewhat worse students, but there is no relationship between Sports Enthusiasm and Academic Performance.

Student Aspirations.

(See Table 5.) For both Past Sports Success and Sports Enthusiasm, increasing athletic involvement is associated with a greater likelihood of giving a lower rank to the goal of being recognized as the top student.

Graduate Study Aspirations.

(See Table 6.) For both Past Sports Success and Sports Enthusiasm, there is no relationship between athletic involvement and plans to continue academic study after college.

Assessment of College Education.

(See Table 7.) For both Past Sports Success and Sports Enthusiasm, increasing athletic involvement is associated with a greater tendency to give an "excellent" rating to one's college education.

The possibility of effects of background and contextual factors on the relationships that were found was considered. Thus, controls for sex and college differences were introduced into the data analysis. Other typical, potentially relevant control factors such as social class and race were not examined because the respondents in this study were quite homogeneous in these respects. They were largely from affluent families, and they were almost all white.

The controls for sex and college suggested the importance of incorporating these factors into future theoretical considerations about relationships between athletics and academics. In a number of cases, the correlations were substantially higher for males than females — i.e., student aspirations, assessment of college education, and student-athlete image (Sports Enthusiasm only) results — and for the liberal arts college than university students — i.e., value work for grades, academic performance, and student aspirations results. In the case of the relationship between past sports success and student-athlete image, it was stronger for females than males. In the case of Value Work for Grades, relationships with both athletic involvement factors existed for the liberal arts college students, but none existed for the university students. Finally, a weak but statistically significant negative correlation between Sports Enthusiasm and Academic Performance existed for the liberal arts college students, while none existed for the university students.

Table 2.   Student-Athlete Image and Athletic Involvement

Student-Athlete Image

		% strongly disagree with stereotype	% agree or disagree with reservations with stereo-type	n	χ^2	df	p	N
Past Sports Success	High	60.7	39.3	163	24.4*	2	<.01	480
	Medium	43.2	56.8	162				
	Low	33.5	66.5	155				
Sports Enthusiasm	High	62.5	37.5	152	28.4*	2	<.01	479
	Medium	44.7	55.3	152				
	Low	33.1	66.9	175				

Note.-The asterisk (*) in this table and subsequent ones indicates that the value of chi-square is statistically significant at the .05 level. In certain cases, percentage totals do not exactly equal 100% due to rounding.

Table 3.   Value Work for Grades and Athletic Involvement

Value Work for Grades

		% always admire	% depends on situation or always dislike	n	χ^2	df	p	N
Past Sports Success	High	49.4	50.6	164	1.51	2	.47	480
	Medium	42.9	57.1	161				
	Low	44.5	55.5	155				
Sports Enthusiasm	High	50.0	50.0	152	4.05	2	.13	479
	Medium	48.3	51.7	151				
	Low	39.8	60.2	176				

Table 4. Academic Performance and Athletic Involvement

		Academic Performance							
		%A	%B	% $\leq$ C	n	χ^2	df	p	N
Past Sports Success	High	10.3	59.0	30.8	117	9.55*	4	.05	358
	Medium	12.3	57.4	30.3	122				
	Low	18.5	64.7	16.8	119				
Sports Enthusiasm	High	12.0	59.0	29.0	100	1.50	4	.83	356
	Medium	13.9	59.1	27.0	115				
	Low	14.9	62.4	22.7	141				

Table 5. Student Aspirations and Athletic Involvement

		Student Aspirations						
		% 1st or 2nd rank	% 3rd or 4th rank	n	χ^2	df	p	N
Past Sports Success	High	48.7	51.3	156	7.81*	2	.02	452
	Medium	55.8	44.2	154				
	Low	64.8	35.2	142				
Sports Enthusiasm	High	49.0	51.0	145	8.86*	2	.01	451
	Medium	55.9	44.1	143				
	Low	65.6	34.4	163				

Table 6. Graduate Study Aspirations and Athletic Involvement

		Graduate Study Aspirations							
		% definitely yes	% probably yes	% no	n	χ^2	df	p	N
Past Sports Success	High	27.3	51.6	21.1	161	5.68	4	.22	474
	Medium	20.6	48.1	31.3	160				
	Low	26.8	45.1	28.1	153				
Sports Enthusiasm	High	24.7	51.3	24.0	150	.28	4	.59	473
	Medium	29.1	43.7	27.2	151				
	Low	22.7	50.0	27.3	172				

Table 7. Assessment of College Education and Athletic Involvement

		Assessment of College Education						
		% Excellent	% Poor-Good	n	χ^2	df	p	N
Past Sports Success	High	44.4	55.6	151	11.4*	2	<.01	449
	Medium	29.6	70.4	152				
	Low	27.4	72.6	146				
Sports Enthusiasm	High	44.9	55.1	138	11.8*	2	<.01	448
	Medium	29.0	71.0	145				
	Low	27.9	72.1	165				

DISCUSSION

Table 8 summarizes the test of the four models proposed in this paper. The conclusion that seems most warranted by the pattern of statistically significant relationships found in this research is that, at the two schools that were surveyed, those more athletically competent and enthusiastic differed in a number of academic respects from their less athletic classmates. That is, the "athletes" on these two campuses were not "ordinary students," as Model 4 implies. If the athletes on these campuses, which were outside the realm of big-time college sports, could not be viewed as ordinary students, then it seems that scholarship athletes in big-time programs would not be likely to fit the assumptions of Model 4 either. But, do any of the remaining three models proposed here provide a coherent and valid picture of the student-athlete relationship on the two campuses that were surveyed?

It appears that neither the set of Past Sports Success results nor the set of Sports Enthusiasm results conforms to any one of the remaining three models. However, since those who were more athletically inclined tended to earn lower grades than their less athletic classmates (especially at the smaller college), the Scholar-Athlete Model seems to be inappropriate for explaining the results. In fact, all of the results, except the absence of significant relationships concerning graduate study aspirations, can be explained either by the Academically Incompetent Jock or Anti-Intellectual Jock Model. To the extent that some combination of the assumptions helps us understand the experience of the athlete as college student, it appears that some degree of conflict or inconsistency between the athlete and student or scholar roles exists. This conflict seemed particularly strong for the males and students at the smaller college in this research, but these patterns were not totally consistent. The effects of sex, college, and other background and contextual factors must be explored further in efforts to formulate more refined models of the student-athlete role relationship. These future efforts should look especially closely at how past sports socialization (reflected here by sex) and

Table 8.   Summary of Empirical Testing of Four Models

	Past Sports Success	Sports Enthusiasm
Student-Athlete Image	More athletic more likely to strongly reject stereotype/ supports Models 1, 2, 3.	More athletic more likely to strongly reject stereotype/ supports Models 1, 2, 3.
Value Work for Grades	No relationship/ supports Models 2, 4 (univ.). For coll., more athletic place more value on work for grades/supports Model 3.	No relationship/ supports Models 2, 4 (univ.). For coll., more athletic place more value on work for grades/supports Model 3.
Academic Performance	More athletic receive lower grades/supports Model 1.	No relationship/ supports Models 2, 4 (univ.). For coll., more athletic receive lower grades/supports Model 1.
Student Aspirations	More athletic rank top student goal lower/ supports Models 1, 2.	More athletic rank top student goal lower/ supports Models 1, 2.
Graduate Study Aspirations	No relationship/ supports Model 4.	No relationship/ supports Model 4.
Assessment of College Education	More athletic give more positive assessment of their college education/ supports Models 1, 3.	More athletic give more positive assessment of their college education/ supports Models 1, 3.

Note.-Model 1: Academically Incompetent Jock;
Model 2: Anti-Intellectual Jock; Model 3: Scholar-
Athlete; Model 4: Athlete as Ordinary Student.

the nature of the participation context (including the level and domain of competition as well as the type of school) shape this relationship.

In conclusion, at least it can be said that the stereotype of the dumb jock is too simple to help us understand athletes as students. Furthermore, nearly 84% of the students surveyed on both campuses in this study either strongly disagreed or disagreed with reservations with the stereotypical statement about athletes as relatively less intelligent and less serious academically than other students. Thus, for the college students, both athletes and non-athletes, in this study, the stereotype had relatively few firm believers. This seems an important insight to keep in mind in future research in this area.

NOTES

[1]The data collection phase of this research was supported by a University of Vermont Institutional Grant. The Sociology Department at Brigham Young University deserves thanks for providing facilities to conduct the data analysis during my sabbatical leave.

REFERENCES

Associated Press (AP)
  1981 "Graduation rate higher for athletes." Reported in Burlington, (Vermont) Free Press, May 17.
Davis, B. E. and R. A. Berger
  1973 "Relative academic achievement of varsity athletes." Research Quarterly 44: 59-62.
Ewing, L. E.
  1975 Career Development of College Athletes: Implications for Counseling Activities. Ed.D. Dissertation, Virginia Polytechnic and State University.
Figler, S. K.
  1981 Sport and Play in American Life. Philadelphia and New York: Saunders.
Hanford, G. H.
  1974 An Inquiry Into The Need For and Feasibility of a National Study of Intercollegiate Athletics. Washington, D.C.: American Council on Education.
Harrison, J. H.
  1976 "Intercollegiate football participation and academic achievement." Paper presented at the Southwestern Sociological Association Meeting, Dallas, Texas.
LeBar, J.
  1973 "An analysis of achievement of selected groups of Duke University graduates." NCPEAM: Proceedings of the 76th Annual Meeting, pp. 22-28.
Rothenberg, F.
  1977 "The academic life of jocks." Associated Press story reported in the San Francisco Chronicle, December 7.
Scholastic Coach
  1978 "College athletics and graduation." March issue, p. 163.

Chapter 16

INTERCOLLEGIATE ATHLETIC PARTICIPATION AND ACADEMIC ACHIEVEMENT

Steven F. Messner and Daniel Groisser,
Columbia University

One of the more important controversies in higher education today concerns the role of intercollegiate athletics. The popular press has unearthed a disturbing number of scandals indicating an overemphasis on athletic goals at the expense of academic ones. For example, some Arizona State football players were recently caught receiving credit for unattended off-campus "extension courses"; the Portland State basketball coach was accused of paying his players as well as taking kickbacks from them; and the use of an ineligible player forced Oregon State to forfeit its lone football victory in a 1-10 season (Axthelm et al., 1981:54). These events, and a plethora of other similar practices such as the encouragement of high school athletes to repeat their last year in high school in order to gain size and experience for future intercollegiate athletics, transcript fixing, recruiting violations, and the award of undeserved grades to athletes, may have encouraged many student-athletes to pin their hopes on an athletic future to the detriment of a normal education. This displacement of academic goals for athletic ones would be truly unfortunate given the fact that the chances for a career in professional sports are exceedingly slim. By way of illustration, in 1980 only 333 out of well over 21,500 intercollegiate football players were invited to try out by professional teams (B. Phillips, 1981:4).

From their inception in 1852, the evolution of intercollegiate sports has been affected by changing institutional philosophies of the relationship between athletics and academics. This process can be understood in terms of four major periods during which the ancillary versus the integral role of intercollegiate sports in the college education of a student has been debated. In the first period, extending roughly from 1852 to 1905, intercollegiate sports were student directed (Sage, 1975). A slow changing of the guard occurred during the second period, 1906-1920, when faculty and administration began half-heartedly to accept the regulation of team sports. It was in this period that the National Collegiate Athletic Association (NCAA) was formed. After this transitional period, the years 1921-1950 produced greater faculty regulations and greater acceptance of intercollegiate athletic activities as an integral part of the program of higher education (Sells, 1959:6-8).

A new debate has been sparked during the fourth period (Sage 1980), 1951 to the present, characterized not so much by a concern for the acceptance of intercollegiate sport as a viable part of a college education but rather by a controversy over the degree and direction this acceptance should take. A wide variety of attitudes has been expressed by various institutions. One position in this debate is that taken by the so-called Ivy League schools: Brown, Columbia, Cornell, Dartmouth, Harvard, Princeton, Pennsylvania, and Yale. These privately funded colleges and universities have insisted that the academic integrity of a school can only be maintained if a concerted effort is made to integrate intercollegiate sport with the needs of a student's academic life.

In 1954, the Ivy schools formed their own athletic conference. While they remain within the superstructure of the NCAA, the Ivy schools have adopted a rigorous set of checks and balances in an effort to secure their academically oriented sports philosophy. These safeguards, which are adhered to by all eight schools, expressly prohibit any type of athletic scholarships, demand roughly comparable admissions requirements for both athletes and non-athletes, limit formal off-season practices, and rule that all intercollegiate athletes must be making normal progress towards a degree at their respective schools. The Ivy agreement explicitly states that the intercollegiate athletic program should "limit undue strain upon players and coaches, permitting them to enjoy the game as participants in a form of recreational competition rather than as professional performers in a public spectacle" (DeMarras, 1980:5).

Yet despite these attempts at Ivy schools to prevent athletics from subverting academic goals, concern has been expressed recently that athletics are getting out of hand even at these institutions. Yale President Bartlett Giamatti has warned that "there is a lack of proportion, an imbalance in the way the programs in athletics in the Ivy Group have been allowed to grow." He continues:

> "The result of this disproportion is, in my opinion, that some students, and not a trivial number, spend far, far too much time, with the encouragement of the institutions, on athletic pursuits; the result is that coaching has gone a long, long way, particularly in some sports, to being a matter of recruiting and not of teaching; the result is that athletics in the Ivy group now hunger for the next event, that sequel, that bigger-league look and feel, that I think violates the essence of what we believe the role of organized athletics in our institutions ought to be" (Giamatti, 1980:21).

Giamatti's warning of a possible imbalance between athletics and academics raises a very important question: do students at these institutions suffer academically because of participation in contemporary intercollegiate athletic programs?

The purpose of this paper is to address this question with data for a sample of students at one Ivy League institution — Columbia College. Columbia certainly is not representative of American colleges generally. Along with its other Ivy counterparts, it is an "elite" institution academically. Admission is highly selective and the emphasis on academic achievement is exceptionally strong. Nevertheless, the very features which make Columbia unrepresentative also make it a particularly interesting and strategic institution for investigating the effects of intercollegiate athletics. The "elite" schools would seem to be the least susceptible to the lure of athletic glory and to any resulting subversion of academic goals by athletic ones. Hence, if an appreciable influence of athletic participation on academic performance can be found in these institutions, it is highly plausible that the effects are even more pronounced in more typical colleges with greater emphasis on intercollegiate athletics.

PREVIOUS LITERATURE

Published research on intercollegiate athletic participation and academic achievement is not very extensive. Many of the available studies are rather dated, and the results of the different studies are often contradictory. Some report that college athletes have lower levels of achievement, as reflected in grade point average, than do non-athletes (Larsen, 1973; Cooper, 1933; and the studies by Sneeden, Savage, Bevier, Phillips, and Foster cited in Davis, 1934). Others report no difference or exactly the reverse (Hanks and Eckland, 1976; Stechleim, 1965; Hindman, Miller, and Finley, cited in Davis, 1934). Comparisons of the grades of college athletes in the athletic season and the off-season are likewise contradictory. Early studies by P. Phillips (1908) and Cooper (1933) suggest that the athlete's grades suffer during the athletic season. In contrast, a more recent study by Stechleim (1965) detects no difference in the GPA of athletes in different seasons.[1]

The inconsistencies in the results of previous studies of intercollegiate athletics may be attributable in part to two common methodological weaknesses. One of these is the failure to control for relevant differences between athletes and non-athletes other than the fact of athletic participation or non-participation (see Stevenson, 1980, for a more extensive critique). A lower or higher grade point average for athletes could easily be due to differences in academic aptitude or socio-demographic background. It is thus critical to control for these factors when attempting to assess the effects of athletic participation per se.

A second serious deficiency in many previous studies is the operationalization of academic performance by means of overall grade point average. The problem with this procedure is that it is insensitive to variation in course difficulty. Students typically have considerable latitude in the formulation of their academic programs, which makes the interpretation of overall GPA highly problematic. An "easy" program can produce a GPA which is misleadingly high, whereas a relatively difficult program can have the opposite effect. The possibility of systematic bias is especially worrisome here — athletes may be induced by overly zealous coaches to enroll in courses of low difficulty in order to protect eligibility. The effect of such course selection would be to inflate the GPAs of athletes and thereby conceal the extent to which athletic participation affects academic achievement. Yet despite the importance of a control for course difficulty, this factor has been taken into account only in the studies of Savage, Snedden (cited in Davis, 1934) and Stechleim (1965). The present study hopes to go beyond previous research by explicitly controlling for all of the relevant factors discussed above, i.e., academic aptitude, socio-economic status, and the level of difficulty of the student's academic program.

THE SAMPLE

Students were selected for the study by means of a two stage sampling procedure. In the first stage, every other name listed on rosters for intercollegiate athletic teams was chosen for inclusion in the sample. The reason for using team rosters as an initial sampling frame was to insure that a sufficient number of athletes would be included in the study for certain detailed analyses. A total of 218 students were selected in this manner.

The second stage of the sampling was based on the student directory compiled by the Office of the Dean of Students. After eliminating the names of those students chosen from the team rosters, a systematic sample of 319 students was taken from the dean's directory. This resulted in a target sample of 537 students to whom questionnaires were sent. The addresses proved to be incorrect for 14 students, leaving 523 who presumably received the questionnaire. Returns were received for slightly over half (50.7%) of these students. Academic records could not be found for 18 of the returns, resulting in a final sample of 247. Since the probability of selection into the sample was not identical for all students, weighting has been performed to permit inferences about the general population. All of the statistical analyses reported below are based upon weighted cases.[2]

The sample students were each assigned an identifying number which was hand written in the upper-left hand corner of the questionnaire. It was necessary to have such an identifier in order to be able to merge information from the student's academic files with the responses to the questionnaire. We were careful to code the returns in such a way that it was not possible to associate specific names with the actual responses. Nevertheless, no effort was made to conceal the identifying number from the students.[3]

VARIABLES

The dependent variable for the study is academic achievement, which has been operationalized by means of two measures. The first is simply overall grade point average (GPA). This is obtained in the usual way by converting letter grades to numerical values on a scale of 0 to 4, adjusting for the number of credits for the course, and then averaging over all courses for which letter grades are given.

The second measure of academic achievement is designed to indicate performance in a program which is roughly standardized in terms of difficulty. Columbia College has a "core" curriculum. Hence, it is possible to restrict attention to grades received in that part of a student's program which is common to all. Three of the core courses have been selected for analysis: "Freshman Composition," "Contemporary Civilization," and "Masterpieces of Literature and Philosophy." The "standardized" measure of academic achievement — GPA REQUIRED — is simply the average grade point computed across as many of these required courses as had been completed at the time of the survey.[4]

The key independent variable is a dummy variable based on self-reported participation in intercollegiate athletics (ATHLETICS). A value of "1" on this variable is assigned to students who report that they have participated in intercollegiate athletics; a value of "0" is assigned to all others. Additional independent variables — the controls — are:

1) SAT TOTAL — the combined score on the verbal and mathematical components of the Scholastic Aptitude test, as recorded in the student's academic files;

2) SES — an index based on self-reported parents' income, father's education, and mother's education;[5]

3) RACE — a dummy variable with "1" designating white and "0" non-white;

4) STUDYHRS — self-reported study hours on a typical day;

5) EXTRACUR — participation in non-athletic extracurricular activities (1 = Yes, 9 = No).

RESULTS

The first step in the empirical analysis is to examine the simple relationships between participation in intercollegiate athletics and academic achievement. This can be accomplished by regressing the measures of grade point average on the dummy variable for athletics. The results for overall grade point average are given in Equation 1. The number in parentheses is the standard error for the regression coefficient.

Equation 1.   GPA = 3.267 − .103 ATHLETICS   N = 246
                         (.069)

The sign of the slope indicates that participation in intercollegiate athletics has a negative effect on grades. Athletes, in other
words, tend to have slightly lower GPAs than do non-athletes.
The magnitude of the effect is modest and since the regression
coefficient is not quite twice its standard error, the simple relationship between GPA and athletic participation is not statistically significant at conventional levels.

The regression results for GPA in required courses are presented in Equation 2. Athletic participation once again has a
modest negative effect on grades, but in contrast with the results
for overall GPA, the regression coefficient in Equation 2 does
exceed twice its standard error. This implies that athletes receive
grades in required courses which are significantly lower (statistically) than those received by their non-athletic counterparts.[6]

Equation 2.   GPA REQUIRED = 3.345 − .141 ATHLETICS   N = 241
                          (.059)

The most obvious possible explanation for the bivariate relationship between athletic participation and academic achievement
in required courses is the one suggested in the literature review,
namely, that it is spurious; that students who decide to participate in athletics are initially different in relevant ways from those
who choose not to participate. There are in fact some relevant initial differences in our sample. Athletes have significantly lower
combined SAT scores than non-athletes (1187 versus 1238), and
they also have slightly lower scores on the SES scale (3.65 versus
3.73).

The results of the multivariate analysis, however, do not
support the interpretation or spuriousness. Although SAT has a
significantly positive effect on both measures of academic performance, the negative effect of ATHLETICS on grades in required

courses is still significant (see Equation 4). In short, even with controls for measures of academic aptitude and socio-demographic background, participants in intercollegiate athletics tend to receive lower grades in required courses than do non-participants.

Equation 3.

$$.088 \text{ ATHLETICS} + .0008 \text{ SAT TOTAL}$$
$$(.070) \quad\quad\quad (.0003)$$

$$.021 \text{ SES} + .142 \text{ RACE} \quad\quad\quad N = 237$$
$$(.031) \quad\quad (.086)$$

Equation 4.

$$.125 \text{ ATHLETICS} + .0009 \text{ SAT TOTAL}$$
$$(.057) \quad\quad\quad (.0002)$$

$$.026 \text{ SES} + .129 \text{ RACE} \quad\quad\quad N = 232$$
$$(.025) \quad\quad (.070)$$

How can we account for the poorer achievement of intercollegiate athletes? A plausible hypothesis is that athletes are unable to devote as much time to their study as their non-athletic colleagues, given the demands of practice schedules. We can evaluate this hypothesis by introducing our measure of self-reported study time. If the hypothesis of a "time constraint" is correct, then study hours should be positively related to academic achievement and, once this variable has been taken into account, athletic participation should no longer exhibit any relationship with achievement.

Equation 5 does not support the "time constraint" hypothesis. The ATHLETICS variable continues to exhibit a significant effect on GPA in required courses despite the control for STUDYHRS.[7] Evidently, the lower grades of athletes in comparison with non-athletes cannot be accounted for simply in terms of a reduction in studying induced by the time demands of athletic participation. Further evidence contrary to a simple "time constraint" interpretation is provided in Equation 6, which includes the measure of participation in non-athletic extracurricular activities as well as the other controls. The results reveal no significant effect of participation in extracurricular activities on grades in required courses, while athletic participation retains its significant negative effect.

Equation 5.

$$.138 \text{ ATHLETICS} + .0009 \text{ SAT TOTAL}$$
$$(.056) \qquad\qquad (.0002)$$

$$.032 \text{ SES} + .088 \text{ RACE} + .043 \text{ STUDYHRS} \qquad N = 220$$
$$(.025) \qquad (.073) \qquad (.017)$$

Equation 6.

$$.141 \text{ ATHLETICS} + .0009 \text{ SAT TOTAL}$$
$$(.058) \qquad\qquad (.0002)$$

$$.032 \text{ SES} + .087 \text{ RACE} + .044 \text{ STUDYHRS}$$
$$(.025) \qquad (.073) \qquad (.017)$$

$$- .010 \text{ EXTRACUR} \qquad N = 219$$
$$(.059)$$

DISCUSSION

The most important finding of this study is the negative association between participation in intercollegiate athletics and grade point average in a sample of required courses. This negative relationship persists despite controls for academic aptitude, socioeconomic status, and race. On the basis of these results, we tentatively conclude that there is a minor academic "cost" of participation in intercollegiate athletics at Columbia.

Our data do not explain just how athletic participation interferes with academic achievement. The most obvious explanation — that participation in athletics takes time away from studying — is not supported by the results. The negative effect of the athletic variable does not disappear when self-reported study time is entered into the regression equation. Furthermore, there is virtually no simple relationship between athletic participation and reported study hours ($r = .03$). It may be that participation in intercollegiate athletics lessens the quality of study time while not affecting its quantity. Such an effect might reflect the fatigue likely to accompany vigorous physical activity. Another possibility is that athletes actually achieve at levels comparable to non-athletes but suffer discrimination in the assignment of grades. Unfortunately, these speculations cannot be addressed with the current data.

The policy implications of these results must, for two reasons, be interpreted cautiously. In the first place, the analysis is cross-sectional in nature, and even though we have employed statistical controls to take into account several relevant differences between athletes and non-athletes, any attempt to draw causal inferences from cross-sectional data is inevitably hazardous. Secondly, the substantive importance of the differences actually observed must not be exaggerated. Although the data indicate that athletic participation has a statistically significant negative effect on achievement in required courses, the magnitude of the effect is indeed quite modest. The estimated "cost" of athletic participation at Columbia is only slightly over one-tenth of a grade point. Conceivably, athletes may receive non-academic benefits from their athletic experiences which far outweigh the modest academic penalties detected in this study. Such benefits might include the development of close friendships, enhanced self-esteem, and simple personal enjoyment.

We have some evidence bearing upon this last item, i.e., personal enjoyment or satisfaction. Students were asked to indicate how satisfied they were with social life and with academic life at Columbia. Contrary to the argument that athletes enjoy higher levels of satisfaction with social life due to their participation in intercollegiate athletics, the differences between athletes and others on this item are insignificant. At the same time, athletes express just as much satisfaction with academic life as non-athletes. This latter finding implies that athletes themselves show no indication of being particularly disturbed by any academic cost of athletic participation.

We do detect one possible problem confronting athletes. Athletes were asked to give their own ratings of the relative importance of academics and athletics as well as their perceptions of their coaches' ratings. Most of the intercollegiate athletes reported that academics are more important to them than are athletics. But, in contrast to their own views, most athletes feel that their coaches value academics and sports equally. This discrepancy between personal values and perceptions of coaches' values could conceivably be a source of tension and strain for the college athlete.

We close with the traditional call for more research. It is our suspicion, as noted in the introduction, that the slight negative effects of athletic participation observed at Columbia would be more pronounced at other institutions with a greater emphasis on athletics. This seems to us to be the most plausible hypothesis, but an alternative hypothesis could be formulated with the opposite prediction. Perhaps negative effects of athletic participation are unique to institutions placing little emphasis on athletics for the simple reason that participation in athletics is demoralizing in such unsupportive environments. Additional research at institutions of varying sizes and with different sport philosphies is needed to resolve these uncertainties and to determine the generalizability of the findings reported in this paper.

NOTES

[1]Since our concern is with the effects of athletic participation on academic achievement in institutions of higher education, the review in the text is limited to studies of college athletes. Research has also been done at the secondary school level. The bulk of these studies suggest that high school athletes obtain higher grades than do non-athletes (Schafer and Armer, 1968; Edwards, 1967; Phillips and Schafer, 1980; see also Snyder and Spreitzer, 1977). The salutary effect of high school athletic participation has been attributed to the fact that athletes are more highly motivated, more goal oriented, less delinquent (e.g., Landers and Landers, 1978), and more likely to aspire to college than are their non-athletic counterparts. Recent studies by Hauser and Lueptow (1978) and Hanks and Eckland (1976) dispute the claim that there is any causal relationship between high school athletic participation and academic achievement. In any event, there is good reason to expect that any positive effects of athletic participation in high school may not be reproduced at the college level. The demands of both athletics and academics are considerably greater in college than in high school, raising the likelihood that one form of endeavor will at some point come into conflict with the other.

[2]Details of the weighting are available from the authors upon request.

[3]The prominent display of the identifying number may have introduced some response bias, but ethical considerations convinced us to use this procedure rather than to attempt any sort of deception.

[4]The number of courses and the specific mix of courses used in the computation of GPA REQUIRED are not necessarily the same for all students. In effect, we are assuming that the three required courses are of roughly comparable levels of difficulty and that the use of a subset of these courses in cases where the student has not yet completed all three will not introduce systematic bias. The grade distributions for these courses in our sample are in fact very similar, although "Freshman Composition" appears to have slightly higher grades on the average. In any case, GPA REQUIRED is no doubt a better measure than simple GPA, which is the usual alternative.

[5]The questionnaire items for father's education, mother's education, and parents' income contained 5 ordered categories. The SES index was constructed by taking the arithmetic average of non-missing values on these items.

[6]Note that the magnitude of the differences between athletes and non-athletes on GPA and GPA REQUIRED is not very great, belying the stereotype of the "dumb jock."

[7]Note that the effect of study hours on overall GPA is not statistically significant, whereas its effect on GPA in required courses is. Assuming that study time should have some bearing on academic achievement, these results support the argument that GPA REQUIRED is the more valid indicator of achievement.

[8]We are very grateful to Deans Roger Lehecka and Ben Lieber for their invaluable cooperation during the data collection phase of this study. The authors alone assume full responsibility for the analyses and interpretations presented herein.

REFERENCES

Axthelm, P. and D. Foote, V. Coppola, J. Kirsch
    1981 "The shame of college sports." Newsweek, September 22, pp. 54-59.
Cooper, J.
    1933 The Effect of Participation in Athletics Upon Scholarship Measured by Achievement Tests. Pennsylvania State College Press.
Davis, E. and J. Cooper
    1934 "A Resume of studies comparing scholarship-abilities of athletes and non-athletes." Research Quarterly 5:68-78.
De Marras, K.
    1980 The Ivy League Record Book, 1980-81. Ivy League Sports Information Directors, pp. 5-8.
Edwards, T.
    1967 "Scholarship and athletics." Journal of Health, Physical Education and Recreation 38:75.
Giamatti, B.
    1980 "Yale and athletics." Transcript of speech given on April 10, 1980.
Hanks, M. P. and B. K. Eckland
    1976 "Athletics and social participation in the educational attainment process." Sociology of Education 49:271-294.
Hauser, W. J. and L. Lueptow
    1978 "Participation in athletics and academic achievement: a replication and extension." Sociological Quarterly 19:304-309.
Landers, D. and D. Landers
    1978 "Socialization via interscholastic athletics: its effects on delinquency." Sociology of Education 51:299-303.

Larsen, S.
1973 A Study of the Academic Achievement of Athletes at the University of Tennessee, Knoxville. Office of Institutional Research, University of Tennessee.
Phillips, B. J.
1981 "Fattening them up for football." Time, March 9, p. 41.
Phillips, P.
1908 "Competitive athletics and scholarship." Science, April 3, 1908, pp. 547-553.
Phillips, J. and W. Schafer
1980 "Consequences of participation in interscholastic sports: a review and prospectus." Pp. 182-190 in G. Sage (ed.), Sport and American Society, 3rd Edition. Reading, Mass.:Addison-Wesley.
Sage, G. H.
1975 "An occupational analysis of the college coach." Pp. 395-455 in D. Ball and J. Loy (eds.), Sport and Social Order. Reading, Mass.:Addison-Wesley.
1980 "The collegiate dilemma of sport and leisure." Pp. 203-210 in G. Sage (ed.), Sport and American Society, 3rd Edition. Reading, Mass.:Addison-Wesley.
Schafer, W. E. and J. Armer
1968 "Athletes are not inferior students." TransAction 6:21-62.
Sells, J.
1959 Analysis of Functions Performed and Competencies Needed to Administer Programs of Intercollegiate Athletics. Unpublished Ph.D. thesis, Columbia University Teachers College.
Snyder, E. and E. Spreitzer
1977 "Participation in sport as related to educational expectations among high school girls." Sociology of Education 50:47-55.
Stechleim, J.
1965 Athletics and Academic Progress. Bureau of Institutional Research. University of Minnesota.
Stevenson, C.
1980 "Socialization effects of participation in sport: a critical view of the research." Pp. 143-159 in G. Sage (ed.), Sport and American Society, 3rd Edition. Reading, Mass.:Addison-Wesley.

Chapter 17

SPORT AND RACIAL INTEGRATION: THE RELATIONSHIP OF PERSONAL CONTACT, ATTITUDES AND BEHAVIOR

Donald Chu, Skidmore College
David C. Griffey, University of Texas

Does interracial participation on sport teams promote positive attitudes and behavior toward other racial groups? Does the player interaction and teamwork required for successful sport participation reduce prejudice and promote interracial harmony? Certainly Gordon Allport (1954:276) believed so when he noted that the type of contact required to reduce prejudice —

> . . . must reach below the surface in order to be effective . . . Only the type of contact that leads people to do things together is likely to result in changed attitudes. The principle is clearly illustrated in the multi-ethnic athletic team. Here the goal is all important: the ethnic composition of the team is irrelevant.

It is the cooperative striving for the goal that engenders solidarity. According to the contact hypothesis, exposure to the interracial contacts under conditions of a) equal status of groups, b) common group goals, c) cooperative interaction, and d) environmental support should generally lead to positive changes in intergroup attitudes and interaction patterns (Braddock, 1980:179). Although at first glance it may appear that these conditions are met in sport settings, research by sport sociologists on the question of sport's contribution to the promotion of integration has led to mixed results. Czula (1978) in his study of adult males in a basketball competition league found little integration and social interaction after the game. Basketball competitions were marked by intraracial loyalty and a great degree of racial rivalry in the daily matches. In an early study, Ibrahim (1968) found no significant difference between the attitudes of athletes and non-athletes toward minorities. If sport helped reduce the prejudices of athletes, no significant differences were noted. Similarly Kraus (1969) found little integration resulting from the community recreation programs studied, and Sargent (1972) concluded that the participation of West Indian boys on school sport teams did not result in increased numbers of friendships or other interactions with whites.

In their reviews of the literature both McPherson (1976) and Coakley (1978) note the very limited degree to which sport participation may promote integration. Integration, if it results at all, may only be evident on the field. Also the friendships developed by elite athletes of different races may not be developed by recreational athletes who do not depend on each other for as high stakes as professional and world class sport participants. Attitudes are highly resistant to change. Potential attitude and behavior altering stimuli gained from inter-racial contacts may be blocked or reinterpreted to reinforce previously held racial stereotypes.

The concern demonstrated by sport sociologists in their evaluations of the contact hypothesis of racial relations has been mirrored by educational researchers studying inter-racial schools. Will such controversial measures as the alteration of school district boundaries and busing promote integration? Such programs depend partly for their justification on the notion that increased personal contact between the races will lead to better attitudes and behavior toward members of other races. Reviews of research by St. John (1975), Cohen (1975) and McConahay (1978), however, have found inconclusive results. The belief that school desegregation will positively change racial attitudes and behavior is at this point based more upon intuition than research findings.

Of interest to researchers concerned with both schools and sport is the recent work of Slavin and Madden (1979). Based largely upon Educational Testing Service data of 1974 (Forehand, Ragosta and Rock, 1976), the study was designed to assess the factors that were associated with alterations in racial attitudes and behavior. Effects of the following school practices directed toward the improvement of student relations were compared:

1) attempts to change teacher or principal attitudes through workshops;

2) attempts to change student attitudes by providing minority history classes, portraying minorities in positive roles in textbooks and in school positions, and discussing race relations in class;

3) heterogeneous grouping, either within or between classes; and

4) attempting to change student behaviors directly by assigning them to work and play in mixed racial groups (Slavin & Madden, 1979:171).

It is especially interesting then that the study by Slavin and Madden (1979), based upon their sample of 2384 10th grade respondents drawn from 51 schools, generally found that "multicultured texts, intergroup relations workshops for teachers and bi-racial advisory committees do not change the way that students interact, and they have weak effects (if any) on inter-racial behaviors and attitudes" (Slavin & Madden, 1979:179). What was found important was the effect of interpersonal interaction on the promotion of positive racial attitudes and behavior. For both whites and blacks, the independent variable of "playing team with members of another race" was most highly correlated with the dependent variables associated with positive racial attitudes and behavior. If indeed sport experience may be demonstrated as an effective aid in the efforts of schools to promote racial relations, then the appropriateness of allocations of scarce funds to athletics and the legitimacy of scholastic sport in general may be enhanced.

METHODOLOGY

Questionnaires were completed by 1082 high school students attending three schools in the upstate New York area. Schools were selected because of their urban public character and the differences in their racial composition. The population of school "A" was 52 percent white and 41 percent black; at school "T," 86 percent white and 12 percent black; and at school "S," 97 percent white and 3 percent black. Samples gathered for this study reflect school racial populations.

Items used in the questionnaire originally appeared in a study by Forehand, Ragosta and Rock (1976) conducted for the Educational Testing Service and appear in somewhat modified form in Slavin and Madden (1979). For the purposes of this study the two behavioral and four attitudinal dependent variables have been slightly modified in order to gain further information.

Behavioral Dependent Variables

— Think for a moment about the three students you talk with most often at school. Are they all the same race as you?

— Have you ever called a student of a different race on the phone? If "yes" approximately how often?

Attitudinal Dependent Variables

— Would you like to have more friends who are of a different race? If "yes" how much?

— If you could choose the kind of school you would go to, would you pick one with a mixture of black and white students?

— In general do you think — A. that white people are more competent than black people; or B. that black people are more competent than white people; or C. do you think that a person's color doesn't have anything to do with how competent they are? Do you feel comfortable around students of a different race? If "no" how uncomfortable?

Independent variables which were examined to assess their correlation to the above items included the following:

Independent Variables

— Individual or cooperative nature of sports played. For example of the sports listed on the questionnaire football and basketball were deemed cooperative sports while gymnastics and golf were deemed individual sports.

— Years of playing experience for each sport.

— Won/lost record for each sport.

— Minority percentage on each team.

— Sex.

— Socioeconomic status. Students were asked to describe the occupation of the head of their household.

In this analysis "athlete" was defined as a student who had engaged in a sport league in or outside of school. Students/athletes who had experience in race relations courses were also asked to compare the effectiveness of such courses with their athletic experiences.

ANALYSES AND RESULTS

Of the 1082 subjects who completed the questionnaire, 1018 indicated that they were athletes or non-athletes by virtue of their response to "have you ever played in a sports league?" Seven hundred four, or 69 percent, said that they had participated in organized sport. The breakdown for sport participation by sex is shown in Table 1.

Students' (1) number of interracial contacts, as indicated by "phone calls to person of another race" and "talk to persons of another race," and (2) their attitudes about multiracial environment as indicated by "would you like to have more friends of a different race?" "would you choose to attend a multi-racial school?" and "do you feel comfortable around students of a different race?" were found to be inter-related as indicated by signifi-

Table 1

Organized Sport Participation by Sex

Sex	Had Not Played	Had Played	Total
Male	88	392	480
Female	226	312	538
Total	314	704	1018

cant intercorrelations in every case. The exact wording of items and correlations between them are shown in Table 2. Substantively, all items are positively related; negative correlations resulted from item wording or data coding.

Interracial Contacts and Attitudes of Athletes and Non-Atheltes

Most students, 76 percent of the non-athletes and 77 percent of the athletes, indicated that the three people they talked with most often at school were the same race as themselves. The results of an analysis of variance for the difference between responses for athletes and non-athletes was not significant, $F = .118$, $p = .73$.

The average number of phone calls to students of a different race, for non-athletes, was 1.9. For athletes, the average was 2.9. This difference was tested with ANOVA and found to be significant at $p < .001$, $F = 17.76$.

Athletes expressed more interest in having more friends of another race than did non-athletes. This difference was slight and not significant, $p = .12$, $F = 2.38$, with subjects feeling, on average, that it was not very important to have more friends of another race.

Eighty one percent of non-athletes and 82 percent of athletes said that they would choose a school with a mixture of black and

Table 2

Intercorrelations Between Racial Attitudes and Contact

	1	2	3	4	5
1. How many times have you called a student of a different race on the phone?	----	----	----	----	----
2. Would you like to have more friends who are of a different race? How much?	-.24*	----	----	----	----
3. If you could, would you choose a school with a mixture of black and white students?	.12*	-.30*	----	----	----
4. Do you feel comfortable around students of another race? If no how uncomfortable?	.15*	-.20*	.28*	----	----
5. Are the three students you talk to most at school the same race as you?	-.24*	.17*	-.15*	-.13*	

* Significant Correlation at $p < .001$

white students. The difference between athletes and non-athletes on this item was not significant, $p = .85$, $F = .04$.

When responding to the question, "do you feel comfortable around students of a different race?" students answered in one of three categories: (1) Very Uncomfortable, (2) Mildly Uncomfortable, (3) Comfortable. The mean response for athletes was 2.77 and that for non-athletes was 2.75, indicating that, in general, subjects were comfortable around students of a different race. The difference in responses for athletes and non-athletes was not significant, $p. = .51$, $F = .43$.

The overwhelming majority of subjects were non-racist in responding to the question about relative competence of blacks and whites. Eleven percent of the subjects felt that one racial group was more competent than the other. When responses were broken down by athletic participation, Table 3, it was found that athletes were significantly ($\chi^2 = 3.87$, p<.05, df= 1) more racist in their responses than were non-athletes.

The relationships of behavior and attitude variables to years of sport participation, win-loss record and percentage of blacks on the team are shown in Table 4.

A significant correlation was found between the percentage of blacks on a team, either individual or cooperative, and the frequency of inter-racial contacts in the school house. A "no" response to the question — Are the three students you talk with most often at school the same race as you — occurred more frequently as the percentage of blacks on the team increased.

Similarly, significant correlations between number of phone calls to students of a different race and percentage of blacks on the team were found. The number of calls also increased as years of

Table 3

Racist Attitudes by Sport Participation

Racism	Non-Athletes	Athletes	Total
One racial group more competent than another	25	85	110
Race not an indicator of competence	295	631	926
Total	320	716	1036

x^2 = 3.87, df = 1, p<.05

Table 4

Intercorrelations of Interracial Attitudes and

Behaviors with Sport Variables

Sport Variables	People you talk with at school	Phone calls to Ss of another race	Like more friends of another race	Choose a multiracial school	Comfortable around Ss of another race
Cooperative Sport					
Years of Participation	-.04	.09**	.06*	-.05	-.01
Win-Loss Record	-.06	.06	.06	.04	.01
Percentage of Blacks on Team	-.14***	.16***	.09*	.04	.01
Individual Sport					
Years of Participation	-.04	.12***	-.02	-.04	.08**
Win-Loss Record	-.07	.00	.04	-.03	-.10*
Percentage of Blacks on Team	-.16**	.26*	-.02	.09*	.09*

*   Significant at p<.05
**   Significant at p<.01
*** Significant at p<.001

participation increased. The longer students were involved in sport, the more often they called persons of a different race.

Individual sport participants also differed from cooperative sport participants on the relationship of choosing a multi-racial school and comfort around students of a different race with years of participation, won-loss record and percentage of blacks on team. The only significant correlation with choosing a multi-racial school was percentage of blacks on individual sport teams. For individual team participants, significant correlations between degree of comfort around students of another race and years of participation, win-loss record and percentage of blacks on the team were found. As length of participation, win percentage and number of blacks on the team increased, so did the degree of comfort around other races expressed by subjects.

Sport and Human Relations Courses

Of the 704 athletes in the study, 211 had taken a race relations course or participated in a race relations program. Thirty-four percent of those felt that the course/program was more effective in improving racial understanding than was sport league participation. Sixty-six percent felt sport was more effective. The difference was tested against the hypothesis that subjects felt courses and sport were equally effective using chi-square. The value, $X^2 = 21.27$, was significant at $p < .001$ indicating that athletes felt that sport was more valuable for improving race relations than courses designed for that purpose.

DISCUSSION

The findings of this research indicate the over-simplicity of the general contact theory presented by Allport (1954) and recently extended by Slaven and Madden (1979). For the population studied there was little found to suggest the consistent validity of the notion that mere contact with members of another race in the sport setting will lead to more positive racial attitudes and behavior. Instead this research suggests that as the environments of sport vary, their effect on inter-racial behavior and attitudes may also vary.

As we have seen, the athletes in this study were not generally less racist than non-athletes. Those who had engaged in organized sport were significantly more racist in attitude on one of the four attitudinal variables measured. While the contact theory would suggest that exposure to members of another race would facilitate more favorable behavior and attitudes for the athletes working with minority team-mates, we have seen that the athletes and non-athletes did not vary significantly in either their inter-racial thoughts or behavior.

The need for further multivariate research is apparent from this study's web of findings. Athletes from individual sport backgrounds differ in many ways from their peers in cooperative sport. Although the contact theory would suggest that the close work and team activity of cooperative sports like football and basketball would be more conducive to positive racial attitudes and behavior, the findings of this research do not bear out this hypothesis. Increases in the proportion of minorities on sport teams and tenure of athletic activity by cooperative sport athletes did not correlate with more positive inter-racial attitudes. The situation is reversed, however, for athletes from individual sport backgrounds such as tennis and track. As years of participation and percentage of minorities on these teams increased, so did their racial attitudes improve.

Future research should continue to examine the multitude of factors that effect and moderate racial attitudes and behavior. It may be that such factors as the structured or unstructured nature of a sport's practice sessions or contests, the warmth or climate of a sport or coach, visibility of evaluation, social class, sex or minority proportion in the organization exert a significant influence on the development of attitudes and behavior.

REFERENCES

Allport, Gordan
    1954 The Nature of Prejudice. Cambridge, Mass.:Addison-Wesley.

Braddock II, Jomills Henry

   1980 "The perpetuation of segregation across levels of education: a behavioral assess-
        ment of the contact hypothesis." Sociology of Education 53: 178-186.

Coakley, Jay J.

   1978 Sport in Society. St. Louis: C. V. Mosley.

Cohen, E. G.

   1975 "The effects of desegregation on race relations." Law and Contemporary Prob-
        lems 39: 271-299.

Czula, Roman

   1978 "A participant observation approach to the study of restricted groups." Paper
        presented at the International Sociological Association World Congress,
        Upsula, Sweden.

Forehand, G., M. Ragosta and D. Rock

   1976 Conditions and Processes of Effective School Desegregation (Final Report), US
        Office of Education, Department of Health, Education and Welfare, Princeton,
        New Jersey: Educational Testing Service.

Ibrahim, Hilmi

   1968 "Prejudice among college athletes." Research Quarterly 39: 556-559.

Kraus, R.

   1969 "Race and sports: the challenge to recreation." Journal of Physical Education
        and Recreation. 40: 32-24.

McConahay, John B.

   1978 "The effects of school desegregation upon student's racial attitudes and behav-
        ior: a critical review of the literature and a prolegomen on to future research."
        Law and Contemporary Problems 42: 77-107.

McPherson, Barry

   1976 "The black athlete: an overview and analysis." Pp. 122-150 in Daniel H. Lan-
        ders (ed.), Social Problems in Athletics: Essays in the Sociology of Sport.
        Urbana, Illinois: University of Illinois Press.

St. John, N. H.

   1975 School Desegregation: Outcomes for Children. New York: John Wiley and
        Sons.

Sargent, A. J.

   1972 "Participation of West Indian boys in English school sport teams." Education
        Research 14: 225-230.

Slavin, Robert E. and Nancy A. Madden

   1979 "School practices that improve race relations." American Educational Research
        Journal 16: 169-180.

IMPACT OF SPORT PARTICIPATION ON YOUTH

Section VI

IMPACT OF SPORT PARTICIPATION ON YOUTH

The chapters in this section provide four interrelated analyses of the nature of youth sport practices in selected North American settings.

After reviewing the literature on professionalization of attitude (from Webb's work to the present), Theberge, Curtis and Brown suggest that the differential emphasis placed on winning by males and females is a result of the higher level of participation among males. Sampling young adults from five countries, they showed that while, in general, males showed a greater winning orientation than females, this difference did not occur in the specific case of elite athletes. However, when professionalization of attitudes between samples of adult and adolescent Canadians were examined, the orientation towards winning between the sexes persisted.

Berlage examines the socializing function of youth sport. The data presented are based on observations and interviews of parents and coaches of children's soccer and ice hockey organizations in Connecticut and New York. Berlage concludes that organized sports for children inculcate attitudes, values and social skills which are congruent with the values and social ethic of the corporate structures of American business, a finding that provides support for earlier work by several other researchers.

Podilchak poses an interesting question regarding the nature of sport organizations. Does the involvement of adults in the organization of youth sport have predictable effects? It is often assumed that peer organized settings (without adult influence) differ from adult organized settings. Since children today participate in both types of settings, it also can be assumed that there might be a transfer of learning from one to the other. Podilchak compared data collected from peer settings with data on two types of adult organized soccer leagues — egalitarian, recreational houseleagues and selective leagues with an elite structure. Podilchak found that boys in the selective leagues emphasized performance, while boys in the houseleagues emphasized sociability. Boys in each league tended to transfer these organization-specific traits to peer-organized settings. In general, boys experienced similar perceptions of the peer setting that were more characteristic of their respective adult setting, i.e., selective or house league. Thus, he concludes that peer setting cannot be compared directly to adult organized settings since a generalized perception of game involvement occurs.

In the concluding paper of this section, Dubois presents a comparative analysis of the behavior of youth sport coaches in a competitive and in an instructional league setting. Consistent with previous studies in the field, the Dubois data indicate "positive" behaviors are more frequently associated with "instructional" than "competitive" settings. Indeed, as Dubois notes, "the instructional league coaches maintain a relatively stable output of . . . positive behaviors irrespective of game outcome or team record, whereas, the competitive league coaches' positive behaviors are clearly linked to team performance." Dubois concludes this chapter with several recommendations for future practices in the coaching of youth sport.

Chapter 18

SEX DIFFERENCES IN ORIENTATIONS TOWARD GAMES: TESTS OF THE SPORT INVOLVEMENT HYPOTHESIS

Nancy Theberge, James Curtis, and Barbara Brown,
University of Waterloo

One often encounters the conventional wisdom that sport is an institution where values of sportsmanship and fair play are emphasized and effectively taught. However, most sociologists of sport would argue that sport has a dominant value of winning however much other values are involved (cf. Webb, 1969; Edwards, 1973:84ff; Sage, 1980a). Winning as a valued goal, it is said, is taught far more assiduously in sport than are other goals. This understanding is perhaps best illustrated in the statement which has been attributed to the late Vince Lombardi, a long-time professional football coach: "Winning isn't everything; it is the only thing." While professional sport may epitomize this orientation, all organized non-professional sport is said to place a great priority on winning. This, it has been argued, is very much in the interest of individual participants because the norms of the adult work world, for which most people must be prepared, place strong emphasis on the principles of competition and success. Sport is seen as one of the major training grounds for the work world (cf. Webb, 1969).

If sport is a socialization agency for the important value of success, females apparently lose out from two standpoints, compared with males. First, it has been shown that females participate less in sport than do males. Second, it has been reported, in a literature building especially from Harry Webb's (1969) work on this topic, that females orient themselves differently toward sport when they do participate in it. Females are less likely than males to see winning as important. The sociological processes which make for these sex differences remain unclear. As a step toward a clearer understanding of them, our purpose in this paper is to consider, conjointly, the two sex differences just mentioned. We ask if sex differences in orientations toward games are, in large part at least, a function of sex differences in extent and types of involvement in sport.

Since we will extrapolate from what has come to be called "the Webb Scale literature," a review of Webb's theory and the results of studies guided by it is in order.

THEORETICAL ARGUMENTS AND HYPOTHESES

Some years ago, Webb (1969) developed a "professionalization scale" for measuring attitudes toward games, and this has been the impetus for most studies of sex differences in game orientations. Webb argued that the ideologies of industrial societies stress achievement criteria rather than ascribed criteria, that they emphasize that allocation to work roles is based primarily upon qualifications or skill not upon ascribed characteristics. Furthermore, he argued that the ideology holds that competition for the roles takes place under conditions that are equitable. In short, the most "highly touted values" are victory.., skill and fairness (Webb, 1969:161). Webb contended that these three values are promulgated in major social institutions, most notably in the economy and schools, *but also in sport.*

Webb believed that the realization of the values is problematic, however, because one value may be in conflict with another. In particular, were one to decide to succeed at almost any cost, then one might set the fairness principle aside. Indeed, he noted that through time society has become increasingly achievement-oriented, and success and the skill needed to achieve success have come to be valued more highly than fairness. Webb went on to say that, as they mature, children come to understand this priorizing of the key values. Their play becomes more oriented toward adult roles as they grow up. Their orientation toward games comes to emphasize success and skill more and to deemphasize fairness. Webb implied that this developing understanding comes about through the influence of adult socializing agents both in sport and outside sport. As far as socialization to the values through sport, he believed that it was most effective where sport was more rationalized, where adults had the greatest influence on the organization of the sport.

Webb believed that no child escapes this experience inside or outside of sport, but that some, such as males, as opposed to females, "are more subject to its strictures than others" (1969:163). He emphasized that the training of females placed less weight on success values because their participation in full-time work is not as likely nor as expected (1969:188).

Webb's research procedure was to ask this question of subjects: "What do you think is most important in playing a game":

a. to play as well as you are able [play]?
b. to beat your opponent [beat]?
c. to play fairly [fair]?

Respondents were asked to rank order the importance of these approaches. There are six possible patterns of responses which he ranked from greater to lesser professionalization. Webb argued that the least professional orientation, which he called a "play" orientation, was in the order of FAIR-PLAY-BEAT. The most professional approach was the "beat" or "win" orientation, with responses in the order of BEAT-PLAY-FAIR. Figure 1 shows his overall scale.

Webb asked his question of U.S. school children from four school grades between 3 and 12. He found consistently higher professionalization scores among males than females at each age level, with the greatest difference among the older students. He

Figure 1

Professionalization of Play Scale[a]

Rank Order of Responses	Scale Values					
	1	2	3	4	5	6
First	Fair	Fair	Play	Play	Beat	Beat
Second	Play	Beat	Fair	Beat	Fair	Play
Third	Beat	Play	Beat	Fair	Play	Fair

[a]Adapted from Webb (1969:166).

also found a positive association between age and professionalization among both boys and girls, supporting his argument that as
children mature their orientations change. Surprisingly, Webb
did not pursue part of the logic of his theory by studying whether
children who were involved in organized sport were higher on
professionalization than were those who were not.

Several researchers have extended Webb's work by adminis-
tering the professionalization scale to different populations, and
most have confirmed the finding of sex differences (Petrie, 1971a,
1971b; Maloney and Petrie, 1974; Loy, Birrell, and Rose, 1976;
Snyder and Spreitzer, 1979; McElroy and Kirkendell, 1980;
Nixon, 1980; and Sage, 1980b; cf. Mantel and VanderVelden,
1971). Some have also explored sport involvement correlates of
professionalization. There have been two studies of youngsters:
Mantel and VanderVelden (1971) administered the scale to 10 and
11 year old boys and found that those who participated in organized sports had more professionalized orientations than those
who did not. Maloney and Petrie (1974) studied English-

Canadian male and female students in grades 8 through 12 and obtained similar results. (There were no controls for sex.) An exception was that intramural athletes were not as high in winning orientation as would be expected.

Still other studies have employed samples of university students and adults. For example, Loy, Birrell, and Rose (1976) examined the professionalization of attitudes of six types of samples in a U.S. community — university students, their parents, intramural sport participants, varsity intercollegiate athletes, married students, and married citizens — and one of their findings was that professionalization was higher in the samples which were more highly involved in sport. The exception was that intramural athletes were comparatively low in winning orientation. These athletes scored lower than persons of the same sex from the community at large, for example.

The study by Loy *et al.* is of special interest because it considered the effects of sex within levels of sport participation. The results showed that varsity athletes and physical education majors had the most marked differences between females and males in ranking winning first (2 per cent vs. 22 per cent and 6 per cent vs. 29 per cent respectively). In another study of this type, Nixon (1980) correlated professional attitudes with three different measures of sport involvement in a sample of university students. He found that, among both males and females, "prior athletic success" was positively related to endorsing a professional attitude. The factors of "sports enthusiasm" and "support for sport's institutional structure" bore a slight positive relationship to professionalization among men but not among women. Regardless of which of the three sport involvement controls were made, males emphasized a winning orientation more than females. Moreover, the higher the involvement, on each measure, the greater the female-male difference in ranking winning first. Snyder and Spreitzer (1979) have also reported that athletes (i.e., those university students who had some experience with interscholastic athletics in high school) showed higher professional orientations than non-athletes. Also, the athletes showed reasonably marked female-male differences in ranking winning first (2 per cent vs. 13 per cent), while there were small female-male differences among non-athletes (2 per cent vs. 4 per cent).

If we took our cue for working hypotheses simply from the previous studies, then, we would have to conclude that there are likely both sex and sport involvement effects on game orientation. We would also conclude that sex differences in sport involvement do not take us very far in accounting for sex differences in game orientation, because sex differences in orientation have been shown to remain after controls for sport involvement. Indeed, as we have indicated, there is evidence that sex differences in support for winning are largest among those involved in sport.

Caution is very much in order here, however. It is very difficult to control precisely on type and extent of experience with sport for females and males, and there is the matter of choosing as a control the particular facets of sport involvement which affect winning orientations. This issue is suggested by the previously mentioned findings on intramural sports. Apparently this type of involvement does not function to increase a winning orientation, and may even blunt it. We know that the involvement of females in sport is generally more of the intramural sort; it is less competitive, less often in highly organized team sports, and less sustained over the life cycle than is the case for the activity of males (cf. Curtis and Milton, 1975; Hobart, 1975; Loy, McPherson and Kenyon, 1978:356ff). If higher competition and organized sports are greater training grounds in winning orientation, and if the extent of contact with such activities is related to subscription to a winning orientation, then women have less opportunity to acquire this orientation. It follows, therefore, that there is a need for the use of control variables when investigating male and female orientation towards sport.

One way of approximating tightly controlled comparisons is to compare males and females with simultaneous controls for numerous measures of the extent and character of sport involvement over the life cycle. We attempt analyses along these lines in this study. We have available, for primary analysis, four samples of adults and adolescents from English Canada and French Canada. Sex differences in orientations toward games will be explored as a function of sport involvement, for each of the four samples.

Another way of approximating these careful controls would be to compare male and female athletes of the same elite stature in a sport requiring similar amounts and types of training for each sex to reach the elite. We are able to speak to such comparisons as well. We are able to compare females and males among the national elite in track and field athletes, and we can make further comparisons with females and males of about the same age from the general population.

Our working hypotheses were as follows: Extrapolating from the literature we expected that, without controls, males would have a stronger winning orientation than females. We also hypothesized that sport involvement, variously measured, would be positively related to winning orientation. We expected that in tightly controlled comparisons, females would not differ, or would differ very minimally, from males in winning orientation. We expected this pattern especially among elite athletes. We wondered if similar findings would be obtained for samples of adults and adolescents if several sport involvement controls were udsed. We expected, minimally, that controls on sport involvement would function to reduce sex differences.

DATA SOURCES AND PROCEDURES

Our findings are taken from data obtained in the International Project on Leisure Role Socialization sponsored by the International Committee on the Sociology of Sport. The data were gathered between 1972 and 1974 from seven countries. In most of the countries, a sample of males and females was drawn from the highest level of elite performers among track and field athletes. Samples of young people and adolescents from the general population were also used in most of the countries. Two equal probability samples (based on census tracts or their equivalent) were drawn for a major city in each country. The samples were for about 500 male and female adults between the ages of 25 and 35 and for about the same number of adolescents aged 16. The respondents were interviewed at home (or in the school in the case of some adolescents). Some elite athletes had questionnaires mailed to them, the others were interviewed. The professionalization scale devised by Webb was included for each sample, and this provided the information for our dependent variables. For countries other than Canada, only marginal responses on the scale, by sex, were available for analysis. For the Canadian samples we were able to do primary analysis of the data.

For Canada, two samples of adolescents and two samples of adults were employed, with one of each for English-speaking persons (Toronto) and for French-speaking persons (Montreal).[1] The adult and adolescent samples were administered separate interview schedules in which many but not all of the questions were identical. Information gathered in the interviews pertained to a range of leisure and sport socialization experiences and social background factors.

The sport involvement variables available for adults in the Canadian samples were present sport involvement, prior consideration of a sport career and mother's and father's encouragement of participation in sport. We would have preferred a more extensive set of variables for controls on sport background, but these allow a rough approximation of the preferred approach described above. Present sport involvement is self-explanatory as a measure of sport involvement. We viewed consideration of a sport career as a measure of intensity of involvement in sport in earlier years. The rationale for studying parental encouragement of sport involvement as a predictor of orientation toward winning derives from two previous bodies of research. The first is the literature on socialization into sport, which has consistently shown that mother's and father's encouragement is a strong correlate of sport involvement for both sexes (cf. Greendorfer, 1978; Greendorfer and Lewko, 1978; Snyder and Spreitzer, 1973, 1978; Theberge, 1977). To date, there have not been studies of the association between parental encouragement and the development of professionalized orientations. Parental encouragement has, however, been shown to affect a related factor, need to achieve (see Birrell, 1979).[2]

The sport involvement variables for the Canadian adolescent samples were similar to those asked of adults. They included present involvement in sport,[3] father's and mother's encouragement of sport participation presently,[4] and age of first sport competition.[5] The question on consideration of a sport career was not asked of the adolescents.[6] It should be noted that the parental encouragement variables, for each sample, refer to the adolescent period of the life cycle. Thus, for the adults these were recall questions and for the adolescents they pertained to the present.

For each of the samples, we also combined all of the single indicators of sport involvement (there were four in the case of each adult and adolescent sample) into a composite index of sport involvement. This involved collapsing each sport involvement indicator into a dichotomy of high vs. low involvement, coded as 1 vs. 0. These scores were then summed to create the index. Thus, the index scores ranged from 0, for no involvement, to 5, for the highest level of involvement. This index was constructed so that we could check on whether the effects of the different types of involvement on orientations were cumulative.

Our data analysis procedures are contingency controls and multiple classification analysis or MCA (Andrews *et al.*, 1973). The latter technique, used in our primary analyses of the Canadian samples, allows a number of controls to be made simultaneously to assess the effects of a primary independent variable on the dependent variable. This technique provides mean values on the dependent variable for each category of the independent and control variables both before and after controls are introduced (these are the figures reported in Tables 5-7). We used MCA to measure changes in sex differences in sport orientations before and after controls for sport involvement, and to ask if there were significant sex differences after appropriate controls.

FINDINGS

Comparing Females and Males in the Samples of Elite Athletes and Adults

Table 1 shows the percentages, by sex, that gave first rank importance to each of the options in Webb's question for samples of elite athletes and young adults from three countries. Actually these elite athlete — young adult comparisons could be made for five countries: Canada, Australia, Germany, Belgium, and Hungary. We have limited our tabular presentation of the data to selected findings, but we will discuss the complete set of results.

As expected the first ranking of winning was greater among Canadian elite athletes than among their counterparts in the adult samples, at least as far as comparisons with English-Canadian adults were concerned. The same pattern held in each of the other four national cases as well. The first ranking of winning was markedly greater among elite athletes than among the adults. This was true regardless of the sex of respondent (except for the females in the French Canadian samples).

In three of the five national cases the sex differences in placing winning first were negligible for the elite athletes. There was a five percent difference or less between females and males in each instance. This pattern was obtained despite the fact that the opportunity for females and males to differ, in percentage terms, was greater among the athletes because of their greater overall tendency to place winning first. The other two nations, Australia and Germany, showed differences of twenty-three percent and ten percent respectively, with males being higher in Australia and females higher in Germany.

The Canadian and other athletes were also more likely to rank playing well first and less likely to rank playing fair first compared with their counterparts in the adult samples for both sexes (but compare the data for Belgium and Australia).

Sex differences in ranking playing well and playing fairly were also minimal among the athletes. The differences were five percent or under in seven of ten comparisons for both sexes in the

Table 1

Sex Differences in First Rank Importance Given to "Beat", "Play" and "Fair" in Response
to Webb's Question, for Various Samples of Young Adults and Elite Athletes from Five
Countries

National Samples and Sex	(N)	First Rank Given to:			M/F on Beat
		Beat %[a]	Play %	Fair %	
Canada (Montreal and Toronto)					
Adult Sample, French					
Females (F)	(315)	18	64	18	+7
Males (M)	(200)	25	59	16	
Adult Sample, English					
Females	(293)	6	61	33	+10
Males	(214)	16	57	27	
Elite Athlete Sample					
Females	(48)	17	75	11	+5
Males	(74)	22	72	8	
Belgium (Antwerp)					
Adult Sample					
Females	(247)	2	54	44	+15
Males	(250)	17	54	29	
Elite Athlete Sample					
Females	(22)	64	27	9	+4
Males	(22)	68	22	9	
Hungary (Budapest)					
Adult Sample					
Females	(258)	14	58	23	+1
Males	(236)	15	47	38	
Elite Athlete Sample					
Females	(32)	34	63	8	-3
Males	(40)	31	63	6	

[a]The percentages do not always sum to 100 percent because of "no answers"; some
respondents did not rank all three items.

athlete samples. There was no clear pattern among the athletes whereby males, or females, gave greater priority to playing well or to playing fair. With the exception of the athletes from Belgium, where winning received a higher emphasis than elsewhere, the common pattern for athletes, of each sex, was to have the greatest proportion rank playing well first, followed by first ranks given to winning, followed by first ranks given to playing fair.

For the adult samples, in four of the five national cases there were sex differences in placing winning first, with the differences ranging from six to fourteen percent. Males were higher in each instance. There was no clear pattern of female-male differences in the rank given to playing well and playing fair. The majority of adults in each nation (with the exceptin of German females and Belgians) gave highest priority to playing well, regardless of sex.

Comparing Females and Males in the French- and English-Canadian Samples

We conducted preliminary analyses of the Canadian data using the detailed variable from Webb's work and a collapsed three-level variable whereby the highest level involves responses which placed winning first and the lowest level involves responses which placed playing fair first. These analyses prompted us to focus on the collapsed variable. In each of the four Canadian samples, for both females and males, the respondents very seldom (six percent or less) gave the answer for scale points #2 and #5 on the Webb Scale. These scale points are for a rank order of "Fair," "Beat" and "Play" (#2) and for "Beat," "Fair," and "Play" (#5). Our interpretation of the limited selection of these answers is that respondents think rather explicitly in terms of a fair-beat opposition or dichotomy and find it difficult to give comparatively high priority to both "Beat" and "Fair" at the same time. Because of this possibility we chose to collapse the scale in a fashion similar to the response patterns, paying attention only to whether winning, playing fair, or playing well was given the highest priority.[7]

Table 2 shows, in another form, the pattern by sex reported earlier for the several nations. Males in both Canadian adolescent samples and both Canadian adult samples had higher Webb Scale scores. The percentage differences (and the differences in means) were statistically significant only for the two English-Canadian samples, though.

Table 3 shows that females and males in the four samples differ in sport involvement levels, with the males being higher. The differences are statistically significant in three of four samples for the sport involvement index. As far as the separate items making up the index go, the most consistent statistically significant differences were for having given consideration to a sport career and for present competition in sport. The females were less involved in each respect.

Table 4 asks if the sex differences in orientation to winning are a function of sex differences in sport involvement, using the sport involvement index. Interestingly, there were no statistically significant relationships between involvement and orientation, for either sex for any sample. The same finding obtained in analyses using the individual item on sport involvement. In thirty-two

Table 2

Orientations Toward Games by Sex for Adult and Adolescent

Samples of French-and English-Canadians

Scores on the Professionalism Scale	Toronto English Samples				Montreal French Samples			
	Adults		Adolescents		Adults		Adolescents	
	Females	Males	Females	Males	Females	Males	Females	Males
N =	(285)	(211)	(208)	(208)	(282)	(189)	(232)	(253)
	%	%	%	%	%	%	%	%
Webb Scale Scores								
1 and 2 (low)	34	27	29	13	18	16	24	20
3 and 4	61	58	63	72	64	60	59	58
5 and 6 (high)	6	15	8	15	18	24	18	23
	***		***					
Grand Mean	1.69	1.88	1.72	1.96	1.82	2.00	1.93	1.97

*** significant at the .001 level. The level of significance is from X^2.

Table 3

Sex and Sport Involvement and Socialization Variables for Adult and Adolescent

Samples of French-and English-Canadians

Sport Involvement and Socialization Variables	Toronto English Samples				Montreal French Samples			
	Adults		Adolescents		Adults		Adolescents	
	Females	Males	Females	Males	Females	Males	Females	Males
N =	(285)	(211)	(208)	(208)	(283)	(189)	(232)	(253)
	%	%	%	%	%	%	%	%
Competes in Sport Presently								
Yes	23	34	58	61	22	38	16	44
No	77 **	65	42	39	78 ***	61	84 *	56
Age of First Sport Competition								
Under 12 Years			22	18			52	31
Over 12 Years			78	82			48 ***	69
Gave Some Consideration to a Sport Career								
Yes	9	32			9	25		
No	91 ***	68			91 ***	75		
Father's Encouragement of Sport Participation								
None or Discouraged	41	32	27	26	46	39	14	14
Occasionally Encouraged	32	32	33	26	20	26	28	25
Frequently Encouraged	27 *	35	40	48	34	35	59	61
Mother's Encouragement of Sport Participation								
None or Discouraged	40	42	25	30	46	44	13	15
Occasionally Encouraged	36	33	35	29	24	27	27	30
Frequently Encouraged	25	25	40	41	30	29	60	54
Sport Involvement Index								
0 (low)	28	18	5	3	34	26	9	7
1	18	18	11	13	19	17	7	8
2	37	35	22	23	39	32	36	22
3	15	21	28	28	6	17	40	35
4	2 ***	8	34	33	2 ***	8	8 ***	28

* = significant at the .05 level; ** = significant at the .01 level; *** = significant at the .001 level. The level of significant is from X^2.

Table 4

Percentages Ranking "Beat" First and "Fair" First by Sport Involvement Levels for Each Sex in Adult and Adolescent Samples of French-and English Canadians

Sport Involvement	Toronto English Samples				Montreal French Samples			
	Adults		Adolescents		Adults		Adolescents	
N=	Females (285)	Males (211)	Females (208)	Males (208)	Females (282)	Males (189)	Females (232)	Males (253)
	%	%	%	%	%	%	%	%
Ranking "Beat" First:								
Sport Involvement Index								
0 (low)	(80) 10	(39) 15	(9) 22	(5) 40	(89) 21	(47) 13	(20) 15	(15) 20
1	(50) 4	(38) 11	(21) 14	(28) 21	(56) 20	(32) 25	(16) 0	(20) 40
2	(107) 2	(76) 16	(46) 9	(46) 20	(116) 16	(61) 28	(83) 22	(55) 24
3	(43) 9	(42) 14	(60) 8	(57) 12	(16) 13	(7) 21	(95) 17	(90) 24
4 (high)	(5) 0	(16) 25	(72) 4	(72) 10	(5) 20	(8) 53	(18) 22	(73) 15
Ranking "Fair" First:								
Sport Involvement Index								
0 (low)	38	39	22	0	36	12	35	40
1	44	24	24	21	23	13	38	15
2	28	26	35	15	15	15	29	26
3	30	24	28	11	6	24	17	21
4 (high)	20	13	28	12	20	20	11	11

Table 5

Orientations Toward Games By Sport Involvement Factors With
And Without MCA Controls For Separate Analyses For
Females and Males From The Toronto Adult Sample

Sport Involvement Factors	Toronto Adult Females			Toronto Adult Males		
	(N)	NC[a]	WC[a]	(N)	NC	WC
Grand Mean		1.67			1.87	
Competes in Sport Presently						
Yes	(173)	1.66	1.67	(146)	1.91	1.90
No	(95)	1.88	1.68	(50)	1.76	1.77
(eta/beta)		(.02)	(.01)		(.10)	(.09)
Gave Consideration To a Sport Career						
Yes	(25)	1.76	1.76	(61)	2.01	1.99
No	(243)	1.66	1.66	(135)	1.80	1.82
(eta/beta)		(.05)	(.05)		(.14) *	(.12) *
Father's Encouragement Of Sport Participation						
None or Discouraged	(111)	1.60	1.59	(64)	1.83	1.76
Occasionally Encouraged	(86)	1.78	1.80	(64)	1.83	1.83
Frequently Encouraged	(71)	1.65	1.64	(68)	1.95	2.01
(eta/beat)		(.12)	(.15)		(.09)	(.16)
Mother's Encouragement Of Sport Participation						
None or Discouraged	(100)	1.64	1.70	(83)	1.89	1.97
Occasionally Encouraged	(95)	1.70	1.64	(63)	1.84	1.84
Frequently Encouraged	(64)	1.67	1.67	(50)	1.88	1.74
(eta/beta)		(.04)	(.05)		(.03)	(.14)

[a] NC signifies that no controls are made. WC signifies that controls have been employed. The controls are made using MCA and in the case of each independent variable in the table all other variables cited in the table are entered as controls.

[b] Etas (for the uncontrolled relationship) and betas (for controlled relationships) are given in parenthesis.

*=significant at the .05 level.

comparisons — involving four alternate measures of involvement for the two sexes in four samples — there were only four statistically significant relationships of involvement and orientation. In each case there was a positive relationship — the higher the involvement, the higher the emphasis on winning. Table 5 shows some of these analyses, for female and male adults in English Canada.

Not surprisingly, given the findings reported above, when we controlled on sport involvement, sex differences in winning orientation persisted. They were only minimally diminished through the controls. Tables 6 and 7 show the results. In Table 6, with MCA controls for the sport involvement index, there were statistically significant sex differences in winning orientation for three of the four samples, and the differences were in the same direction in the four samples. Males had higher scale scores than females. Table 7 shows the same pattern after simultaneous controls for each of the single item sport involvement variables.[8]

CONCLUSIONS

Our analyses have considered hypotheses for three relationships: (1) sex and orientation toward winning, (2) sport involvement and orientation toward winning and (3) sex and orientation toward winning as a function of sport involvement. Our findings are somewhat different depending on which of the two sections of our analysis is involved, so we will deal with the sections separately. First, our comparisons of the results from the different national studies gave several tests of each of the hypotheses. We found, as expected, support for the proposition that there are sex differences toward winning, at least as far as adults in the nations studied are concerned. This was not true of the top-flight athletes in these countries, however. Females and males among the elite athletes were similar in their orientations toward winning. It appeared that there was a homogenization of the orientations toward winning, skill and fairness among females and males with elite-level involvement and certainly compared to their counter-

Table 6

Sex and the Sport Involvement Index as Predictors of Orientations Toward Games

Before and After Controls (MCA) for Adult and Adolescent Samples

of French-and English-Canadians

Predictors	Toronto English Samples						Montreal French Samples					
	Adults			Adolescents			Adults			Adolescents		
	(N)	NC[a]	WC[a]	(N)	NC	WC	(N)	NC	WC	(N)	NC	WC
Grand Mean	1.76			1.80			1.86			1.95		
Sex												
Females	(293)	1.68	1.69	(219)	1.70	1.70	(315)	1.79	1.80	(236)	1.91	1.93
Males	(214)	1.87	1.86	(270)	1.90	1.90	(200)	1.97	1.89	(259)	1.99	1.97
(eta/beta)[b]		(.14)	(.13) **		(.15)	(.15) **		(.10)	(.09) *		(.05)	(.03)
Sport Involvement Index												
0 (low)	(123)	1.69	1.71	(16)	1.87	1.90	(16)	1.69	1.70	(39)	1.62	1.62
1	(90)	1.69	1.69	(52)	1.84	1.83	(94)	1.89	1.89	(36)	1.98	1.98
2	(84)	1.80	1.80	(99)	1.75	1.75	(188)	1.93	1.94	(142)	1.90	1.90
3	(89)	1.77	1.76	(173)	1.81	1.81	(52)	1.92	1.88	(187)	2.00	2.00
4 (high)	(21)	2.06	2.01	(149)	1.80	1.80	(20)	2.25	2.19	(91)	2.06	2.05
(eta/beta)		(.12)	(.11)		(.04)	(.05)		(.16)	(.15) *		(.16)	(.16)

[a]NC signifies that no controls are made. WC signifies that controls have been employed. The controls are made using MCA and in the case of each independent variable in the table all other variables cited in the table are entered as controls.

[b]Etas (for the uncontrolled relationship) and betas (for controlled relationships) are given in parenthesis.

*= significant at the .05 level; **= significant at the .01 level; ***= significant at the .001 level. The level of significance is from an analysis of variance procedure accompanying MCA.

Table 7

Sex and Orientations Toward Games With and Without MCA Controls for Sport Involvement

Factors for Adult and Adolescent Samples of French-and English-Canadians

d Sport ement s	Toronto English Samples						Montreal French Samples					
	Adults			Adolescents			Adults			Adolescents		
	(N)	NC^a	WC^a	(N)	NC	WC	(N)	NC	WC	(N)	NC	WC
Mean		1.76			1.84			1.89			1.95	
es	(268)	1.68	1.70	(194)	1.72	1.73	(274)	1.82	1.82	(208)	1.93	1.95
eta)^b	(196)	1.88	1.85	(195)	1.96	1.95	(178)	2.00	2.00	(217)	1.97	1.95
		(.15)	(.11)		(.18)	(.17)		(.11)	(.11)		(.03)	(.01)
			**			***			*			
es in Sport tly	(345)	1.78	1.77	(230)	1.86	1.86	(106)	1.97	1.96	(133)	2.01	1.98
	(162)	1.71	1.74	(159)	1.81	1.81	(409)	1.87	1.94	(292)	1.92	1.94
beta)		(.05)	(.02)		(.03)	(.04)		(.05)	(.01)		(.06)	(.02)
First Sport tion 12 Years 12 Years				(79)	1.88	1.88				(173)	1.84	1.86
				(310)	1.83	1.83				(253)	2.01	2.00
beta)					(.03)	(.03)					(.01)	(.05)
onsideration to t Career	(86)	1.95	1.89				(67)	2.04	1.99			
	(378)	1.72	1.73				(385)	1.93	1.94			
beta)		(.14)	(.10)					(.05)	(.02)			
's Encouragement of Participation or Discouraged ionally Encouraged ently Encouraged	(175)	1.89	1.77	(99)	1.90	1.82	(195)	1.72	1.90	(55)	1.76	1.90
	(150)	1.80	1.82	(116)	1.75	1.76	(100)	1.88	1.91	(111)	1.91	1.90
	(139)	1.80	1.80	(174)	1.86	1.90	(157)	1.99	1.86	(259)	2.01	1.98
beta)		(.09)	(.11)		(.09)	(.09)		(.09)	(.03)		(.12)	(.06)
's Encouragement of Participation or Discouraged ionally Encouraged ently Encouraged	(192)	1.75	1.85	(106)	1.94	1.95	(208)	1.82	1.87	(59)	2.19	2.11
	(188)	1.76	1.74	(124)	1.79	1.84	(113)	1.83	1.87	(124)	1.95	1.99
	(114)	1.77	1.71	(159)	1.81	1.77	(131)	2.06	2.15	(247)	2.00	1.97
beta)		(.01)	(.10)		(.09)	(.11)		(.14)	(.16)		(.13)	(.09)
			*						*			

gnifies that no controls are made. WC signifies that controls have been employed. The controls are made
MCA and in the case of each independent variable in the table all other variables cited in the table
ntered as controls.

(for the uncontrolled relationship) and betas (for controlled relationships) are given in parenthesis.

nificant at the .05 level; **= significant at the .01 level; ***= significant at the .001 level. The
of significance is from an analysis of variance procedure accompanying MCA.

parts among young adults in the general population. There was also evidence, as expected, that those involved in elite sport place far more emphasis on winning than young adults in general, whether males or female. It is also noteworthy that even the elite athlete samples did not give their highest priority to winning; playing well was consistently ranked higher than winning by each sex.

When we turned to analyses within the four samples of adult and adolescent Canadians, looking at different sport involvement measures as correlates of a winning orientation, we found as follows: Females were lower on emphasis given to winning (and lower on the professionalization scale) than males; the sport involvement indicators had little relationship to orientations toward winning (and professionalization), and sex differences in orientations were barely reduced with controls for sport involvement.

How are we to interpret the different sets of results on the role of sport involvement in the two types of analysis? There are a number of possibilities, among which we favor the following: We began by saying that comparisons of females and males on only a few indicators of sport involvement are problematic because they may not entail controls for the correct factors among the probably rich set of differences in experiences with sport by females and males. By "correct factors" we mean those aspects of sport involvement that are related to acquiring an emphasis on winning. These may, of course, differ for females and males as well. It is an empirical question in which particular aspects of sport involvement are implicated in socialization to winning attitudes. Our analyses of the Canadian adult and adolescent samples probably provides an illustration of the problems of selecting the appropriate factor. We had available four different types of indicators of sport involvement for each sample. Yet these seldom predicted orientations, for either females or males. Further research will have to determine which aspects of sport involvement are related to game orientations among women and men. It may be that only in highly competitive and sustained involvement in sport do females receive the training in winning that males receive more generally in sport. We are prompted to urge that further research on this issue be done not so much by the results from the Canadian adult and adolescent samples, but by those from comparisons of the elite and young adult samples. We would no doubt have concluded somewhat differently if we had only had the one set of analyses in hand. One of our recommendations here, therefore, has to be that triangulation on a research problem such as this, using different measures and different types of samples, is advised.

We have interpreted the similarity in orientations among females and males in the elite athlete samples as resulting from the near-common experiences of women and men with competition in this sport. While this is likely the case, there is another possibility that warrants attention as well. It is possible that the female and male athletes are highly similar in their responses because of selection, not because of their common experience with sport (cf. Stevenson, 1975:297ff). It may be that these athletes differ from others and are quite similar regardless of their sex because persons with winning attitudes are recruited into the sport. Perhaps those who can best survive selection procedures, early competition and the rigors of training programs are those who, whether female or male, placed a higher emphasis on winning even before they entered the sport. Also, perhaps there is an underlying, as yet undetermined, personality correlate of winning attitude (such as N achievement) which is shared by most persons recruited to elite athlete status. These are reasonable hypotheses for further research, but it seems unlikely that such selection processes operate alone in making the two sexes similar among the athletes, without significant socialization effects coming from the organization of the sport. Certainly, though, what is "selection effect" and what is "sport experience effect" should be explored in further research. This will require expensive and time-consuming longitudinal designs.

What is required is that we proceed to the mapping of precisely what it is about sport, at the elite or mass level, that socializes one to an emphasis on winning and how these influences differentially affect females and males. For the time being, our results make the case for studying the sex differences and the sport involvement differences as related phenomena by showing the apparent persistence of sex and involvement differences cross-culturally and by showing that the sex differences do not extend to the highest levels of sport involvement.

NOTES

[1] For more details on the studies, see McPherson (1978) and Kenyon and McPherson (1978).

[2] As Birrell (1978) has shown, this literature has focused almost exclusively on the need to achieve among males.

[3] Both the adolescent and the adult respondents were asked to name their favorite sports and whether (and how often) they were involved in these sports and in track and field and hockey (if the latter two were not named initially by the respondent). We have recoded the responses as involved in one or more sports vs. not involved.

[4] Both the adult and the adolescent samples were asked: "Now we would like to ask you about the encouragement or discouragement you may have received from some of these people or groups (father, mother . . .)." The responses were recoded as "discouraged" or "never encouraged" vs. "occasionally encouraged" vs. "frequently encouraged" or "encouraged me at every opportunity."

[5] The adolescents were asked at what age they began to "participate in organized competition" in their favorite sports or in track and field and hockey (if the latter were not named by the respondent). The responses were arbitrarily coded as aged 12 or younger for one or more sports vs. after age 12 for first competition.

[6] The adult respondents were asked: "Did you ever think of seeking a career in sport" (and in which sport(s)? The responses were coded as "yes" for one or more sports considered vs. "no" for none.

[7] While we report results only for the three-level variable, we did conduct analyses using both versions of the scale as dependent variables, and near-identical results obtained in the two sets of analyses.

[8] The effects of the social status backgrounds of the samples were also checked on. We looked at relationships of the Webb Scale responses (the three- and six-level versions) with father's occupational status, father's education and mother's education for the adolescent samples and respondent's education and occupation of the main wage earner for the adult samples. The females and males did not show statistically significant differences for the different samples (except that female adults were less likely to be working). These female-male similarities are to be expected for representative samples of young adults and adolescents. Among the adults, the occupational status and education variables were positively related to present sport involvement for each sex. Among the adolescents the social status factors showed no clear pattern of relationship to involvement. The only statistically significant relationships of the social status factors to professional orientations were for occupational status among females and males in the English-Canadian sample, where there were curvilinear relationships — middle status persons showed lower professionalization scores than those with lower and higher status. When the types of analyses in Table 6 and 7 were reproduced, but with controls for the social status factors,

the directions and significance levels of the findings were the same as reported in these tables.

REFERENCES

Andrews, F. M., J. N. Morgan, J. A. Sonquist and L. Klem
  1973 Multiple Classification Analysis. Ann Arbor: University of Michigan.
Birrell, S.
  1978 "Achievement related motives and the woman athlete." Pp. 143-71 in Carole A. Oglesby, (ed.), Women and Sport: From Myth to Reality. Philadelphia: Lea and Febiger.
Curtis, J. E. and E. G. Milton
  1976 "Social status and the 'active' society: national data on correlates of leisure-time physical and sport activities." Pp. 302-29 in R. S. Gruneau and J. G. Albinson (eds.), Canadian Sport: Sociological Perspectives. Don Mills, Ontario: Addison-Wesley.
Edwards, H.
  1973 Sociology of Sport. Homewood, Ill.: Dorsey Press.
Greendorfer, S. L.
  1978 "Children's socialization into sport: a conceptual and empirical analysis." Paper presented at the 9th World Congress of Sociology, Uppsala, Sweden.
Greendorfer, S. L. and J. H. Lewko
  1978 "Role of family members in sport socialization of children." Research Quarterly 49(2):146-152.
Hobart, C. W.
  1975 "Active sport participation among the young, the middle-aged and the elderly." International Review of Sport Sociology 10(3-4):27-44.
Kenyon, G. S. and E. D. McPherson
  1978 "The sport role socialization project in four industrialized countries." Pp. 5-34 in F. Landry and W. Orban (eds.), Sociology of Sport. Miami: Symposia Specialists.
Loy, J., S. Birrell, and D. Rose
  1976 "Attitudes held toward agonetic acitvities as a function of selected social identities." Quest Monograph 26:81-93.
Loy, J. W., B. D. McPherson and G. S. Kenyon
  1978 Sport and Social Systems. Reading, Mass.: Addison-Wesley.
Maloney, T. L. and B. M. Petrie
  1972 "Professionalization of attitude toward play among Canadian school pupils as a function of sex, grade, and athletic participation." Journal of Leisure Research 4:184-195.
Mantel, R. C. and L. VanderVelden
  1971 "The relationship betwen the professionalization of attitude toward play of pre-adolescent boys and participation in organized sport." Paper presented at the 3rd International Symposium on the Sociology of Sport, Waterloo, Canada.
McElroy, M. A. and D. R. Kirkendall
  1980 "Significant others and professional sport attitudes." Research Quarterly 54 (4):645-53.
McPherson, B. D.
  1978 "The sport role socialization process for anglophone and francophone adults in Canada: accounting for present patterns of involvement." Pp. 41-52 in F. Landry and W. Orban (ed.), Sociology of Sport. Miami: Symposia Specialists.

Nixon, H. L.
  1980 "Orientation toward sports participation among college students." Journal of
       Sport Behavior 3(1):29-45.
Petrie, B. M.
  1971a "Achievement orientations in adolescent attitudes toward play." International
        Review of Sport Sociology 6:89-99.
  1971b "Achievement orientations in the motivations of Canadian university students
        toward physical activity. Journal of the Canadian Association of Health, Phys-
        ical Education and Recreation 37(3):7-13.
Sage, G. H.
  1980a "Sport and American society: the quest for success." Pp. 112-22 in G. H. Sage
        (ed.), Sport and American Society. Don Mills, Ontario: Addison-Wesley, 3rd
        edition.
  1980b "Orientations toward sport of male and female intercollegiate athletes." Jour-
        nal of Sport Psychology 2:355-62.
Snyder, E. E. and E. Spreitzer
  1973 Family influence and involvement in sports." Research Quarterly 44(3):249-
       255.
  1978 "Socialization comparisons of adolescent female athletes and musicians."
       Research Quarterly 49(3):342-350.
  1979 "Orientations toward sport: intrinsic, normative, and extrinsic." Journal of
       Sport Psychology 1:170-75.
Stevenson, C. L.
  1975 "Socialization effects of participation in sports: a critical review of the research."
       Research Quarterly 46(3):287-301.
Theberge, N.
  1977 "Some factors associated with socialization into the role of professional woman
       golfer." Pp. 215-21 in Proceedings of the Ninth Canadian Psycho-Motor Learn-
       ing and Sport Psychology Symposium, Banff, Alberta.
Webb, H.
  1969 "Professionalization of attitudes toward play among adolescents." Pp. 161-187
       in G. Kenyon (ed.), Aspects of Contemporary Sport Sociology. Chicago: Ath-
       letic Institute.

Chapter 19

ARE CHILDREN'S COMPETITIVE TEAM SPORTS SOCIALIZING AGENTS FOR CORPORATE AMERICA?

Gai Ingham Berlage, Iona College

Since World War II children's play has been transformed from informal games to highly organized sporting events. Adults now organize and direct most sports programs for children from Little League baseball to youth soccer. Today these programs mirror professional teams. Each team has a coach, a manager, uniforms and an official schedule. Scoreboards, official league standings, and tournaments now determine success. Trophies and newspaper coverage now signify winners. The play ethic associated with childrens' games of playing to have fun, to relax and let off steam has shifted to teaching skills, developing character, developing scholarship winners and professionals.

More and more children's sports resemble training grounds for the adult world and for business rather than games for fun. Beisser, for example, sees sports as a useful bridge between child play and adult work.

Work has already lost many of its traditional characteristics and so has play. Play has become increasingly transformed into organized sports, and sports, in turn, increasingly resemble work in the arduous practice and preparation they require, in the intense involvement of coaches and athletes in the spirit of work . . . (1973:94-95).

Today sports may serve to socialize children in values, attitudes and behavior suited to corporate jobs. Several organizational studies on women in corporations suggest this. They cite women's lack of experience with team sports as one reason they have not been more successful in the corporate world. Harragan, for example, discusses the similarities between the corporate group and the competitive sport team. She exlains why men's participation in team sports socializes them for the corporate world.

> The traditional boy's games are far from pointless childish pursuits. They are training grounds for life, preparation for adult imperatives of working with others, practical education for the discipline of business. The most popular games of baseball, football, and basketball are all team sports, and a structured, organized team is a well-defined social unit. . . . each player knows exactly what his duties are and how they dovetail into the operations of the rest of the team; . . . and each player knows that he has to perform smoothly and cooperatively with the others if he wants to retain his place on the team. If there's a conflict between individual glory and the greater glory of the team, then personal virtuosity must be sacrificed. (1977: 50).

Various sociologists such as Edwards, Page and Schafer have commented on the role of sports as a socializing agent for American society.

> . . . the social world of sport, although clearly distinguishable, is an inseparable part of the larger society; its cultural characteristics reflect the more inclusive culture and in turn, help to shape society's standards and style of life (Page, 1973: 35).

However, traditional American values as expressed in the Protestant Ethic may have changed to what Whyte in the 1950s called the "social ethic." The social ethic according to Whyte could also be called an organization or bureaucratic ethic. The social ethic has three main propositions: "a belief in the group as the source of creativity; a belief in 'belongingness' as the ultimate need of the individual; and a belief in the application of science to achieve the belongingness (Whyte, 1957:7).

Scott and Hart (1979:52) state that a new "organizational imperative" has replaced the Protestant Ethic of the past.

The organizational imperative, while originally a subset within the context of the overarching social value system, has now become the dominant force in the homogenization of organizational America, displacing the more individualistic values of the past.

Margolis (1979:267) in her study of corporate managers in one community, also emphasizes how corporate values are affecting the whole community and not just those employed by the corporation. Giant corporations appear to be setting the style and dictating the terms of life for those they do not employ almost as much as they do for those in their pay.

Today American cultural values have become more and more oriented to a corporate economy, and the values of children's organized team sports may reflect these changes. Competitive team sports may have become socializing agents for corporate America.

This research was designed to explore the question: Are children's competitive team sports socializing agents for corporate America?

Two basic issues were explored:

1. Does the structural organization of children's competitive sports programs resemble the structural organization of American corporations?

2. Are the values of children's competitive sports programs similar to corporate values?

METHOD

Data were based on examining the structure and organization of children's soccer and ice hockey organizations in the Connecticut and New York metropolitan area. Information is based on observations as well as interviews with parents and coaches of children both at the intramural and travel league divisions.

Questionnaires were also distributed to 222 Connecticut and New York metropolitan area fathers' with sons on soccer and ice hockey travel teams. The reason why questionnaires were distributed to fathers' of elite or travel team players was that it was felt that if the values of competitive team sports are similar to corporate values that fathers would be most salient at the highest levels of competition. The socialization process at the travel team level would be more intense than at the house league or recreational league level.

The hockey sample consisted of fathers who had sons competing in the Pee Wee Level Division III Connecticut State Tournament. The Pee Wee division is comprised of boys 11 and 12 years of age. All fathers of participants were asked to fill out questionnaires. No one refused to participate. However, some boys' fathers were deceased, divorced or unable to attend the tournament and therefore, responses were collected from 107 fathers. These fathers were from various parts of Connecticut since ten teams finishing the season at this level were invited to the tournament. The data were gathered in March, 1981.

The soccer sample consisted of fathers who had sons competing in a local Connecticut soccer tournament. Teams were drawn from communities in New York and Connecticut which are part of the New York metropolitan area. The teams were comprised of boys ages 11 and 12. As with the hockey sample, all fathers of participants were asked to fill out the questionnaires. A total of 115 fathers completed questionnaires. The data were gathered in June, 1981.

Although the sample is comprised of fathers from all educational and occupational levels, the majority of fathers were college graduates with white-collar jobs. This is probably the result of two factors: one the nature of the socio-economic backgrounds of people living in the New York metropolitan area and in Connecticut and two, the high cost of participating on a travel team. Similar research should be conducted with a working class population.

FINDINGS

The structural organization of children's competitive soccer and hockey sports programs resembles the structural organization of American corporations. Even on the community level, many sports organizations clearly resemble bureaucratic or corporate structures. The adult organizational structure for the youth soccer program in Wilton, Connecticut, a suburban community with a population around 15,000, has a board of directors, executive officers, management heads for publicity, procurement, community relations, travel teams and intramural teams. With a few label changes, the chart of the soccer hierarchial structure could easily be that of many corporations.

The organizational structure indicates how bureaucratically and formally organized children's team sports have become. No aspect of the organization, from public relations in the community to the actual composition of teams, is left to chance. There is a hierarchy of responsibility.

The chart is illustrative of Merton's (1968:249) definition of a bureaucracy as "a formal, rationally organized social structure [with] clearly defined patterns of activity in which, ideally, every series of actions is functionally related to the purposes of the organization."

At the bottom of the hierarchy are the coaches of the actual teams. Even within the team divisions there is a hierarchy defined by age and skill differences. Within each age division are travel teams and house league or intramural teams. For example, at the D division level the 11 and 12 year old division, there is a hierarchy of teams. The intramural teams are at the bottom level, then D3 travel, then D2 travel; the most elite travel team is D1. Every year each boy is also assigned by his coach a skill assessment level from 1 to 5. The higher the number, the more skilled the player. In other words, players are constantly evaluated for performance. However, travel team players, once they make the team, are rarely dropped by the coach. In a way, making a travel team is similar to gaining a promotion in a corporation. Prestige in the league and in the community at large accompanies travel team attainment. Other rewards are special travel team uniforms, travel to other communities, increased newspaper coverage and a chance to win state tournaments and trophies. The youth become classified as a sports elite similar to corporate executives.

The values stressed in children's competitive sports are also similar to corporate values. One of the major values of the "social ethic" according to Whyte is a belief in the group as a source of creativity. Team sports epitomize group effort over individual effort. A team player whether within a corporation or in a youth team sport is inculcated with the belief that the team effort is something greater and better than the sum of the individual player's effort.

Fathers' of soccer travel team players were asked to check off the three attributes that sports develop that they thought would be most important for a youth to develop to be successful in business. The most important attribute according to these fathers was teamwork. Sixty-seven percent of the fathers selected teamwork from the list of ten items. The top four were teamwork, self-discipline, leadership and competition. (See Table 1.)

Table 1

What Hockey Fathers' Consider as the Most Important
Attribute Sports Develop for Business

Teamwork	(77) 67%
Self-Discipline	(71) 62%
Leadership	(65) 57%
Competitiveness	(58) 50%
Honesty	(20) 17%
Respect for Authority	(15) 13%

Physical Fitness	(11)	10%
Sportsmanship	(11)	10%
Political Awareness	(8)	7%
Masculinity	(0)	0%
Other	(1)	%1

Hockey fathers were asked to list the three attributes that sports develop that they considered the most important. The words "for business" were not included. Teamwork was listed by 71% of the fathers. (See Table 2.)

Table 2

What Hockey Fathers Consider as the Most Important
Attributes Sports Develop

Teamwork	(76)	71%
Self-Discipline	(65)	61%
Sportsmanship	(50)	47%
Competitiveness	(48)	45%
Leadership	(26)	24%
Physical Fitness	(26)	24%
Respect for Authority	(11)	10%
Honesty	(7)	7%
Political Awareness	(2)	2%
Masculinity	(0)	0%
Other	(3)	3%

The importance of learning to be a part of a team was a constant theme of both soccer and hockey fathers. Fathers seemed to want to inculcate in their sons the idea that the product of a team's effort is greater than the sum of the individual participants and that team cooperation is more important than any individual performance. Comments such as the following were common: "The concept of one team pulling together applies in both (business and sports) situations"; "he learns the benefits of working with and depending on others"; ". . . learning how to work together as a team and the recognition of what can be accomplished through group effort"; "he learns to play as part of an organized group — knows doing his job helps the team to win"; ". . . an early realization of a level of interdependency, plus a satisfaction from self-discipline."

Teamwork was a central theme of the fathers. No one spoke of making a star but rather that the group effort was more important. This value is congruent with Whyte's notions about the "social ethic." Whyte (1957: 21) stated: "The man of the future, as junior executives see him, is not the individualist, but the man who works through others for others."

Whyte also stresses the importance of self-discipline in the "new" corporate ethic.

> As organization men see it, through an extension of the group spirit, through educating people to sublimate their egos, organizations can rid themselves of their tyrants and create a harmonious atmosphere in which the group will bring out the best in everyone (1957: 54).

The top two values that the majority of fathers considered important for their sons to learn from playing on a team (teamwork and self-discipline) are the same two that Maccoby describes as central to the new corporate top executive.

> The new corporate top executive . . . is a team player whose center is the corporation. . . . Thus he thinks in terms of what is good for the company, hardly separating that from what is good for himself . . . He has succeeded in submerging his ego and gaining strength from his exercise in self-control" (1977: 41).

The new leader of corporate America according to Maccoby (1977: 24) is not the jungle-fighter industrialist of the past who was driven to build and preside over empires but rather the man who is a good team organizer.

Coaches, too, want dedicated team players not individualistic stars. Players who don't conform and don't submit to practice schedules or team assignments and who don't get along with team members are dispensible. No one is indispensible. If the youth isn't totally dedicated to the team effort, he can be replaced.

As the coach emphasizes the need for the child to commit himself totally to the team and to be loyal and dedicated to the team, so does the corporation. As Whyte (1957: 6) states: "Social ethic (corporate ethic) rationalizes the organization's demands for fealty and gives those who offer it wholeheartedly a sense of dedication in doing so. . . ."

As corporations demand total commitment to the organization on the part of the worker, travel team coaches constantly stress the importance of the child's total commitment to the team. Practices and games take precedence over family dinner hours, family activities and other social events. For the corporate man, the company comes first and dominates his life; the team comes to dominate the child's. As wives and children learn that the husband often has to work late or travel on business trips and miss family and school occasions and they have to mold their schedule around the husband, the family also molds their schedule around the travel team player. Many parents of travel team players for both hockey and soccer reported that the child's participation interfered with dinner, vacations, family activities and even with school.

Eighty-four percent of soccer fathers said soccer interfered with dinner hours; 46% said it interfered with family vacations; 77% said it disrupted family activities; and 16% even said it interfered with school.

Hockey fathers reported similar accounts. Eighty percent said hockey interefered with dinner hours; 44% with family vacations; 72% with family activities and 28% with school.

One may wonder why parents let their children's sports interfere with family activities. The reasons are similar to the reasons company men let the corporation interfere with their family life. Being on a travel team is prestige-conferring for the child and his family. As social prestige for the father revolves around his work, for the child social prestige at school and in the community often is a product of his sports participation (Gordon, 1957; Coleman, 1961). As families often bask in the reflected status of the corporate husband, parents bask in the reflected status of having an athletic son or daughter.

Another reason parents may want their child to participate on the travel team is that they may see this participation as the first step toward an amateur sports career. For example, in the hockey sample 94% of the fathers hoped that their sons would play high school hockey and 86%, college hockey. For soccer fathers, it was 99% for high school soccer and 95% for college soccer.

If one doesn't allow his son or daughter to meet his or her commitment to the team, some other parent will, and the child will be dropped. Control by the coach is maintained much the same way a boss maintains control in a corporation — one can be fired or let go.

In interviews with parents, they would often comment on how they planned family weekend activities around the child's travel games. Several commented on that when they took their sons to visit relatives out of state, they had asked the coaches' permission. No one expressed the idea that family trips, even at Thanksgiving or Christmas, took precedence over travel games.

Harragan, in her discussion of corporate gamesmanship for women, explains this analogy between the control of the labor force in business and team members in sports.

> First off, team membership is voluntary, as is employment, but must be requested or applied for. To secure a place on a choice team, the applicant has to offer a needed skill or the potential for usefulness. Once accepted, the rookie agrees to abide by the formal rules of the game and the team. A novice who does not measure up to expectations, or does not follow the coach's directions, can be dropped and replaced with a more amenable candidate (1977: 44-45).

The coach as boss, mentor and arbitrator of values has become a dominant figure in the eyes of his team and their parents. A child learns that loyalty and devotion to the team is important, and he becomes proud to be associated with and known as a member of a particular team. Team membership becomes a part of his self-identity. Commitment and loyalty to a team is similar to loyalty to a company.

As a child knows that a coach's command is to be obeyed, so does a corporate person know that the order of a superior is to be obeyed. At an early age, these team players learn to accept an authoritarian structure and to learn that a team is not a democratic organization. Even parents, as was noted before, grant and accept the coach's authority since it is the coach who determines who plays, how long one plays and what position.

As Al Rosen (1967: 26) has stated about organized youth sports, "Organized sports are not democratic nor should they be. They teach respect for authority, discipline, and the individual's role in a group activity."

The emphasis on teamwork, obedience, and dispensability in sports are some of the same values that Scott and Hart speak of when they discuss the changes in American values from that of the Protestant Ethic to that of the "organizational ethic or imperative." The change in values has been "from innate human nature to malleability, from individualism to obedience; from indispensability to dispensability; from community to specialization; from spontaneity to planning; from voluntarism to paternalism" (Scott and Hart, 1979: 53).

These changing values are evident in business as well as team sports. The concept that athletes are made not born is widely accepted today. The malleability of the individual or athlete is what training is all about. Good training, good coaches, hard work and dedication make a winning player and winning team.

At earlier and earlier ages youth in sports are asked to specialize not only in a particular sport but in a particular position. Already at the mite level, eight years and under, in ice hockey, travel team players are designated as defensemen or forwards. These positions become more and more fixed as the youth move up through the league.

Soccer players too at fairly early ages become designated as defensemen or attackers. Boys and girls at fairly early ages (7 or 8) refer to themselves as goalies, fullbacks, halfbacks, centers and so forth. A child often feels that if he changes positions, he won't make the team the following year because he hasn't had as much practice in that position as someone else.

Children at early ages may have difficulty in trying to play seriously more than one sport. This is because the seasons for the various sports overlap creating conflicts with other sports.

Specialization by boys is evident in both the hockey and soccer samples. In the hockey sample, the mean age that boys started playing in an organized program was age 6½. These boys by Pee Wee level, ages 11-12, had been playing an average of 4½ to 5½ years. They were already veterans on the ice. In order to perfect their skills further, 70% of the fathers planned on sending their sons to summer hockey camp.

For soccer, the findings were similar except that soccer has both a fall and spring season in the Connecticut and New York area. So soccer youth have more months of organized play than do hockey players. Still, 45% of fathers of soccer players planned on sending their sons to summer soccer camp. The mean age that boys began playing organized soccer was 7 years.

Ingham (1975: 363) has stated that "Sport is ideologically bolstered by the performance principle, a principle which suggests that athletes are recruited and maintained on the basis of their merits."

American businesses or corporations also operate on the "performance principle." Both the businessman and the athlete must play by the rules to win whether it be winning a game or an economic profit. However, the ideal and the reality are not always synonomous. The ideology is to play by the rules.

However, as Brower (1979: 44-45) states when discussing the professionalization of organized youth sports, the reality of the situation is

> using all "reasonable" tactics to win. Getting away with
> undetected rule infractions and taking advantage of an

umpire's mistake has become institutionalized as "part of the game."

Business tactics also include being shrewd and taking advantage of a competitive situation. The rules can be bent if one makes a profit. The belief is that if you don't take advantage of the situation, the competition will.

Competition in business and in youth sports sometimes gives rise to politics. Ideally, the selection process for making the team is based purely on performance. For the majority of youth this is probably the case; however, favoritism sometimes exists whether it be the coach's child or that of a large contributor. Favoritism also exists at times in business with "the bosses son." The expression "It's not what you know, but who you know," although not the case most of the time, has some basis in reality.

When fathers were asked if the selection process for travel teams was based on skills, politics and skills, or politics, 39% of the soccer fathers and 51% of the hockey fathers said politics and skills.

One hockey father made this rather pessimistic comment about what he thought youth learned from competitive hockey.

We think that instead of providing a focus for development and happiness during the important years between eight and twelve, youth hockey quickly became a harbinger of events that probably would occur in adult life. (Politics, the best man doesn't always get the job, etc.)

The majority of fathers, however, felt that politics played a very small part if any in the selection process. Fifty-nine percent of soccer and 49% of hockey fathers felt that the selection process was based on skills only.

On the whole, fathers held positive attitudes toward competitive youth sports. The majority of both hockey and soccer fathers believed that their son's playing competitive sports would be an advantage to their child in later years in a business career. Ninety-three percent of hockey fathers and 88% of soccer fathers

believed that a boy has an advantage in business if he has played
competitive sports. When fathers were asked why they thought
sports were important, the majority emphasized teamwork, com-
petitiveness and tenacity.

Some of the comments made on why sports were important
for training a youth for business are listed below.

> A marketing manager: "Life is competitive. Groups are
> teams organized to achieved goals."

> A banker: "Business by its nature is competitive and involves
> interaction with other people."

> A vice-president of a corporation: "Competition is a fact of
> life, at least in the U.S., where to win is foremost."

> A tool and die maker: "Sports develop competitiveness and
> self-confidence."

> A cabinet maker: "He can learn how to handle disappoint-
> ment and success, gain a realistic approach to life."

Fathers' beliefs that sports foster values and skills that are
important in the business world are supported by testimonials of
famous Americans and even sociologists. The following examples
are found in Tutko and Bruns' book, *Winning is Everything*
(1976: 41-42).

> General Douglas MacArthur: "(Sport) is a vital character
> builder. It molds the youth of our country for their roles as
> custodians of the republic . . . Fathers and mothers who
> would make their sons into men should have them partici-
> pate in (sports)."

> Sociologist David Riesman: "The road to the board room
> leads through the locker room."

> Gerald Ford: "Broadly speaking, outside of a national char-
> acter and an educated society, there are few things more
> important to a country's growth and well-being than com-
> petitive athletics."

One father of a soccer player stated another reason why sports are important is that "recruiters like athletes." Whether or not recruiters favor athletes is a moot question, but the idea that athletics are important is one universally held.

Indicative of this belief that sports aid one in getting a job are the responses of soccer fathers to the following questions. One, "In applying for jobs do you think that a person has an advantage if he can say he has played varsity high school or college team sports?" Seventy-four percent of fathers stated, "yes," to this question. Two, "Hypothetically, if you had two equally qualified applicants for a job would the fact that one played varsity high school or college sports make a difference in your opinion as to which one to hire?" Fifty-seven percent stated that they would be more likely to hire the one who played varsity sports. Forty-two percent said that it would make no difference. Only one person said that he would be more likely to hire the non-athlete.

Harragan describes why fathers may hold these beliefs. She believes that men see team sports as training grounds for business. She states:

> (Corporate Men) have gone through preliminary training on the school teams and Pee Wee leagues years before; they sense what is expected of them; they are bonded in a familiar male camaraderie. They feel they have finally grown up "to be a man" and made it into the major leagues — the wage-earners' team (1977: 45).

Whether or not athletes become managers because recruiters are more likely to hire them or because their personalities and skills are types that are valued in business, there is some evidence that athletes often become managers. Maccoby (1977: 29), when he studied managers in technical corporations, found the typical manager to have been a high school athlete. "Most (75 percent) played on high school teams and 64 percent played in college."

All the evidence seems to point to the fact that children's competitive team sports are socializing agents for corporate

America. From testimonials to corporate studies, athletes are shown to have advantages in business careers.

The research in this study of children's soccer and ice hockey associations supports the view that the attitudes, values and skills inculcated in the training of team athletes more and more mirrors the corporate structure, its values and ethic. From observations and interviews, it appears that parents and coaches accept and want their children to be socialized in these values. These values are now seen as basic to American society.

REFERENCES

Beisser, Arnold
1973 "Modern man and sports." Pp. 85-96 in J. Talamini and C. Page, (eds.), Sports and Society: An Anthology. Boston: Little, Brown.
Brower, Jonathan
1979 "The professionalization of organized youth sport: social psychological impacts and outcomes." Annals, AAPSS 45:39-46.
Coleman, James
1961 The Adolescent Society. New York: The Free Press.
Gordon,C. Wayne
1981 The Social System of High School. Glencoe, Ill.: Free Press.
Harragan, Betty
1977 Games Mother Never Taught You: Corporate Gamesmanship for Women. New York: Rawson.
Ingham, Alan
1975 "Occupational subcultures in the work world of sport." Pp. 337-389 in D. Ball and J. Loy (ed.), Sport and Social Order: Contributions to the Society of Sport. Reading, Mass.: Addison-Wesley.
Maccoby, Michael
1977 The Gamesman: The New Corporate Leaders. New York: Simon and Schuster.
Margolis, Diane
1979 The Managers: Corporate Life in America. New York: Wm. Morrow.
Merton, Robert
1968 Social Theory and Social Structure, enlarged edition. New York: Macmillan.
Page, Charles
1973 "Pervasive sociological themes in the study of sport." Pp. 14-37 in J. Talamini and C. H. Page (eds.), Sport and Society: An Anthology. Boston: Little, Brown.
Rosen, Al
1967 Baseball and Your Boy. New York: World.
Scott, William and David Hart
1979 Organizational America. Boston: Houghton Mifflin.
Tutko, Thomas and William Bruns
1976 Winning is Everything and Other American Myths. New York: Macmillan.
Whyte, Jr., William H.
1957 The Organization Man. Garden City, NY: Doubleday Anchor.

Chapter 20

YOUTH SPORT INVOLVEMENT: IMPACT ON INFORMAL GAME PARTICIPATION

Walter Podilchak, The University of Calgary

Play behavior has traditionally been viewed as an activity in which the child practices broader social roles. Historically, the socialization of play behavior was 'child-centered' where children learned and interacted among themselves. This continues to occur. However, adult interaction has increased considerably in this setting. Would this adult-child interaction result in a unique perception of a game when compared to a game perception of an informal game setting? Presuming a unique quality in the peer setting which developed as a result of the children's interactions in a setting devoid of adults, one may assume a 'children's culture' specific to the participants' needs. Socialization influences should then be different from the adult setting, which emphasizes dominant cultural values.

Research findings suggest that adult settings and peer settings may have different criteria by which the individual is evaluated. For example, Clausen (1968:5) suggested that, in general, socialization is measured by adult performance standards. One would assume that this would be more prevalent in children's interactions with adults. Alternatively, Ingham, Loy and Berryman (1972:250) noted that "unlike the adult world where identities are ascribed, in the world of one's peers, identities are achieved." This suggests that socialization in the adult setting emphasizes social learning to predetermined standards required by society, whereas, in the peer setting, socialization emphasizes the particular emergent needs of the peer group.

A game activity occurs in both the adult and peer organized setting. As children are now participating in both settings, there should be a transfer of learning. Assuming the adult setting is more important, perceptions of game involvement in this setting should influence informal game interactions. While the peer setting and adult organized setting create a continuum of social institutionalization of a game, it would be interesting to investigate the effects of participating in an organized structure upon the peer setting. In adult structures, the game has been institutionalized to be 'real' (a word used by some players to differentiate an adult from a peer organized game). Upon isolating boys' perceptions of their involvement in the adult and peer organized settings, comparisons could be made of 'selective'[2] and 'houseleague' players within the peer setting to isolate institutionalization effects of the same phenomenon: play behavior in a game.

Within the adult-controlled leagues, sport organizations may have different structures to facilitate children's involvement: selective and houseleague. Soccer developed initially as a recreational league in the area under study, with the emphasis on providing opportunities for boys to play soccer. As more boys (and girls) began to play the sport, the shift from an egalitarian approach was expanded to include an elite structure.

A summary of the social organization of a game is provided in Figure 1. As the game becomes more institutionalized, the child has less and less control of the game. How will increasing institutionalization influence the child's perception of the informal game occurrence?

REVIEW OF THE LITERATURE

The institutionalization of children's play and games is largely a twentieth century phenomenon (cf. Ritchie and Koller, 1964:205). Analysis of this phenomenon has primarily been doc-

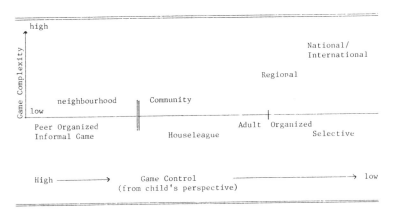

FIGURE 1: Social Organization Of A Game

umented through the popular literature (Eitzen, 1979; Martens, 1978; Michener, 1976). These articles are generally emotive. The authors generally assume that if sport involvement was 'good' for them, it must be the same for children now. What they fail to account for is the possibility of changes in the social complexity of the game.

Socialization

In reviewing the literature, Clausen (1968) noted that researchers such as Elkin and Child emphasize the learning by the child; while others such as Alberle put stress on the social apparatus which influences the individual's learning and defines for him the range of what is acceptable. Socialization implies that the individual is induced in some measure to conform willingly to the ways of society as measured by adult performance standards.

Researchers have turned their attention to influences of socialization into and through sport involvement. Goldstein and Bredemeier (1977) noted that "values transmitted by structured athletics are more conservative than those of society at large" (cf. Iso-Ahola, 1980:131). Children are socialized to conformity. Stevenson (1975) questions assumptions made on differences in populations of athletes and non-athletes. The treatment population must experience satisfactory exposure to the socialization agency in length and intensity to ensure that a consequent socialization effect might reasonably be expected. Stevenson, in a later article (1976:65), noted that the "interaction" concept of socialization demands that the socialization effect must of necessity occur as a consequence of participation in sport. He suggests an "institutional socialization" model which posits its locus of socialization external to the social structure.

Watson (1976) noted three modes of studying games and socialization: (1) interactionalist, (2) conflict, and (3) spontaneous involvement models. He believed the latter is the most appropriate as the children have no control of the rules in adult organized sports (the interactionalist model assumes the individual has a say in rules, team selection, and so on), and organized sports can heighten conflict instead of allowing for its expression in a "buffering learning" setting (the conflict model assumes the individual can act out his conflicts from real life in game settings). Socialization for children is viewed as a temporal sequence of initial "attraction," the "impact' of involvement and the outcome of involvement ("training effect").

Within the highly organized structure, the coach is isolated as a strong socializing agent representing the dominant cultural values; parents and spectators represent community values. The participants are socialized by these agents in an "interactive" model alongside peer socialization which adopts these adult attitudes and values within the organized context of sport. The diffuseness of these attitudes and values is situationally dependent.

Peer Influences

As games involve groups of individuals, one would expect that some socialization effect occurs among peer participants. Sport participation within the group serves two functions: as a source of pleasure for the participant, while playing the game, and a means of status definition. Kenyon and McPherson (1974) noted that peer aggregates are particularly influential in creating a propensity for sport involvement in general. Ingham, Loy and Berryman (1972) cited distinct socialization effects. In the peer world, socialization consists of adhering to emergent rules and learning to perform adequately in roles which are part of the emergent structure. Unlike the adult supervised world where identites are ascribed, in the world of one's peers identities are achieved. Hartup (1970:290) cited research by himself and Coates which may help explain this interaction effect of adult culture upon peer interactions: "A child's previous interactions with the model (adult) and his history of interaction in the peer group affect his susceptibility to peer modelling." In a study of adults, Spreitzer and Snyder (1976:242) noted that perceived athletic ability was the strongest factor for both males and females as a measure of sport involvement. They noted that perceived ability apparently does not develop merely from parental encouragement; rather it develops by actual childhood and adolescent autotelic participation and others' evaluations of ability. Polgar's (1976) observational study of game playing behavior of sixth grade boys in free play in the school yards and in formal physical education classes noted that the peer group context appears to develop an egalitarian consensual model concerned with means, while the authoritarian and imposed adult structure is concerned with ends.

Informal Game Socialization

Research in informal game behavior has not developed to the same extent as sport socialization research. Methodological difficulties in studying informal groups probably account for this deficiency. Much of the research into children's sport draws "nostalgic" comparison to "days gone by." Opie and Opie (1969:4) studied children's game in informal settings in Great Britain, and noted that children became "self conscious" about the games they play on their own more quickly than they used to; and "discard" them two to three years earlier than they did in the "days before" the introduction of organized sport. Another interpretation by Eifermann (1971:291) suggested that there was no "challenge" in "games with rules" in the informal setting. Informal games are liked when they "move in stages, in which each stage, the choosing of leaders, the determining of which side shall start, are almost games in themselves" (Opie and Opie, 1969:2). Devereaux (1976) compared socialization patterns in adult and peer organized settings, and noted that children no longer develop various social interaction skills.

'Professionalization' Research

The 'professionalization index' is another research tradition which attempts to measure the influence of sport participation on value formations. Webb (1969) developed the index to rank values of equality, performance and outcome. He discovered that children in grade three initially emphasize ascriptive criteria such as "likeability," "neighborhood residence" and so on: all related to fairness. Children in grades five and six began to emphasize skill. Mantel and VanderVelden (1971:7) tested the 'professionalization' index on ten and eleven-year-old middle-class boys, comparing boys involved in organized sport for at least two years with peers not involved, and concluded that the "professionalization of parents and coaches may be as important, if not more important, than the actual participation in the game sport.

Kidd and Woodman (1975) applied a phenomenological model to the three stages of sport involvement: (1) to have fun, (2) to play well, (3) to win. The aims of stage one are to develop social contacts and have fun in sport. Stage two results in a sense of pride as skill develops. After the competitor plays well for a considerable time, he becomes committed to the sport activity, and, to enjoy the activity, he must play well. Winning becomes the motivational goal in stage three. Kidd and Woodman concluded that the play-well stage may be a generalized acceptable norm.

Snyder and Spreitzer (1979) further used the three processual stages from above, extending the model to five stages. They hypothesized that stage one is usually of an informal nature where the motivation is primarily intrinsic. In stage two, extrinsic dimensions "began to intrude," where in the third stage the primary motivation is extrinsic. Individuals may revert back to the stage of fun and sociability after "peaking" at a particular sport. Coakley's (1979) approach established the characteristics of the social contexts in which the activities occur and the meaning that the children themselves assign to their experiences. Each activity offers a unique and necessary but incomplete set of developmental experiences. Informal games activities are dependent on abilities to manage competitive interpersonal relationships, and they provide experiences with a combined emphasis on expression, personal involvement and controlled uncertainty. Organized sport is a structurally stable activity providing experiences focusing on role learning, performance and outcome. Thus, socialization experiences are different, depending on settings.

Researchers have noted the importance of discussing the social context of the game activity. The theoretical basis of ludic order (Goffman, 1961; Ingham and Loy, 1974) may be perceived as being similar, irrespective of setting. However, the social conditions at the various organizational levels appear to influence strongly the possible range of acceptable behavior, especially rationalized behavior (Lüschen, 1967; Heinila, 1973; Cheek and Burch, 1976; Lenk, 1977). In youth sport, a similar process may be developing whereby ranges of behavior are allowed, however simultaneously changing the generalized notion of a game.

METHODOLOGY

The subjects for this study included boys, aged seven to twelve years, who played in a selective or houseleague summer soccer season. The selective team consisted of the best players at the age level who were chosen after the tryout season. This team represented the association in competition at various regional, provincial and national playoffs. The houseleague team generally consisted of less skillful players. They competed only at local league playoffs.

The importance of this study was theory development, and as such, theoretical sampling, as suggested by Glaser and Strauss (1967), was of primary concern rather than any confirmatory (and subsequently a larger sample) methodological design. Four teams were selected, two each from the under-ten and under-twelve level. Field observations were undertaken of the under-ten teams while they participated in the adult organized setting. Twenty-six boys were observed. For the formal interview, eleven boys were chosen from each of the four teams, for a total of forty-four boys.

General Sport and Leisure Participation

The following section provides a description, albeit brief, of the boys' sport and leisure participation. The subjects predominantly played hockey and soccer in adult organized leagues. As there was a one- to two-year difference between under-ten and under-twelve players, one would expect the older boys to have a longer period of sport involvement. However, this was not the case as both selective groups participated longer than the house-league players.

Hockey, soccer, baseball and football were the sports predominantly played by the boys in the peer-organized setting. Hockey and soccer were most frequently cited by all boys (39 and 36, respectively) followed by baseball and football (29 each). These sports and others were cited thirty-eight times by the 'selective' under ten, forty-three times by 'selective' under twelve, thirty-seven by 'houseleague' under ten and thirty-one by 'house-league' under twelve players. In sum, 'selective' players played more sports in the peer setting than did the 'houseleague' players. This suggested that 'selective' players continued to play a greater range of sports informally as they grew older, while 'houseleague' players participated in fewer sports.

Average peer organized group sizes were similar for the boys of 'selective' and 'houseleague' teams. When formally asked, all boys said peer group sizes generally consisted of nine or ten players.

During informal field interviews about the previous days' informal sport involvement, the boys noted that informal games generally occurred in school yards, roads and backyards. Participants were more heterogeneous in age, sex and skill levels. It became evident that informal peer group sizes were generally smaller (4 to 5) than that reported above. During the summer, games are harder to organize, for as more than one boy remarked, "There isn't anybody around." The larger peer group sizes probably related to school times when there were more children available. Although inconclusive, it appeared that boys in 'house-leagues' played more peer-organized sports in the summer than did 'selective' players, but the latter group participated more often in the adult setting and were generally too fatigued to play sports with friends. Many of the 'selective' under-ten players also stated that they were practicing ice hockey for the upcoming season. Practices began in August and were generally in the evenings. Normally more 'houseleague' players reported they or their friends organized a game, while the 'selective' players "went to an area where a game will occur," such as a school field.

Boys in both age groups mentioned other activities they enjoyed doing in their leisure time. Although patterns of leisure involvement were difficult to compare, a distinction appeared in the under-twelve groups. Twenty-four activities were cited by the 'houseleague' group, whereas, sixteen were cited by the 'selective' group. This suggested that 'houseleague' boys participated more often in a variety of leisure activities than did the 'selective' boys.

DISCUSSION

The discussion will focus upon differences between 'house-league' and 'selective' boys' perceptions of their informal game participation. Similarities in these boys' perceptions of peer organized sports were dealt with elsewhere (Podilchak, 1981). The eight categories: 'separateness' of game, team creation, rules governing action, role of participants, participant interaction pattern, abilities required for action, results or 'pay-off' and reasons for game involvement were theoretical categories for analyzing a game phenomenon. They were partially based on Avedon's (1971) structural model of a game. Abilities required for action and results or 'pay-off' were not discussed in this paper as there were no differences between 'selective' and 'houseleague' boys, but rather only setting differences.

Throughout the discussion, age differences will also be presented as this factor may also help explain some of the institutional effects. In general, younger boys (under 10) expressed similar patterns to the houseleague boys, while older boys (under 12) generally followed selective patterns. A maturational effect may also be operating.

'Separateness' of Game

This section concerns the times associated with a game phenomenon, but not the actual game behavior: pre-game, breaks and post-games. The importance of the game may reflect in these various times.

The pre-game period was perceived to be more friendly before an adult than a peer-organized game for all boys. However, houseleague and under-ten players perceived very little difference between friendliness in settings. This suggests that 'houseleague' boys approached a game activity with similar expectations, irrespective of setting. 'Selective' boys differentiated a game. In the peer setting, varying methods of deciding to take "breaks" were employed by the boys (see Table 1 below). A 'group decision' process was employed by most players; a group consensus was made when to take a 'time-out.' A difference was found between the selective and under-twelve players in comparison to the houseleague and under-ten players. Thus, a 'group decision' (or a normative basis from prolonged participation in sports) was used by older boys and selective players much more than other methods of deciding to take a break. An 'individual decision' (players deciding by themselves to take a break while activity continues) was

Table 1
Means of Taking "Breaks" in Peer Organized Games

Methods[1]	Selective (N=22)	Houseleague (N=22)	Total (N=44)
(1) Individual decision	5	10	15
(2) Group decision	13	7	20
(3) Best player or captain decision	4	2	6
(4) Individuals take turns	3	1	4
(5) Somebody times	0	4	4

[1]Methods are interdependent.

used more by the houseleague players. This suggested a lack of any normative base.

Once the game ended, most boys thought it was more "friendly" after a peer organized game (31 of 44 boys said this setting) than an adult organized game (12 said this setting). (One player said it was the same.) This was important for both the selective and houseleague players and the age groups when comparing the adult and peer settings. Thus the social organization of an informal game was more important in fostering a friendly atmosphere.

Team Creation

The selection of teams is an integral part of a game. In theory, teams are created as equal as possible so both teams have equal opportunity to win (cf. Ingham and Loy, 1974:38).

In the peer settings, teams were generally temporary, though a few boys have started their own "league" in the neighborhood or at school. Team selection appeared to be a function of skill evaluation and friendship patterns. Table 2 outlines the methods by which boys chose teams. There are inter-related methods which the boys used and described in team selection. Captains generally chose teams and normally chose the better skilled players first. The older boys emphasized the importance of skill in choosing players. 'Selective' boys stressed the use of the "stick" method. Thirty-two percent of the subjects also emphasized that teams were chosen fairly. Teams are chosen on the basis of skill in both the peer and adult setting. However, there appeared to be a stronger tendency by the older boys and those of the 'selective' leagues to want to keep the better skilled players together. Here is how one boy described the "stick" method:

> "Well, sometimes we have stick teams. Like there's about fifteen players there and we play us against you nine or whatever. (Why does that happen?) Because we just like to pick the best six people. Six people get together and they're good

Table 2

Methods of Team Selection in Peer Organized Games

Methods[1]	Total (N=44)
(1) Captain decides	35
(2) Group decision	4
(3) Better skilled chosen first (or tryouts for positions)	23 (8,15)[a]
(4) Smallest and/or youngest players chosen first	3
(5) "Stick" (a few better players against all others)	5 (5,0)[b]
(6) Fairly (boys said teams were chosen fairly	14

[1]All methods are interrelated and can occur concurrently

[a]Raw scores for -10 and -12

[b]Raw scores for selective and houseleague

players and the rest are, you know, fair players. And that makes it sorta fair teams because six versus nine or whatever you know. (Why do the best players want to get together?) Well, it's more fun when you have it like that. Because when you've been playing with the other people sometimes they're making, well everybody is making mistakes, but they're making a lot of mistakes and they don't try and it bothers me sorta. And when you get six people it makes the other people try too . . ."

Rules Governing Action

In the peer organized game the participants themselves regulated the game. The categories of responses are summarized in Table 3. In general, all participants were the rule enforcers. There was also a strong emphasis by fifteen players that one was supposed to play to the rules. 'Selective' players also differed from 'houseleague' players in stating there were "no rules" in the peer setting. Twenty-one players (14 'selective' and 7 'houseleague') said not having a referee was the reason for cheating, while eleven

Table 3

Rule Enforcers in a Peer Organized Game

	Categories	Total (N=44)
(1)	Everybody	26
(2)	You're supposed to play by rules	15
(3)	Captain and/or better player	9
(4)	Other (non-playing)	3
(5)	No rules	5[a]

[a]All selective players.

players (8 'selective' and 3 'houseleague') said having "no rules and doing what you want" was the other general reason. Cheating was situational and learned. For example, when players had to make a decision about a goal or penalty, the team which lost the decision would think that the other team was cheating. There was no external judge (referee), as in the league game, to decide the issue. Different perceptions among boys in a peer organized game also caused cheating. However, participants in the peer setting allow cheating to occur to create a 'fun' atmosphere.

All participants were potential rule enforcers in the peer organized setting. However, in this setting, rule enforcement depended on interpersonal relationships as the individual who thought a foul occurred had to persuade the other participants that action should be taken. Although roles in the peer setting were generally pre-established (for example, in soccer one was supposed to kick the ball and attempt to score), the participants molded the rules to suit the situational needs (for example, how large a net should be or if hand balls should be called). In general "everything goes" until an infraction occurred, at which time the participants discussed whether or not a rule should be added to the game.

Not having a referee was perceived as being a problem in rule management. However, the 'selective' players particularly noted not having a referee and no rules in peer organized games were causes for cheating. 'Houseleague' players on the other hand probably understood the rules in the peer organized game were different than the adult game and generally did not state any problems in absence of rules. They appeared to emphasize the use and manipulation of rules to create humorous situations.

It may have been possible that 'selective' players in the peer setting wanted to play the same as in the adult organized league. However, others may not have necessarily enjoyed that type of game and manipulated the rules to meet such requirements of the peer group as, for example, "to have fun." Further research is needed in this area to find out if 'selective' boys can no longer manipulate the rules to have fun in a peer setting. They may not have developed the skills of "timing" or "hidden meanings in the rules" discussed by Devereaux (1976:49).

Roles of Participants

Soccer rules, except for the institutionalized role of the coach, were similar in both settings. There were no differences between 'selective' and 'houseleague' with respect to choosing positions. As discussed in team creation, the emphasis in role selection was generally on evaluation of skill. The strongest difference from the adult setting was that boys had an opportunity to choose their favorite positions. This appeared to be a complex process which was situationally dependent upon the individual and his interactions in the group. The player may have been allocated a certain position initially (by the captain or self selection) but as the game continued boys played "wherever the action was."

The captain's role was that of an organizer in both settings. However, the role was generally a position for status attainment awarded to the best player in the adult-organized setting. In the peer-organized setting, the role was functional. The captain's responsibility was generally limited to choosing teams. The role was shared by most participants in the peer setting as various mechanisms (such as 'call out') provided opportunities for participants to be captains, irrespective of their skill level. The role was temporary in order to create teams. His authority was then dependent on his ability to maintain that status through interpersonal abilities.

'Selective' under-twelve players thought there was no need for a captain in the peer organized setting. 'Selective' under-ten boys said too many arguments erupted when captains were selected. One possible explanation for this could be the association of the captain role with status attainment. 'Selective' players may not have understood the need for a captain to select teams so that the game could occur. Arguments in deciding who was to be captain suggested that the role was still perceived as one for status attainment. However this may not have been appropriate to the peer setting. Conflicts in captain selection made it difficult to start the game as one or two person(s) have to emerge in a group when team selection had to occur.

Soccer skills were taught predominantly by the coach in the adult setting. How was the learning process carried out in the peer-organized setting? Table 4 summarizes the methods by which boys learned sport skills in peer settings. The boys noted that simultaneous observation and participation with peers was the general method by which they learned to play their peer organized games. 'Houseleague' players tended to involve themselves in group formation of teams and rule discussions by members on what should be done. 'Selective' players tended to adapt knowledge learned from watching sports on television. Seven 'selective' under-ten players also noted that they adopted the rules of the adult-organized setting to the peer setting. In general, 'houseleague' boys tended to discuss among themselves, whereas 'selective' boys carried sport-learning skills from the adult setting.

Table 4

Methods of Sport Skill Learning in Peer Settings

Methods	Total (N=44)
(1) Observation and participation with peers	30
(2) Group formation, with rule discussion	12 (2, 10)[a]
(3) Learning from experienced, older individual	12
(4) Adapt knowledge from organized setting	13
(5) Watching sports on television	6 (5, 1)[a]

[a]Raw score for 'selective' and 'houseleague'.

Participant Interaction Patterns

All boys said more laughter occurred in the peer setting than in the adult organized setting. 'Houseleague' boys generally laughed more at funny situations in the peer setting than did the 'selective' players. However, 'selective' boys laughed more at errors and poorer players in the peer setting. Thus it appeared that the adult-organized setting was too serious for laughter to occur; especially with the selective league. The peer setting allowed players to create humorous situations which resulted in laughter among participants. However, selected players tended to laugh more at errors and poorly skilled performers.

Criticism among teammates was heard in the adult setting, though, as expected, it also occurred in the peer setting. Twenty-seven boys criticized teammates in the adult setting and twenty-five said the same for the peer setting. 'Selective' and under-twelve players, and 'houseleague' and under-ten players showed similar patterns across settings. The former groupings tended to criticize more in each setting. Errors were generally criticized in both settings. Moreover, "wanting to win" was the reason errors were criticized in the adult setting, while a disruptive player (over-successful player or "hog") was criticized in the peer setting. However, when comparing settings, most boys (31) perceived more criticism in the peer setting than in the adult setting (12).

Descriptions of fun could generally be classified with Watson's (1976) four potential reward systems: (1) social reciprocity (playing with friends); (2) intrinsic motivation (nature of the game); (3) achievement-mastery (exerting effort and winning); and (4) extrinsically rewarded behavior which is applied to institutionalized games. Although Watson focused on institutionalized games, the reward systems could also be applied to both settings. Boys of the 'selective' league generally differed from the houseleague players in achievement-mastery (exerting effort and winning). Thus Watson's categories must be applied in specific reference to league type. In the peer organized setting, intrinsic motivation was important for fun to half the boys. Social reciprocity and achievement-mastery (in particular, winning) were significantly emphasized by the under-twelve boys. It was concluded that intrinsic motivation was the major reward system until the age of twelve, then social differences were shown as working class boys in comparison to middle class boys, emphasized achievement. This study suggests that the importance of achievement could also be extended to the middle class for boys in peer organized games. Moreover, achievement-mastery was found to have been stressed in younger age levels — under ten in the selective leagues. Thus achievement (winning) may be more of a socialization influence of selective league participation than age.

Adult and peer games were generally seen as having the potential to be equally boring. Eighteen boys said the former was more boring, whereas twenty judged the latter, and six said games were not boring. 'Selective' boys generally differed from the 'houseleague' boys in stating that peer organized games were boring.

Reasons for Sport Involvement

The 'professionalization index' research provides a general measure of sport-related values and could be used as a measure of socialization influences. A four-way analysis of variance with repeated measures on two factors revealed a significant interaction between groups (league: select or house, and age) and within groups (settings: adult- and peer-organized and professionalization index). The subjects were asked to rank the following three choices: to play fair, to play your best or to win, in order of importance. The responses were assigned values of 1, 2 and 3. The means were established independently for the choices for the groups. Both settings were discussed to draw comparisons and subsequent differences of the peer setting.

Selective and under-twelve boys expressed similar ranking patterns in the adult- and peer-organized setting (see Figure 2) — best, fair, and win was the order in ranked importance. However, the distinctions of the ranks are negligible in the peer-organized setting. While playing fair remained relatively consistent in both settings, playing your best was stressed in the adult setting and playing to win was stressed in the peer organized game. Thus while the pattern was the same, it remained so only within settings. Selective and under-twelve players tended to view the adult and peer setting with sharp differences in attitudes of 'professionalization' of play (the importance of performance over equity). Houseleague and under-ten boys differed in ranking to the selective and under-twelve and revealed very slight differences in their patterns across settings. Fair, best and win was the ranked order for houseleague and under-ten boys in the adult setting, but shifted slightly for the under-tens in stressing playing your best more than playing fair. In peer organized settings the 'houseleague' had the same pattern in the peer setting as occurred in the adult setting. This suggested that the game was generally played the same way for the houseleague and under-ten, while selective and under-twelve boys were involved in the adult organized game to play their best, and played peer organized games to win.

There was also a significant interaction between setting: adult and peer-organized and the professionalization index. The ranking for the adult setting was best, fair and win (means of 1.5, 1.7 and 2.8 respectively.) The ranking for the peer setting was the same though with different means (1.8, 1.9 and 2.3 respectively). In general, playing your best and playing fair are stressed in the adult and peer setting. However, their importance is stronger in the adult setting, while playing to win was stronger in the peer setting.

CONCLUSION

To measure what effect participation in adult organized setting had upon the peer setting, boys' perceptions of the two settings were compared. Besides organizational differences between the settings, the degree of institutional involvement resulted in different perceptions of the peer organized games. A brief summary of the selective and houseleague game occurrence will be provided, upon which comparisons can be made of the respective peer-organized settings.

The adult organized settings stressed competition for social status in evaluating the quality of performance. Players within the selective league were chosen from candidates who exhibited superior athletic ability. Participants had to compete for starting positions and played only when the coach evaluated their performance in relation to the other players. Substitution was common when an individual's performance did not reach the coach's expectations. The role of the captain was awarded to the player who exhibited the best performance. The houseleague setting, on the other hand, generally emphasized the roles and position of the players, though once the game began, the players did not follow their assigned positions.

In the peer organized setting, a similar occurrence with role and positions was also found. The captain's role was functional in organizing the participants into teams. This role was shared by most participants at various times.

In the selective league, all participants generally had a more serious or 'professionalized' attitude towards their actions. Attention was constantly focused on playing proper positions, executing skills correctly and adhering to the coach's commands. The parents often interacted with the boys in this setting. There was very little talk or laughter amongst the selective players. Performance and winning were most important.

In the houseleague setting, there appeared a more 'relaxed' atmosphere with respect to the game. Parents did not interact to the same degree, preferring to be spectators. The coach stressed game objectives to teach the boys appropriate behaviors, but it was not a serious matter. They laughed, talked and teased each other constantly. The game was, however, competitive as both teams tried to win, but the game was quickly forgotten once concluded. Thereafter, boys continued to express 'playful' behaviors with each other.

Moreover, there appeared to be a transfer of learning across settings. Sociability was emphasized by the houseleague boys in

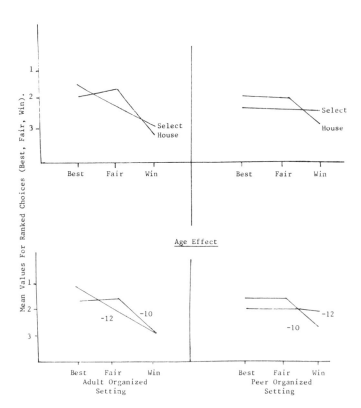

FIGURE 2:   Interaction Effects of League (House or Select), Age (Under Ten and Under
            Twelve) and 'Professionalization' Index (Best, Fair, Win)

both settings, whereas performance was emphasized by the selective boys in both settings.

Game involvement cannot be studied by separating characteristics of various settings. One would expect to find differences in adult and peer settings and selective and houseleague settings within the former setting. However, the importance of the research was the distinctions expressed by the boys in evaluating their peer involvement. In general, the boys expressed perceptions of the peer setting that were characteristic of their respective adult setting, in selective or houseleagues. Game involvement cannot be discussed generally, irrespective of the social context; neither could a peer setting be directly compared to the adult setting. A generalized perception of game involvement occurred. Players of selective leagues emphasized performance in both settings: a greater rationalized perspective influenced by sport participation which is highly organized. Players of the houseleague emphasized sociability in both settings: a more affective perspective sustained by sport participation in less formal social organizations.

NOTES

[1]This research was completed while at Dalhousie University. I thank Dr. J. C. Pooley for his assistance. Special thanks to Dr. Bob Bratton, University of Calgary, for his suggestions and presentation of this paper.

[2]The single quotations around selective or houseleague will be used when discussing boys' perceptions of the peer organized game. The quotations emphasize the adult organizational structure from which the samples were drawn.

REFERENCES

Avedon, Elliott M.
    1971 "The structural elements of games." Pp. 419-426 in Elliott M. Avedon and Brian Sutton-Smith (eds.), The Study of Games. Toronto: Wiley.
Cheek Jr., Neil H. and William R. Burch Jr.
    1976 The Social Organization of Leisure in Human Society. New York: Harper and Row.
Clausen, John A.
    1968 "Socialization as a concept and as a field of study." Pp. 3-17 in John A. Clausen (ed.), Socialization and Society. Boston: Little, Brown.

Coakley, Jay J.
  1979 "Plays, games and sport: developmental implications for young people." Paper presented at the annual meetings of the American Alliance for Health, Physical Education and Recreation, New Orleans, March 15-20.
Devereaux, Edward C.
  1976 "Backyard versus little league baseball: the impoverishment of children's games." Pp. 37-56 in Daniel M. Landers (ed.), Social Problems in Athletics. Urbana: University of Illinois.
Eifermann, Rioka
  1971 "Social play in childhood." Pp. 270-297 in R. E. Herron and B. Sutton-Smith (eds.), Child's Play. Toronto: Wiley.
Eitzen, D. Stanley
  1979 Sport in Contemporary Society. New York: St. Martin's.
Glazer, B. G. and A. L. Strauss
  1967 The Discovery of Grounded Theory: Strategies for Qualitative Research. Chicago: Aldine-Atherton.
Goffman, Erving
  1961 "Fun in games." Pp. 17-84 in Erving Goffman (ed.), Encounters. New York: Bobbs-Merrill.
Goldstein, J. H. and B. J. Bredemeier
  1977 "Sports and socialization: some basic issues." Journal of Communication 27: 154-59.
Hartup, Willard W.
  1970 "Peer relations." Pp. 265-294 in Thomas D. Spencer and Norman Kass (eds.), Perspectives in Child Psychology, Research and Review. Toronto: McGraw-Hill.
Heinila, K.
  1973 "Citius-Altius-Fortius: the Olympic contribution to the professionalization of sport?" Pp. 351-355 in Ommo Grupe, Dietrich Kurz and Johannes Marcus Teipel (eds.), Sport in the Modern World — Chances and Problems. Heidelburg: Springer-Verlag Berlin.
Ingham, Alan, John W. Loy and Jack W. Berryman
  1972 "Socialization dialects, and sport." Pp. 235-276 in Dorothy V. Harris (ed.), Women and Sport: A National Research Conference. Penn State HPER Series No. 2.
Ingham, Alan G. and John W. Loy
  1974 "The structure of ludic action." International Review of Sport Sociology 1(9):23-62.
Iso-Ahola, Seppo E.
  1980 The Social Psychology of Leisure and Recreation. Dubuque, Iowa: Brown.
Kenyon, G. S. and Barry D. McPherson
  1974 "An approach to the study of sport socialization." International Review of Sport Sociology 1(9): 127-139.
Kidd, Thomas R. and William F. Woodman
  1975 "Sex and orientations toward winning in sport." Research Quarterly 46(2):476-483.
Lenk, Hans
  1977 "Against the new socio-philosophical criticism of athletes and achievement." Pp. 167-180 in Hans Lenk (ed.), Team Dynamics. Essays in the Sociology and Social Psychology of Sport Including Methodological and Epistemological Issues. Champaign, Ill.: Stipes.

Lüschen, G.
1967 "The interdependence of sport and culture." International Review of Sport Sociology 2:127-139.
Mantel, R. and L. VanderVelden
1971 "The relationship between the professionalization of attitudes toward play among pre-adolescent boys and participation in organized sports." Abstracts III, Third International Symposium on the Sociology of Sport, University of Waterloo, Canada, August 22-28.
Martens, Rainer
1978 Joy and Sadness in Children's Sports. Champaign, Ill.: Human Kinetic.
Michener, James A.
1976 "Children and sports." Pp. 93-119 in James A. Michener (ed.), Sports in America. New York: Random House.
Opie, Joan and Peter Opie
1969 Children's Games in Street and Playground. London: Oxford at the Clarendon Press.
Podilchak, Walter
1981 "Boys' perceptions of adult and peer organized games." Paper presented at the First Regional Symposium of the International Committee for the Sociology of Sport, Vancouver, B.C.
Polgar, Sylvia Knopp
1976 "The social context of games: or when is play not play?" Sociology of Education 49:256-271.
Ritchie, O. and M. R. Koller
1964 Sociology of Childhood. New York: Appleton.
Snyder, Elton E. and Elmer Spreitzer
1979 "Toward a natural history of lifelong involvement in sport." Pp. 190-204 in March L. Krotee (ed.), The Dimension of Sport Sociology. New York: Leisure Press.
Spreitzer, Elmer and Eldon E. Snyder
1976 "Socialization into sports: an exploratory path analysis." Research Quarterly 46(2):238-245.
Stevenson, Christopher L.
1975 "Socialization effects of participation in sport: a critical review of the research." Research Quarterly 46(3):287-301.
1976 "An alternative theoretical approach to sport socialization: a concept of institutional socialization." International Review of Sport Sociology 1(11):65-76.
Watson, Geoffrey G.
1976 "Reward systems in children's games: the attraction of game interaction in little league baseball." Review of Sport and Leisure 1(Fall):93-121.
Webb, Harry
1969 "Professionalization of attitudes toward play among adolescents." Pp. 161-178 in Gerald S. Kenyon (ed.), Aspects of Contemporary Sport Sociology. C.I.C. Symposium on the Sociology of Sport, University of Wisconsin. Chicago: Athletic Institute.

Chapter 21

THE BEHAVIOR OF YOUTH FOOTBALL COACHES

Paul E. Dubois, Bridgewater State College

The consequences for children involved in organized youth sports programs are contingent upon many factors. Some of these include personal attributes, the influence of parents, the physical and contextual setting during game play, league structure and policies, and rewards. However, perhaps the most vital factor in this equation is the coach (Gould and Martens, 1979; Smoll and Smith, 1980). The notion of the coach as a significant other in the lives of young athletes has both theoretical and empirical support (McElroy and Kirkendall, 1980; Pooley, 1981; Scanlan, 1978; Scanlan and Passer, 1978).

Given the crucial role of the coach in the athletic experiences of young people, it is important to develop an understanding of coaching behaviors and their impact upon youth sport athletes. Efforts toward this end have been slow to develop, but the recent interest in youth sports by social scientists has brought about considerable progress in this area.

Writers and scholars have employed a variety of strategies in an effort to profile the behavior of youth sport coaches. An initial strategy was a journalistic one which often consisted of a case study of a single coach and team (Burchard, 1979; Ralbovsky, 1974). This approach was, no doubt, largely responsible for the current popular stereotype of the youth sport coach as a self-centered ogre who, in the quest for victory, dehumanizes team members, opponents and officials alike.

A second and more systematic strategy involves data collection via interview schedules and questionnaires. Studies of this nature include both self reported behaviors and perceptions of others, most notably players, concerning coaching behaviors. As might be expected, self reported behaviors are of questionable validity. For example, Smith and his associates (1978) found a significant positive relationship between *observed* and *coach-perceived* behaviors for only one of twelve behavior categories identified in their research. Furthermore, self perceptions are also likely to be biased in favor of the coach: when 421 coaches in eight sports were asked to indicate their agreement ratings on twenty attitude items for *their specific program* and for the *sport in general*, the coaches rated their programs as superior on all but one item. On the item concerning "too much emphasis on winning," for example, the agreement rating was 73% for the sport in general and only 49% for their particular program (Gould and Martens, 1979).

Other survey studies reveal a broad range of perceptions about coaching behaviors. An extensive research project conducted by the state of Michigan (Seefeldt, 1978) reported that most athletes and parents felt youth sport coaches generally treated their players well, attempted to comply with program purposes and "always" stressed winning only 6 percent of the time. However, this same study revealed that 10 percent of the coaches never played everyone when games were close, that they "always" displayed good sportsmanship only 60 percent of the time, and "never" argued with officials only about 35 percent of the time.

Equally diverse findings can be noted in other data comparisons. For example, Purdy et al. (1981) found that coaches were more sensitive than parents concerning competitive pressures felt by young athletes, whereas several studies indicate that athletic drop-outs often suggest overly competitive, negative and unconcerned coaches as a primary cause in their decision to withdraw (Orlick, 1976; Pooley, 1981).

A third strategy for gaining an understanding about coaching behaviors involves direct observation and coding of those behaviors. In addition to achieving a complete accounting of a coach's behaviors, this method, because the data generated is quantitative in nature, enables researchers to analyze the behaviors statistically in conjunction with other variables of interest. Pioneer work using this method was conducted on Little League baseball coaches by a team of behavioral scientists led by Smoll and Smith from the University of Washington. Their data (Smith, et al., 1978) indicated the coaches were generally very positive in their behaviors. However, when the more positive coaches were compared with those who were less positive, it was found the former group was better liked and had players with (1) more positive attitudes toward sport and team, and (2) higher levels of self esteem. This relationship between positive/negative coaches and self esteem was also supported by Sander's (1981) study of high school basketball coaches. Controlling for the won-lost record of the team and each player's total points and quarters played, Sanders found that after four months the athletes of positive and of negative coaches displayed self esteem that went in predictably opposite and statistically significant directions.

In another aspect of their research, Smoll and Smith (Smith, et al., 1978) reported a significant negative relationship between games won and negative behaviors, a finding also reported by Dubois (1981).

To date, the behaviors of youth football coaches have not been analyzed via the quantitative coding method. Thus, it was the intent of this study to (1) describe the nature of youth football coaches' behaviors, and (2) to examine if relationships exist between these behaviors and team performance and competitive orientation.

METHOD

Subjects selected for this study consisted of the entire population of volunteer coaches in an eight-team, 10-13-year-old-age-group tackle football program. The program was located in a medium-sized, predominantly working class city in Southeastern

Massachusetts. The teams were equally divided into an "instructional" league, which consisted of the younger and smaller athletes, and a "competitive" league for the more mature and skilled athletes.

As the labels suggest, the instructional league games occurred in a less "professionalized" context than did those of the competitive league. For example, the instructional league played its games under modified rules which eliminated kickoffs and punts and permitted coaches to move freely on the field to provide on-going, hands-on instruction to their players. Furthermore, the instructional league scheduled games on Saturday mornings at a junior high field, while the competitive league countered with Sunday afternoon games in the high school stadium.

The physical trappings of the two leagues were also quite distinct. The competitive league clearly reflected the professional model: games came complete with program, national anthem, electronic scoreboard, public address system, announcer, four uniformed referees, and cheerleaders. By contrast, the typical instructional league game was embellished with only one or two referees and an occasional cheerleader squad. Finally, the competitive league received media coverage in the city newspaper, and players competed for end-of-year awards and trophies; the instructional league engaged in neither of these practices.

The data collection instrument was a modified version of event-recording devices used to gather information about in-class teacher feedback to students (Siedentop, 1976). As a consequence of field tests conducted over four games, a total of eight different coaching behavior categories were identified on the instrument: four dealt with behaviors directed toward player or team, two with behaviors directed toward opponents and officials, and two with miscellaneous behaviors. The categories were equally divided between "positive" and "negative" behaviors. The eight categories and a brief description and example of each are provided in Figure 1.

The reliability and validity of the instrument were determined by use of the agreement-with-expert technique. A class of

Behavior Directed Toward Player or Team

Positive

(1)   Encouragement - - Spontaneous supportive behavior ("C'mon, you
             can do it").
         Positive feedback - Positive response to something done well or
             correctly ("Nice lead pass, Sue").
(2)   Instruction - Spontaneous behavior concerning how a skill should
             be performed ("Both feet on the ground for the throw
             in, John").
         Positive corrective feedback - Responding to a player's performance
             error with information about how he/she can correct
             that error ("Next time that happens, come out of the
             goal mouth more").

Negative

(3)   Negative feedback   -   Direct criticism, usually in response to a
             performance error ("That was a lousy block").
(4)   Negative corrective feedback   -   Similar to positive corrective
             feedback except that its intent is seen as punative
             rather than instructive. Corrective feedback is
             categorized as negative when it is delivered in a
             harsh or sarcastic manner ("Give with the ball
             when you trap it!").

Behavior Directed Toward Opponents and Officials

(5)   Positive - Any behavior that demonstrates support, appreciation
             and/or respect for opposing team or officials ("He
             ran a great pass pattern").
(6)   Negative - Any behavior that demonstrates disrespect or malice
             toward opposing team or officials ("Get some
             glasses, ref!").

Miscellaneous Positive and Negative Behaviors

(7) & (8) Any positive or negative behavior by the coach not falling into one
             of the above categories (E.g. complimenting the bench
             warmers for "yelling it up" during game play).

Figure 1. Categories Used to Code Coaching Behaviors [a]
(Numbers delineate the categories)

a.   Taken from Dubois (1981)

undergraduate Sociology of Sport students was first given a forty-five minute presentation concerning the nature and use of the instrument. Following this classroom session, the students went through field training which lasted a total of three quarters of one game. During the same week, the students and an "expert" on the use of the instrument (the author) recorded a coach's behavior throughout an entire game. It was found that the agreement-with-expert scoring of six randomly selected trainees was 97 percent and 89 percent for the positive and negative categories, respectively.

Each coach was observed during a total of four games, and observations were equally dispersed throughout the beginning, middle and end of the season. With the exception of one game which the author coded, all data were collected by the trained undergraduate students. Observers would arrive at an assigned game a few minutes early to record such information as the competitive orientation of the league, (i.e. competitive or instructional), the team name, and the team's current won-lost record. Only the during-game behaviors of the coaches were recorded. Because the instrument was prelabeled with each of the eight behavior categories, the actual mechanics of recording the coaches' behaviors simply consisted of staying within hearing distance of the coach and making tally marks below the appropriate label.

Based on prior evidence that some coaches emitted well over two hundred distinct behaviors during the course of a game, observer fatigue was a concern. Thus, it was decided that all observers would take a five-minute rest (running time) after the completion of the first and third quarters.

FINDINGS AND DISCUSSION

A total of 95 percent of all coaching behaviors[1] were player or team directed. Since such behaviors reflect a concern for skill performance, it appears the coaches were very much "on task" as concerns their mentor role. Somewhat more of the player/team directed positive behaviors were in the technically oriented instruction and corrective feedback category (43%) than in the more general encouragement/positive category (33%), a finding consistent with a companion study (Dubois, 1981) conducted on male youth soccer coaches. The nearly 20 percent player/team directed negative behaviors were equally divided into negative corrective (9.9%) and negative (9.5%) behaviors. Although few (3%) of the coaches' behaviors were directed toward opponents or officials, most (2.4%) of these were in the negative category. Two percent of the behaviors fell under the miscellaneous categories.

The percentages for the combined positive and negative behavior categories for all coaches totaled 77.2 percent and 22.8 percent, respectively. These figures correspond very closely to those obtained by the aforementioned study of youth soccer coaches (Dubois, 1981), but they do not compare favorably with the 96 percent positive behaviors of coaches in Smoll and Smith's Little League study (Smith et al., 1978). In defense of the football and soccer coaches, however, the authors of the Little League study speculate the extremely high ratio of positive to negative behaviors they obtained was due to the refusal of thirteen suspected "negative" coaches to join the study.

In Table 1, positive and negative behaviors are broken down by league orientation. Note that the instructional league coaches average ten percent more positive behaviors than those in the competitive league. This finding suggests that the positive relationship between professionalization of attitudes toward play and age of athlete, as reported by Webb (1969), may be partly attributable to the athlete's exposure to progressively more harsh and critical (i.e., win-oriented) coaches from one year to the next.

The increasingly professionalized context of the competitive league is further highlighted by Tables 2 & 3. Note that the instructional league coaches maintain a relatively stable output of about 80 percent positive behaviors irrespective of game outcome and team record,[2] whereas, the competitive league coaches' positive behaviors are clearly linked to team performance. In both tables, the percentage of positive coaching behaviors changes from the low 80's to the low 60's when better performing teams are compared with poorer ones. Such sensitivity to team performance suggests these coaches are fostering a winning-is-everything competitive ethic among their athletes. The data also suggests that the coaches' willingness to support and encourage athletes is contingent upon game results and team record.

What might account for the substantial difference in behaviors between the instructional and competitive league coaches? I would contend that the answer can be found in the widely discrepant physical and social contexts in which the games of the two leagues are played. First, an important though latent function of the instructional league is to serve as a minor league "feeder" for the competitive league. Thus, it is primarily in the competitive league that coaching reputations and social status are gained and lost. Second, and as previously identified, the instructional league has few of the professionalized trappings of the competitive league. Attendance figures and television coverage notwithstanding, the competitive league mirrors quite accurately the scene at an NFL game. Placed in this kind of environment, it is difficult to imagine any coach *not* becoming susceptible to behaviors which emphasize winning at the expense of other values.

RECOMMENDATIONS

Youth sports programs should be designed to be both fun and educational. If such objectives are to be realized, the findings of this study suggest the need for some coaches involved in these programs to modify their behavior. Specifically, it is recommended that coaches like those analyzed here eliminate the tendency to display performance-contingent behaviors while at the same time work to minimize negative behaviors. As previously indicated in this presentation, the coach who is consistently positive in interactions with his/her players seems to produce athletes (1) who enjoy the sport experience more (i.e., they drop out less, like the coach and teammates more, etc.) and (2) who display higher levels of self esteem than athletes who must work with

TABLE 1. COACHES' COMBINED POSITIVE AND NEGATIVE
BEHAVIORS BY LEAGUE ORIENTATION

	POS.	NEG.
INSTRUCTIONAL	82.5	17.5
COMPETITIVE	72.1	27.9

$x^2 = 3.08$, p $<$ .10

TABLE 2. PERCENTAGE OF COACHES' POSITIVE BEHAVIORS BY
INSTRUCTIONAL ORIENTATION AND GAME OUTCOME

	INSTRUCTIONAL	COMPETITIVE
WON	81 (N=7)	82 (N=7)
TIED	79 (N=2)	
LOST	85 (N=7)	63 (N=9)

TABLE 3. PERCENTAGE OF COACHES' POSITIVE BEHAVIORS BY
INSTRUCTIONAL ORIENTATION AND TEAM RECORD

	INSTRUCTIONAL	COMPETITIVE
WINNING	86 (N=8)	80 (N=6)
500	64 (N=2)	70 (N=4)
LOSING	84 (N=6)	64 (N=6)

negative coaches. In addition, the coach who gives more praise and positive criticism may be less likely to socialize athletes into a competitive orientation that equates success with winning and views the opponent only as an enemy to be overcome (Dubois, 1980a).

What strategies can be used to increase positive behaviors among coaches? One technique which has met with success is a direct approach involving instructional workshops, behavioral feedback from others, and/or self monitoring (Smoll and Smith, 1980; Dubois, 1980b). A second and more indirect technique is to lower youth sports' "fidelity" to the professional leagues by eliminating such program elements as uniformed referees, scoreboards, cheerleaders (especially if they are only female), and published league standings. As evidenced by this research, the degree of fidelity of youth sports programs to the professional model may be a variable affecting the coaches' ratio of positive:negative behaviors. If in fact the overall context of the sport setting is a primary cause of coaching behavior, the latter technique may actually be more effective than the former in bringing about lasting change in behavior.

A final recommendation is intended for future research in this area. One weakness of the quantitative data gathering method employed in this study is its failure to measure the intensity of behaviors. A second weakness is its narrowness of scope: social situations in youth sports which impact upon the athlete are not limited to coach-player interactions. To reduce these weaknesses, it is recommended that field notes supplement the purely quantitative data of the type collected for this research.

NOTES

[1]The average frequency of during-game behaviors was 124, with minimum and maximum frequencies of 54 and 228, respectively.

[2]The 64 percent positive behaviors in the .500 team record category is difficult to explain. The figure may simply be an aberration. A second possibility is that even in a "low key" instructional league, the motivation for coaches to achieve a minimal threshold of respectability (defined as a .500 season) supercedes the motivation to always behave in the young athletes' best interests.

REFERENCES

Burchard, H.
  1979 "Boys play the men's game." Pp. 130-33 in A. Yiannakis, T. McIntyre,
        M. Melnick and D. Hart (eds.), Sport Sociology: Contemporary Theme, 2nd
        ed., Dubuque: Kendall-Hunt.
Dubois, P. E.
  1980a "Competition in youth sports: process or product?" Physical Educator
        37:154.
  1980b Unpublished data, Bridgewater State College.
  1981 "The youth sport coach as an agent of socialization: an exploratory study." Jour-
        nal of Sport Behavior 4:95-107.
Gould, D., and R. Martens
  1979 "Attitudes of volunteer coaches toward significant youth sport issues." Research
        Quarterly 50:369-80.
McElroy, M. A., and D. R. Kirkendall
  1980 "Significant others and professionalized sport attitudes." Research Quarterly
        51:645-53.
Orlick, T. and C. Botterill
  1976 "Why eliminate kids?" Pp. 106-09 in A. Yiannakis, T. McIntyre, M. Melnick
        and D. Hart (eds.) Sport Sociology: Contemporary Themes. Dubuque:
        Kendall-Hunt.
Pooley, J. C.
  1981 "Drop-outs from sport: a case study of boys age group soccer." Paper presented
        at the AAHPERD National Conference, Boston, MA., April.
Purdy, D. A., S. E. Haufler and D. S. Eitzen
  1981 "Stress among child athletes: perceptions by parents, coaches, and athletes."
        Journal of Sport Behavior 4:32-44.
Ralbovsky, M.
  1974 Destiny's Darlings. New York: Hawthorne.
Sander, R. L.
  1981 "Coaching style and the athlete's self concept." Athletic Journal 46:66-67.
Scanlan, T. K.
  1978 "Social evaluation: a key developmental element in the competition process."
        Pp. 131-147 in R. A. Magill, M. J. Ash and F. L. Smoll (eds.), Children in
        Sport: A Contemporary Anthology. Champaign, Il.: Human Kinetics.
Scanlan, T. K. and M. W. Passer
  1978 "Anxiety inducing factors in competitive youth sports." Pp. 108-22 in F. L.
        Smoll and R. E. Smith (eds.), Psychological Perspectives in Youth Sport.
        Washington, D.C.: Hemisphere.
Seefeldt, V. (ed.)
  1976 Joint Legislative Study of Youth Sports Programs. (Phase II). State of
        Michigan.
Siedentop, D.
  1976 Developing Teaching Skills in Physical Education. Atlanta: Houghton Mifflin.
Smith, R. E., F. L. Smoll and B. Curtis
  1978 "Coaching behaviors in little league baseball." Pp. 173-201 in F. L. Smoll and
        R. E. Smith (eds.), Psychological Perspectives in Youth Sports. Washington,
        D.C.: Hemisphere.

Smoll, F. L., and R. E. Smith
  1980 "Techniques for improving self-awareness of youth sport coaches." Journal of
       Physical Education and Recreation 51:46-49, 52.
Webb, H.
  1969 "Professionalization of attitudes toward play among adolescents." Pp. 161-78 in
       G. S. Kenyon (ed.), Aspects of Contemporary Sport Sociology. Chicago: Ath-
       letic Institute.

CURRICULUM ADVANCES IN THE SOCIOLOGY OF SPORT

Section VII

CURRICULUM ADVANCES IN THE SOCIOLOGY OF SPORT

The final section of this volume is a synopsis of the contributions to a workshop for the exchange of ideas concerning curriculum and teaching in the Sociology of Sport.

As part of a national survey of teacher preparation curriculums, Southard presents some revealing data on the teacher preparation coursework, desired student competencies, and relative program importance of sociology of sport offerings within a large number of physical education programs at American colleges and universities. Southard's results show that a rather low level of importance is presently attached to the sociology of sport within physical education curricula. For example, "a look at the sociology of sport data on a state by state basis shows that none of the 50 states has a status mean greater than an elective level." While these results portray a less than optimistic picture of the state of the art nationally, it is nonetheless valuable for an emerging subdiscipline such as ours to appreciate both the curricular impact the field has realized to date, and the need for future gains.

In an era of increased concern with educational accountability Dunleavy, Landwer, and Rees utilize a rational reconstruction of the foundations of the university in the western world as the basis for judging the legitimate focus and location of courses concerned with the sociological study of sport. The questions raised by this brief, creative treatise should promote significant and serious debate. For example, in light of the framework presented by Dunleavy et al., it is interesting to evaluate the role of courses described by Melnick, VanderVelden, and Hellison in this section. In addition, it would seem that efforts toward program accreditation, as are being undertaken by such organizations as NASPSPA and AAHPERD, ought to be founded in such rational reconstructive thinking.

While Dunleavy, Landwer and Rees speak to general programmatic concerns within the university setting, Melnick, VanderVelden, and Hellison present three rather different approaches to teaching specific courses in the sociology of sport. While Melnick and Hellison both incorporate field experiences as a significant component of their respective course activities, they differ markedly in disciplinary approach. Hellison follows a strongly interdisciplinary style while Melnick presents a more traditional sociological approach. In addition, the humanistic style of Hellison is in contrast to the more traditionally theoretical approach taken by both Melnick and VanderVelden. Of particular interest is the manner in which VanderVelden has attempted to provide a balanced course curriculum with appeal to both kinesiological science majors and general university students.

Despite their differences, Melnick, VanderVelden, and Hellison have each responded to student needs within their local university setting, while not sacrificing what they, explicitly or implicitly, believe to be a worthwhile approach to teaching the sociology of sport. Each departs significantly from traditional teacher education approaches and, therefore, each provides colleagues with stimulating ideas for curriculum innovation within the sociology of sport.

Finally, at a more technological level, Bryant reports on the development of an educational television series which deals with many of the contemporary topics in the sociology of sport. He explains the derivation and format of the series and illustrates some of its curricular uses. In a time when most of us have the facilities for such communication advances, Bryant's work has considerable potential for advancing teaching within this and other sport sub-disciplines. Given the increasing budgetary restrictions and our resultant inability to bring visiting scholars and public figures physically to the classroom, programs such as VTR should have broad appeal.

Chapter 22

A NATIONAL SURVEY: SOCIOLOGY OF SPORT WITHIN AMERICAN COLLEGE AND UNIVERSITY PHYSICAL EDUCATION PROFESSIONAL PREPARATION PROGRAMS

Dan Southard, Texas Christian University

The intent of this presentation is to share with you the Sociology of Sport data collected as part of a national study of teacher preparation curriculums conducted in spring, 1981. The purposes of that national study were to: (1) assess and categorize selected teacher preparation curriculums according to the importance attributed to competencies for future teachers to attain; (2) determine the relative importance of each of the selected competencies and categories; and (3) determine if the coursework offered in curriculums of teacher preparation reflects the importance of corresponding competencies for teachers. Sociology of Sport was one of the 20 selected competencies included in that study. Therefore, the data collected concerning the Sociology of Sport may also accomplish three parallel purposes, to: (1) determine the perceived importance of sociology of sport relative to the remaining 19 competencies within the study; (2) determine the status of sociology of sport courses in programs of teacher preparation; and (3) determine if the status of sociology of sport courses reflect the importance attributed to sociology of sport competencies.

The collection of data involved the use of two questionnaires, a competency questionnaire and a content questionnaire. The competency questionnaire contained 20 selected competencies. Respondents were instructed to rate each of the competencies on a five point semantic differential scale. A rating of one indicated "no importance" and a rating of five indicated "very important" for a teacher of physical education to attain. The competencies were placed in random order and no association was made between competencies and related courses. The competency questionnaires were mailed to the 682 four-year colleges and universities listed as offering a major in physical education by the 1980-81 college Bluebook. Usable competency questionnaires were returned by 606 (89%) of the potential respondents. To avoid questionnaire bias the second content questionnaires were mailed to each of the 606 respondents two weeks following the receival of competency questionnaires. The content questionnaire listed the courses which correspond to the 20 competencies on the first questionnaire, plus other courses which might be offered in programs of teacher preparation. Respondents were instructed to indicate the status of each course in their curriculum by responding: (1) not offered; (2) offered as an elective, but in combination with other subject matter; (3) offered as an elective; (4) required, but in combination with other subject matter; or (5) required. Usable content questionnaires were returned by 536 (88%) of the participants.

Because of the diverse nature of career options available to today's physical education major, a discriminant analysis was performed on both the competency and content data to determine the validity of responses specific to curriculums of teacher preparation. Questionnaires from 21 institutions which did not discriminate in favor of programs for teacher preparation were removed from further analysis. Therefore, the sample size was reduced from 606 to 585.

The validity of the content questionnaire was determined by correlating 50 randomly selected college/university catalog listings with questionnaire responses. Application of the Pearson-

TABLE 1

Individual Competencies And Corresponding Course Scores

VARIABLE	IMPORTANCE		STATUS	
	$\bar{X}$	RANK	$\bar{X}$	RANK
MOTOR LEARNING	4.7	1.5	2.8	17
PHYSIOLOGY OF EXERCISE	4.7	1.5	3.9	5.5
FIRST AID	4.6	3.5	3.9	5.5
TEACHING METHODS	4.6	3.5	4.3	1
ANATOMY	4.5	5.5	4.1	2
BIOMECHANICS	4.5	5.5	3.7	7.5
TEACHING LIFETIME SPORTS	4.5	7	3.0	13.5
MEASUREMENT AND EVALUATION	4.4	8.5	4.0	3.5
TEACHING TEAM SPORTS	4.4	8.5	3.6	9
TEACHING INDIVIDUAL SPORTS	4.3	10	3.7	7.5
ORGANIZATION AND AD	4.1	11	4.0	3.5
PSYCHOLOGY OF SPORT	4.0	12	2.3	18
SOCIOLOGY OF SPORT	3.9	13	2.1	19
COACHING INDIVIDUAL SPORTS	3.8	14.5	2.9	15.5
COACHING TEAM SPORTS	3.8	14.5	3.2	11.5
COACHING THEORY	3.7	16.5	3.0	13.5
DANCE	3.7	16.5	2.9	15.5
PHILOSOPHY OF P.E.	3.6	18.5	3.2	11.5
RESEARCH INTERPRETATION	3.6	18.5	1.8	20
HISTORY OF P.E.	3.3	20	3.5	10

product resulted in a coefficient of .82. The reliability of both competency and content questionnaires was determined by the test-retest method (two-week interval). The responses of 52 randomly selected respondents to the competency questionnaire resulted in a coefficient of .88. The responses of 45 randomly selected respondents to the content questionnaire resulted in a coefficient of .82.

Factor analysis of the competency responses resulted in five factors which explain the interrelations within the data. The variables which loaded significantly for each factor served as a basis for the taxonomy of each factor. The five factors were: I Pedagogy; II Science of Movement; III Coaching; IV History and Philosophy of Physical Education; and V Sociology and Psychology of Sport. Sociology of Sport and Psychology of Sport are the only variables loading on Factor V; therefore educators perceive the importance of these two as related but separate from the other listed competencies and categories.

The mean of scores for the Sociology and Psychology of Sport Factor was ranked third behind Pedagogy and Science of Movement. On an individual basis rankings for means of scores for importance showed that Sociology of Sport was 13th. On the other hand, rankings for means of scores for the status of courses showed Sociology of Sport ranked as 19th. It would appear justifiable to state that the status of Sociology of Sport courses does not reflect the importance attributed to Sociology of Sport competencies for professional preparation.

To determine if, in fact, such a statement is justified, a canonical correlation was performed between the importance attributed to competencies and the status of corresponding courses. Canonical correlation takes as its basic input two sets of variables, each of which can be given theoretical meaning as a set. The basic strategy of the analysis is to derive linear combinations from each of the sets in such a way that the correlation between the two linear combinations is maximized. For this study, data concerning the importance attributed to competencies explains, as much as possible, the status of coursework in curriculums. Of principle

TABLE 2

Varimax Rotated Factor Matrix

VARIABLE	FACTORS					COMMUNALITY
	I	II	III	IV	V	
TEACHING TEAM SPORTS	.82	.04	.22	.06	.00	.73
MOTOR BEHAVIOR	.15	.48	.03	-.05	.17	.28
ORGANIZATION AND AD	.16	.12	.21	.09	.20	.13
SOCIOLOGY OF SPORT	.07	.13	.04	.29	.58	.45
TEACHING LIFETIME SPORTS	.79	.10	.15	.05	.07	.67
HISTORY OF P.E.	.13	.08	.16	.55	.22	.40
TEACHING METHODS	.25	.25	.02	-.01	.18	.16
TEACHING INDIVIDUAL SPORTS	.76	.16	.27	.00	.09	.68
ANATOMY	.03	.58	.07	.29	.00	.43
COACHING	.11	.10	.68	.11	.12	.51
PHYSIOLOGY OF EXERCISE	.02	.63	.00	.19	.03	.43
FIRST AID	.29	.33	.12	.11	.01	.23
RESEARCH IN P.E.	-.02	.46	.05	.41	.11	.40
PHILOSOPHY OF P.E.	-.01	.21	.07	.65	.18	.51
BIOMECHANICS	.09	.68	.05	.02	.16	.50
COACHING TEAM SPORTS	.25	.00	.90	.06	.03	.87
MEASUREMENT AND EVALUATION	.20	.45	.06	.12	.21	.30
DANCE	.35	.24	.14	-.02	.34	.32
PSYCHOLOGY OF SPORT	.01	.23	.09	.26	.64	.53
COACHING INDIVIDUAL SPORTS	.25	.04	.82	.08	.05	.75
EIGENVALUE	4.68	2.17	1.23	.77	.48	
% TOTAL VARIANCE	50.1	23.2	13.2	8.2	5.2	

TABLE 3

Mean Scores For Categories

CATEGORY	IMPORTANCE $\bar{X}$	STATUS $\bar{X}$
SCIENCE OF MOVEMENT	4.4	3.4
PEDAGOGY	4.3	3.6
SOCIOLOGY/PSYCHOLOGY OF SPORT	4.0	2.2
COACHING	3.8	3.4
HISTORY/PHILOSOPHY	3.4	3.4

TABLE 4

Canonical Correlations Between The
Competency Set And Coursework Set

Canvar[a]	R_C	Chi Square	DF	P[b]	R_C^2
1	.430	680.21	430	.0001	.19
2	.413	564.60	390	.0001	.17
3	.360	459.18	352	.0001	.13
4	.340	380.47	316	.002	.11
5	.224	118.21	166	.012	.05
6	.202	80.03	142	.002	.04
7	.181	65.50	120	.0001	.03
8	.151	46.67	100	.0001	.02
9	.122	33.54	82	.0001	.01

[a]Canvar = Canonical Variate

[b]Only Canonical variates significant at the .05 level of probability
are reported here.

interest is the question: Do competency variables, which load high on variates of the first set correspond to the loadings of related courses on variates of the second set? Examination of the nine significant canonical variates revealed that the matching variables with significant loadings for both sets were those from only the Pedagogy and Coaching categories. In other words, the status of Pedagogy and Coaching courses reflects the importance attributed to competencies within each category, but there is a discrepancy between the importance attributed to the remaining three categories (including sociology of sport) and their status in curriculums. On a national basis, educators for teacher preparation perceive Sociology of Sport competencies as important for teachers to attain but do not require future teachers to complete such courses in their curriculums, if indeed they offer them at all.

In fact, a look at the Sociology of Sport data on a state-by-state basis shows that none of the 50 states has a status mean greater than an elective level. Forty-two percent of the responding schools do not even offer a course in Sociology of Sport. Since respondents had the opportunity to at least include that Sociology of Sport was taught in their curriculum but included with other subject matter, one could deduce that at those institutions there is no direct student contact with Sociology of Sport.

When viewing the data according to the size of programs, I expected to see that the smaller programs would be chiefly responsible for the low status means. However, the smallest and largest programs have the same means in reference to status of coursework.

The conclusions are quite apparent: (1) teachers of physical education are not offered courses in accordance with the competencies viewed as important by curriculum planners; and (2) educators need to either re-prioritize course offerings or upgrade the status of coursework if curriculums of teacher preparation are to match the importance attributed to corresponding competencies.

TABLE 5

Frequencies Of Responses For Sociology Of Sport

RESPONSE	N	%	$\bar{X}$
COMPETENCY			
1	0	0	
2	13	2	
3	152	26	3.9
4	291	49	
5	129	23	
STATUS			
NOT OFFERED	213	42	
ELECTIVE COMBO	41	8	
ELECTIVE	124	24	2.1
REQUIRED COMBO	96	19	
REQUIRED	40	7	

TABLE 6

Responses To Competencies And Coursework
According To Size Of Programs

SIZE OF PROGRAM	COMPETENCIES: NUMBER OF RESPONDENTS	$\bar{X}$	COURSES NUMBER OF RESPONDENTS	$\bar{X}$
LESS THAN 20	36	3.9	30	2.6
21-50	116	3.9	103	2.2
51-100	172	3.9	146	2.3
Over 100	259	3.9	234	2.6

Chapter 23

SOCIOLOGICAL KINESIOLOGY: PERSPECTIVES ON PROGRAM DEVELOPMENT

Aidan O. Dunleavy, Gerald E. Landwer and
C. Roger Rees, Texas Christian University

Some four years ago a small group of faculty at TCU undertook a rational reconstruction of kinesiological studies, i.e., that field of knowledge the focus of which is play-based human behavior. From these reconstructive efforts emerged new graduate and undergraduate programs in kinesiological studies, an effective distinction between kinesiological studies and physical education, and some interesting conclusions about the nature of the "Sociology of Sport."

Out of beliefs about the values, ethical and operating principles, and functions of the university in the western world, we argued that the field of knowledge which was our concern was unique by virtue of its focus. Nobody else was directly and solely concerned with the study of play-based human behavior (including sport, which we viewed as fundamentally a play-form). For two reasons, this focus was viewed as most appropriately pursued through a cross-disciplinary approach (Henry, 1964; Renshaw, 1973). First, human play impacts all disciplines. Second, the university holds unified knowledge as one of its values. Consequently, a university program which integrates realms of meaning (disciplines as they exist in universities) is richer than one which does not. From this perspective, then, we felt that our degree programs should be characterized by this cross-disciplinary commitment and that all our course offerings should be directed toward the examination of this one focus.

A further significant understanding to emerge from our deliberations was the distinction between kinesiological studies and physical education. Whereas, kinesiological studies is solely directed to the advancement of understanding about play-based human behavior; physical education exists to serve the central purposes of school-centered education. Consistent with the fundamental nature of the university, kinesiological studies is free of any immediate or binding concern with the application of knowledges generated within the field. However, the same may not be said of physical education which *actively* serves the goals of school-centered education. Physical educators pursue these goals through a physical activity medium and utilize kinesiological knowledge in the pursuit of these goals; it is not their *charge* to generate such knowledge.

The conclusions which we reached in our deliberation presented some interesting implications for "Sociology of Sport" within our program. First, what were we to regard as the appropriate description for our various sub-fields (in this case the Sociology of Sport)? Since we have concluded that all course offerings, and indeed all pursuits, should reflect our defined focus, we must then regard ourselves as kinesiologists. However, we bring differing realms of meaning to bear on our common focus, in our case a sociological realm of meaning. Unlike mainstream sociologists, whose concern with selected forms of human play, e.g., sport, is to provide a testing ground for social theory, the kinesiologist is solely concerned with the advancement of kinesiological theory. A logical *descriptor*, and one relatively consistent with the reasoning presented by Martens (1974) in his paper "Psychological Kinesiology: An Undisciplined Sub-discipline," was that of *sociological kinesiology*.

Consistent with earlier reasoning it was further concluded that course offerings within the kinesiological studies core must be broad in concern, i.e., not narrowly focused on any one play form, for example, sport. Furthermore, such course offerings should not be narrowly applied nor issue-oriented; rather, courses should be primarily directed toward the study of kinesiological theory and the implications of such theory.

This approach to program development obviously had an impact upon our students. For example, before taking the core course in Sociological Kinesiology, they were required to have taken Introduction to Sociology, Foundations of Social Theory, and Foundations of Kinesiological Studies. Also, courses such as Understanding and Managing Youth Sport would carry a physical education prefix, e.g., P.Ed. 2423, and not a kinesiological studies prefix. Such courses as P.Ed. 2423 are concerned with the application of kinesiological knowledge to the solution of educational problems and not with the generation of such knowledge.

The Kinesiological Studies major at TCU need not take physical education certification and, therefore, need not take physical education courses. On the other hand, physical education certification students must first take the kinesiological studies core (28 credit hours), for if they are to utilize kinesiological knowledge then they must first be exposed to such knowledge.

Another programmatic decision of some interest was the manner in which we, as a department, responded to such course offerings as "Sport in Russia," and "Analysis of Contemporary Revenue Athletics." These examples are relatively narrow in focus when compared to Sociological Kinesiology, and would, therefore, not be offered as core requirements within our program. Such courses could be taken as elective credit within a "Social and Behavioral Studies" cognate (22 hours) required of kinesiological studies majors. Where these courses were taught, i.e., within which department, was of no consequence.

In reflection, the process of building a program of this nature was, admittedly, fraught with various "cans of worms," all of which had to be dealt with, but the experience was most rewarding. We are, of course, still in the process of evaluation and adjustment and, as you might expect, still very much under critical review. However, if the fields of kinesiological studies, in general, and sociological kinesiology, in particular, are to grow in a rational manner, then such reconstructive efforts must be both widespread and subjected to serious critical review.

REFERENCES

Henry, Franklin M.
  1964 "Physical education: an academic discipline." Pp. 6-9 in Proceedings of the 67th Annual Meeting of the NCPEAM, Dallas.
Martens, Rainer
  1974 "Psychological kinesiology: an undisciplined sub-discipline." Paper read at the Annual Meeting of the NASPSPA, Anaheim, CA.
Renshaw, Peter
  1973 "The nature of human movement studies and its relationship with physical education." Quest 20:79-86.

Chapter 24

NOTES ON TEACHING SOCIOLOGY OF SPORT

Merril J. Melnick, SUNY College at Brockport

Sociology of sport at State University College at Brockport is a three-credit, upper division, elective offered in and taught by the Department of Physical Education. At least one section of this course has been offered every semester since it was first introduced into the physical education major curriculum 11 years ago. Its prerequisite is a required two-credit physical education major course entitled "Sociocultural Perspective" which explores in broad, contemporary terms the interdependence between sport and culture in North American society. Approximately 70% of the students enrolled in any given section of sociology of sport have taken at least one course in a sociology department, e.g., introduction to sociology, sociology of the family, etc.

I joined the Brockport faculty in 1971 and over the past 10 years have taught a total of 20 sections of sociology of sport to over 500 students. My approaches to the course have run the gamut from a Rogerian-inspired open classroom, to contractual teaching, to small group discussion, to straight lecturing. Student assignments have included such diverse tasks as book reports, annotated bibliographies, critiques, field observations and term papers. My grading systems have reflected a mind-boggling array of assorted evaluative criteria, percentage weightings and mathematical formulae. However, rather than present a detailed description of what it is I'm presently doing in the classroom, I would like instead to share with you some guiding principles which I strongly believe in and endeavor to incorporate into my teaching. These principles, three to be exact, have direct implications for (1) the presentation of course content; (2) class organization; (3) course assignments; and (4) student evaluation. The practical applications of these principles, both in and outside the classroom, have been well received by my students, which leads me to believe that they're worth sharing.

GUIDING PRINCIPLES

1. Students Should be Given the Opportunity to Experience Firsthand What it is Sport Sociologists Do

If our students are to acquire an appreciation for the sociological perspective, and the many ways it can illuminate and explicate the sport phenomenon, I firmly believe that they need to participate actively in the research process, to experience, however modestly, the consummate adventure of asking and answering a sociologically-informed, sport-related research question. Eight years ago, I developed what I euphemistically refer to as the *SOS Research Project Assignment*. And while many students have had cause to signal a dire SOS along the way, most of my students have enjoyed and expressed pleasure in completing this assignment. Of course, the work is frequently uneven, ranging from "very poor" to "outstanding." This is to be expected since few of my students have had a formal course in research methods. In any case, I am usually pleasantly surprised by the thought, effort and thoroughness which my students put into their projects. Essentially, the assignment requires each student to identify a research question, conduct a modest review of the pertinent literature, choose an appropriate research methodology, select and/or construct some type of data-gathering instrument, collect and analyze data and set forth one or more conclusionary statements. Survey research, as expected, is the most popular of the research methodologies chosen. However, field observation, participant observation, secondary data analysis, content analysis, sociometry and role analysis have all been used with some degree of success.

For example, role analysis has been successfully employed to gain insight into such sport-related work roles as female high school basketball officials, college swimming coaches, high school team managers, college baseball umpires, and Little League baseball coaches. Observation and participant observation have been successfully used to gain a better understanding of a wide variety of sport subcultures including harness racing, male bowling leagues, an urban poolhall, motorcross devotees, rugby footballers, the karate dojo, sports gamblers, weight lifters, women body builders and elite racquetball players. Sociometric tests have been used to answer research questions about team friendship patterns, cohesiveness, social structure, leadership and prestige hierarchies. Survey methodology has provided answers to questions about athlete's superstitions, sport consumption patterns, special problems faced by minority group athletes, motives for sport participation, effects of losing on peer group status, drug use, dating patterns of athletes, homosexuality and hero worship. Secondary data analysis studies have employed a variety of library reference materials to find answers to questions about managerial succession in the National Football League, geographical origins of National Basketball Association players, the academic performance of high school athletes, the relationship between crowd size and team performance and the relationship between race and batting average in major league baseball.

To be sure, much of the research I've made reference to has been atheoretical, descriptive and based on convenience sampling. And I say "So what?" For most if not all of my students, this course will be their last formal contact with the subfield. It seems fitting, therefore, that their sociology of sport education include at least one opportunity to undertake an independent research assignment that conforms to the basic canons of social scientific inquiry and which, at the same time, allows them to acquire new knowledges and understandings through a learning experience of their own design.

2. Students Should be Encouraged to Take an "Active" Role in Course Decision-Making and Class Organization

The body of knowledge of sociology of sport is such that the selection of topics, units and/or themes for classroom presentation and discussion can prove most perplexing. Such popular textbook favorites as "Women in Sport," "Aggression and Violence in Sport" and "Sport and the Mass Media" surely have to be included. But then what about "Sport and Social Stratification" and "Sport and Social Deviance" — and everyone's favorite "Sport and Politics"? In the final analysis, the selection of content for an introductory course in sociology of sport is an arbitrary one, based more, I suspect, on the personal biases and research activities of the instructor than anything else. Because my personal teaching philosophy encourages me to make some effort to share the burden of responsibility for the success or failure of the course with my students, I have, in recent years, provided several opportunities for them to take an active role in their own learning. For example, following the first or introductory part of the course in which I discuss with them the social phenomenon of sport, sociology of sport as an academic subfield, and research methodology and techniques of data collection appropriate to the sociology of sport, I have my students complete a student interest questionnaire, the results of which I then use to select the remaining discussion topics for the course. I should hasten to point out that I do impose some structure on their decision-making. Borrowing to some extent from the conceptual framework offered by Loy, McPherson and Kenyon (1978), my students choose their topics from several possibilities listed under each of several broad subject categories. These categories include: "Sport Groups," "Sport Organizations," "Sport Subcultures," "Sport and Social Institutions," "Sport and Social Stratification," and "Sport Problems." Those topics judged by the class to be of greatest interest within each of these categories collectively represent the remaining content of the course. In this way, students have the feeling that they have really participated in shaping the direction of the course. I have found that this sense of active involvement in course planning pays dividends in terms of better class attendance, greater motivation for learning and higher quality work. In addition, each student is required to assist in the development and conduct of a group presentation on one of the discussion topics chosen by the class. In order to help with this task, I organize my students into small groups based on their responses to a group presentation interest questionnaire. I then turn over to each group one or two class periods for their presentation. The latter can and does take many forms, e.g., a question and answer session with one or more invited guests, a panel discussion, a debate, the showing of a movie, etc. Formal peer evaluation following the conclusion of each presentation determines the grade that each group member receives.

Unlike other subfields of sociology, e.g., medical sociology, industrial sociology, sociology of religion, etc., sociology of sport is usually taken by students who have had extensive contact with the phenomenon under investigation. In my case, many of the students I teach have spent more than half their lives actively engaged in both formal and informal sport. They have experienced, firsthand, adult intrusion in their play experiences; they have enjoyed the personal satisfaction that comes with making a valued high school team and the concomitant peer group status that attends such an accomplishment; they have participated in their share of compatible and incompatible coach-athlete dyads; they have worshipped sports heroes; they have used lucky charms and engaged in fetishes and rituals to enhance their chances for success; and, they have been influenced to consume sport by a variety of significant others.

With respect to the affective domain, these students have experienced sport in very personal and powerful ways — they have been cheered, they have despaired, they have exalted in success, they have had to deal with painful defeat. In short, I am very much in agreement with sport sociologist David Whitson's (1976, 1977) arguments in behalf of a "person-centered" approach to sociology of sport in the classroom. I am firmly convinced that the social circumstances surrounding student experiences and the attendant feelings engendered are worth drawing out and examining in the classroom. They deserve as much attention as the appropriate scientifically-based research literature. In my judgment, the conjoining of the student's experiential world with the related theoretical and empirical work of the subfield makes for a winning classroom combination.

3. Observe and Study Sport with Your Students in Natural Settings

I plan with my students at least one field trip each semester which allows us to observe and study sport in a natural setting —away from the classroom, the blackboard and the overhead projector. Invariably, these trips and the discussions they provoke prove to be the highlights of each and every semester. Of course, time, expense, accessibility and transportation can often prove to be formidable obstacles. However, if sport is as pervasive a phenomenon as we sport sociologists would like to believe, then identifying field trip sites within one's own community may not prove that great a challenge. For example, consider all of the following possibilities which should be available close to home. (1) Observe a recess period at a local primary school and note the types of informal play activities preferred by the children; (2) Attend a Saturday morning youth football game at a local field and study the nature of adult intervention and control; (3) Join a Friday night high school football pep rally to gain an appreciation of the role and function of sport in the adolescent subculture.

Of course, where there is accessibility to professional sports events, the opportunities increase considerably. In recent semesters, my classes and I have taken advantage of our proximity to Rochester, New York and have observed as a group the "rites of reversal" characteristic of roller derby; the staging and impression management characteristics of professional wrestling; and, the organizational survival techniques of the Rochester Zeniths, an entry in the new but struggling Continental Basketball Association. More ambitious efforts have taken us to Batavia Downs

(Batavia, New York) to study the subculture of harness racing; admittance into Elmira State Prison (Elmira, New York) to observe the role and function of sport in a penal institution; and a weekend spent in Toronto, Canada to observe sport from a cross-cultural perspective.

As a first step towards implementation of this guiding principle, a compilation of all the sports sites, sports events and sports teams within one's immediate area should be undertaken. This effort will in all probability produce some interesting, exciting and surprising possibilities. Financial and transportation assistance may be available from one's institution and should definitely be looked into. Where none is available, car pooling, dormitory and/or fraternity lodging (when it is necessary) and other low budget arrangements can help keep expenses down. Group-rated ticket prices and other kinds of educational discounts for some professional sports events are sometimes available from sport management and should not be overlooked. Considerable class discussion should precede the actual observation. This discussion should mainly focus on the types of social behavior that will be investigated. Provisions should be made for identifying, recording and interpreting these behaviors on location. The overall evaluation of the field trip should be taken up at the next regularly scheduled class meeting.

If you want to add considerable spice to your sociology of sport course, I strongly recommend the inclusion of some type of group field experience. Given sufficient planning, preparation and a little bit of luck, such an experience can add an exciting dimension to your course by making your students confront sport not as we would like it to be but as it really is.

To summarize, I think it is important for teachers of sociology of sport to provide their students with opportunities to describe the richness and complexity of sport in any and all of its natural habitats. We must recognize the fact that many of our students already possess a certain amount of "expert knowledge" about sport and, with proper guidance and supervision, are capable of studying it in their own ways and on their own terms.

Finally, the field trip experience offers our students one of the grandest opportunities to observe and converse with those social actors who constitute the real social world of sport. Some may ask, "Is this what sociology of sport should be?" For me, the answer is a resounding "yes," and I draw my strength of conviction from sociologist John O'Neill's (1974) short but stimulating book *Making Sense Together* and the arguments he puts forth in behalf of doing "wild sociology." To paraphrase O'Neill,

> It is only through a concern for the ritual wholeness of daily sport particulars that students of sport sociology can experience the suffering and celebration which attend the sport phenomenon. Let's not study sport in order to define its completion through dominating generalizations, ambitions of control and the usurpation of relevance, but rather, to generate the care and concern which can help create the human sport community.

NOTE

Copies of each of the course handouts referred to in this article are available from the author.

REFERENCES

Loy, J. W., B. D. McPherson, and G. S. Kenyon
  1978 Sport and Social Systems. Reading: Addison-Wesley.
O'Neill, J.
  1974 Making Sense Together: An Introduction to Wild Sociology. New York: Harper Torchbooks.
Whitson, D. J.
  1976 "Method in sport sociology: the potential of a phenomenological contribution." International Review of Sport Sociology 11:53-68.
Whitson, D. J.
  1977 "An introduction to experimental research in physical education." Canadian Association for Health, Physical Education and Recreation. Journal 43:39-45.

Chapter 25

SPORT AND AMERICAN SOCIETY: A COURSE FOR KINESIOLOGICAL SCIENCE MAJORS, AND GENERAL UNIVERSITY STUDENTS

Lee VanderVelden, University of Maryland

The Sport and American Society undergraduate course at Maryland was developed in 1972; a consequence of both the movement to make physical education more academic and the anti-establishment *zeitgeist* in America during the late 1960's and early 1970's. Moreover, the publication of Jack Scott's *The Athletic Revolution* (1969) posed for sport the kind of questions being asked of other social institutions: How is sport organized? How does it work? Whom does it benefit? Whom should it benefit? How can it be improved?

Neither specifically planned for nor required of prospective teachers, the course is designed to investigate the structure of sport in American society, how it works, and what its consequences are (discipline orientation) rather than to show how sport can be used to educate or to change behavior (professional orientation). Twenty students, most of them non-majors, comprised the first class in 1972, while approximately 120 students now enroll in the three sections of the course offered each semester. Only recently made a requirement for kinesiological sciences majors — it is not required of prospective teachers — the course still attracts more non-majors than physical education majors. Such an enrollment pattern was reinforced one year ago when

Sport and American Society was included as an option within the Social and Behavioral Sciences Division of the University Studies Program, forty credits of restrictive electives required of all undergraduates at Maryland. Each student must take a minimum of six credits from each of four divisions in addition to completing separate mathematics and English requirements.

This approach to studying sport as a social institution provides an examination of sport somewhat different from that with which the students are familiar. Before attending the class, the views of students toward sport stem from their involvement as participants in and spectators of organized sport at the youth, secondary, collegiate, and professional levels. For the most part their attitudes are positive; they accept sport as it is — myths and all — never asking why sport is the way it is. In addition, those athletes who enroll — another minority group — have experienced organized sport first hand, and their views of sport are primarily from an athlete's perspective. Thus, comparing the benefits a school receives from intercollegiate athletics with those enjoyed by the athletes themselves is revealing to most students, including athletes. Similarly, explaining the behavior of professional sport organizations in terms of a profit maximizing motive, pointing out the social functions (dysfunctions) of amateurism, and using an "institution versus an instrument" conflict model to explain such developments as the old NFL-AFL football war in the mid 1960's and the professional versus amateur hockey series between Canada and Russia are approaches used to present sport as a social institution. The usual student response to such presentations, "I never thought of it that way before, but it makes sense," attests to the educational value of this non-normative, debunking orientation.

At the same time, however, considerable effort is made to maintain a balanced view of sport, apart from the extreme, negative, and muckraking approaches used by some. For example, although it is pointed out that the sports business is not organized to maximize the benefits to the participants (athletes), organized sport is not condemned. Students are never told what to think, which position is the "correct" one, or what to say to earn a passing grade. After studying sport during the semester, students must decide for themselves which views of sport to accept, which to reject. Correspondingly, one feature of the course requires students to prepare a short paper defending a position on some controversial issue in sport. Students choose both the issues and the positions to defend and a frequent question/comment directed to the instructor is, "What do you think about this issue? We do not know what your position is on *(any issue)*." Such responses suggest some success with this evenhanded approach, especially since most of the issues had already been discussed in class.

Finally, students like the course. During the ten years it has been offered, the course evaluations have varied little. The typical response is, "I liked the class, I learned a lot, but I had to work harder than I thought I would." No teacher should have to apologize for that evaluation.

In summary, the course is designed to study sport as a social institution, to provide a balanced, realistic examination of organized sport for kinesiological sciences majors and general university students. Thus, it has a more discipline orientation than a professional teacher training focus. Furthermore, the course has been successful, growing from one to three sections per semester and receiving high marks from students.

INTRODUCTION

School	University of Maryland, College Park
Course Prefix & No.:	PHED 287
Title:	Sport and American Society
Credit Hours:	3
Requirement:	Kinesiological Sciences
Restricted Elective:	University Studies: Social and Behavioral Sciences Division
Prerequisites:	None

Course Objectives:

1. To develop a greater understanding of the social significance
   of sport by:
   a)   explaining sport in light of other social systems and
           subsystems, e.g., how do athletes and fans become
           socialized into sport, and
   b)   explaining the nature of other social systems through
           their relationships with sport, e.g., what is the polit-
           ical function of international amateur sport?
2. To become more aware of the positive and negative consequences of the way sport is organized in America.
3. To demonstrate the utility of the sociological perspective as a
   means to understanding American sport as well as other parts
   of the social world.

Course Readings:

In general, required readings include two textbooks, several
outside readings on reserve in the Undergraduate Library and a
number of articles, summaries, and diagrams distributed in class.
The specific readings required have varied each semester since
1972. As the body of knowledge in the Sociology of Sport grows,
new textbooks, essays, research reports, etc., become available
and additions and deletions are made to improve the course content. During the most recent two semesters the two required textbooks have been:

> Eitzen, D. Stanley and George Sage. *Sociology of Ameri-*
> *can Sport*, Dubuque, Iowa, Wm. C. Brown, 1978, pp. 337.
> Michener, James. *Sports in America*, Greenwich, Con-
> necticut, Fawcett Crest Publications, 1976, pp. 576.

Course Requirements:

1. Three examinations (80 points): two one-hour exams plus a
   two-hour final examination. Examinations are composed of
   true-false, multiple choice, completion, and identification
   items.

2. A position paper on some controversial issue within sport (20 points).

Course Methodology:

Lecture-discussion format with occasional guest speakers from the Washington Metropolitan Area. Classes are limited to 40 students to facilitate discussion. Recent speakers have included Herbert Brown, former Chairman, University of Maryland Board of Regents; Robert Gluckstern, Chancellor, University of Maryland-College Park Campus; and Ed Garvey, Executive Director National Football League Players Association.

Course Content

1. *Nature of Sport* — Attempt is made to define a sport or sports and to contrast the fundamentals of simple sport with the attributes of highly organized, institutionalized sport. A conceptual framework is presented to illustrate the structure and the relationships among the components of institutionalized sport.

2. *Heritage of Sport* — The discussion is designed to show how the "Man," the national character of Americans, and the "Times,"the events, movements, ideas, technology, etc., have shaped the nature, the form, and the function of contemporary sport.

3. *Amateurism and Professionalism* — A logical outgrowth of the Heritage of Sport Section, the discussion of amateurism focuses on the social origins and functions of this attitude toward play. Contemporary concern for amateurism is directed to the more practical question of eligibility and ultimately leads to the issue of whether or not amateurism is a philosophy worth preserving.

4. *Politics and Sport* — The use of sport as a political tool at the local, national and international levels and the politics within sport itself are discussed within the context of the Olympic Games, the premier political sporting event.

5. *Socialization and Sport* — The discussion of socialization *via* sport emphasizes the role of sport as a socializing agent teaching valuable lessons for life. In short, "Are Sports Educational?" Socialization into sport is concerned with the processes of becoming involved in sport, e.g., athlete, coach, referee, fan or cheerleader.

6. *Social Stratification and Mobility and Sport* — One aspect of socialization, stratification in sport is concerned with the social origins of participants in various sports and leisure activities. The patterns of sport participation for males and females, black and whites, and the various social classes and ethnic groups are examined. In addition, the myth that sport is a viable avenue for social mobility in American society is challenged. Special attention is given to the impact of sport on blacks and other disadvantaged groups.

7. *Sport and the School* — The role of athletics in education is discussed by comparing the functions and dysfunctions of school sports both for the participant and for the institution. Other topics include the relationship between certain attributes of schools and their varying emphases on athletics and a comparison of the academic and athletic prowess of athletes.

8. *Sport and the Economy* — An attempt is made to demonstrate the economic significance of sport and to point out the economic structure of sport at the secondary, collegiate, and professional levels. The discussion includes a description of the peculiar economics of sport and several illustrations of a profit motive accounting for more of the behavior of school and professional sport groups than does an emphasis on winning motive.

9. *Sport and the Media* — A natural sequel to the economy discussion, this section contains an examination of the relationship between the media and organized sport. The specific roles of the "Press" and the "Electronic Media" are compared and contrasted within the frame, "Who needs whom the most?" The economic bonds between sport and electronic media are discussed.

10. *Segregation and Discrimination and Sport* — Description of the patterns of sports participation among blacks and women are presented and possible explanations for the seemingly discriminatory patterns are discussed.

11. *Sport and Deviancy* — Discussion includes four sub areas: (a) "Drug Use in Sport" is discussed from the perspective that using drugs in sport is a form of cheating; (b) "Cheating in Sports" is presented with the proposition that "sport teaches one to cheat"; (c) "Sport as a Deterrent to Delinquency" is treated as another of the myths of sport with little evidence to support the adage, "stay out for sports and stay out of courts"; and finally, (d) "Player Violence" is examined for both its antecedants and consequences.

12. *Collective Behavior and Sport* — The behavior of spectators is studied in response to the question, "To what is the fan entitled when he purchases a ticket to a sporting event?"

13. *The Future of Sport in America* — Time is given to speculation about the nature, form, and function of sport in the Twenty-First Century.

Chapter 26

SPORT SOCIOLOGY: A HUMANISTIC PERSPECTIVE

Don Hellison, Portland State University

The undergraduate course that I offer, and which our School of Health and Physical Education requires of all majors, is titled "Physical Education and Humanity: Contemporary Concepts." This title is appropriately fuzzy, because the course is intended to provide an overview of social science and to some extent humanities concepts that have crept (catapulted?) into our professional awareness over the past two decades. The faculty's decision to create this course could be viewed as a "foot in the door" for social science inasmuch as most of the required courses have a basis in the physical sciences. Our majors, who are overwhelmingly practitioner-oriented (some five per cent are currently enrolled in our "research" track), tend to view this kind of course as irrelevant to their needs. They lend credibility to Broekhoff's (1979) observation that for most majors "the academic subject matter will remain just that: academic." However, I did not agree to develop and teach this course either to get social science's "foot in the door" of physical education at Portland State or to help our majors grasp the importance of academic subject matter. Instead, I wanted to introduce a humanistic perspective to our students.

Humanism comes in a wide variety of forms and is therefore an ambiguous term. However, recent sociological thought — influenced by C. Wright Mills, Alvin Gouldner, Peter Berger, Alfred McClung Lee and others — has staked out some groundrules for a humanistic perspective. These scholars contend that sociology is not a value-free enterprise, that personal experiences and feelings matter, and that sociology ought to be committed to serving humanity. Melnick (1975), Ingham (1979), and Yiannakis (1979) have helped to interpret these groundrules for physical education.

My own interpretation is that physical education ought unabashedly to commit to helping others and that the academic subdisciplines ought to support and serve this moral commitment. If "the center of gravity of our profession lies in the act of teaching" (Broekhoff, 1979) in a wide variety of settings, as I think it does, a commitment to the act of helping is further clarified and focused. Further, sociological (and other subdisciplinary) concepts which contribute to the improvement of teaching need to be analyzed and compared to personal experiences, feelings, and values if a humanistic perspective is to become a reality.

"Physical Education and Humanity: Contemporary Concepts" is an attempt to introduce this humanistic perspective to our majors. Concepts are regularly reviewed for their relevance to the improvement of teaching, and a variety of strategies are employed to encourage our majors to evaluate each concept in terms of their personal experiences and values. Introductory concepts are intended to help students comprehend the relevance of the social sciences and humanities for physical education practice and to help them better understand the power of their own experiences in their beliefs and behavior. The cultural concepts section, draws heavily from sociology, is designed to help students understand the context within which the conduct of physical education takes place. The motivation concepts section draws from the psychosocial literature and is designed to help students understand the importance of personality, reinforcement, and needs in the practice of physical education. The ethics concepts section draws from philosophy and social science and is designed to help students understand the role of ethical behavior and character in physical education.

COURSE OUTLINE

I. Introductory Concepts
1. The academic disciplines and physical education
2. The role of affect: personal truths
3. The role of affect: value orientations
4. Teacher and coach artistry
5. The defensibility of one's program

II. 1. The socialization process
2. Cultural change: our low context culture
3. Sex roles
4. Alienation
5. Competition
6. play
7. Aggression as social learning

III. 1. Locus of control
2. Personality traits
3. Reinforcement
4. Survival and security
5. Affection
6. Body image
7. Self esteem and identity
8. Stimulation
10. The "Zen" movement

IV. 1. Ethics: a definition
2. Developmental factors in ethical behavior and character
3. Ethics: school and society
4. Ethics in physical education

REFERENCES

Broekhoff, J.
1979 "Physical education as a profession." Quest 31:244-54.
Ingham, A. G.
1979 "Methodology in the sociology of sport: from symptoms of malaise to Weber for a cure." Quest 31:187-215.
Melnick, M. J.
1975 "A critical look at the sociology of sport." Quest 24:24-47.
Yiannakis, A.
1979 "From the editor." NASSS Newsletter:1-2.

Chapter 27

THE USE OF SPORT IN SOCIETY VTR'S IN THE SPORT SOCIOLOGY CURRICULUM

James E. Bryant, Metropolitan State College

The development of an educational television series (VTR Programming) entitled SPORT IN SOCIETY was conceived initially to provide a format for discussion for the course "The Sociology of Athletics in American Society" offered in the Physical Education Department at Metropolitan State College. The course was an upper division required course for sports communication majors, recreation sports majors, non-teaching physical education majors, and coaching minors.

The course format included lectures and discussion classes covering current topics in sport sociology. The enrichment of the course was supplemented by expert guest speakers who were, on occasion, not as knowledgeable as they appeared on the surface, who sometimes couldn't be depended on to appear in class on the scheduled time, and who monopolized class time through their presentation hence eliminating other areas that could also have been included in the course. As a result of a self-initiated instructor evaluation of the course, it was determined that students could better be served in the existing course through outside class assignments that required the video tape viewing of interviews with experts in sport sociology either as professional sport sociologists or as expert sport-related professionals. A further observation was made that other sport sociology courses throughout the country could also benefit from a prepared program of viewing sport as it relates to society, particularly if study and instructor's guides were developed for use with each program in the series.

The curriculum usage of the SERIES was limited originally to class assignments in the original course, but other possibilities surfaced including the use of excerpts (or the total program) in the course for immediate feedback in discussion, and then the use of the 21-series program as a course in itself, using the television media as the main portion of the prepared course. All three of the curriculum plans are presented in some greater detail later in this paper. Another use that served as spin off of the SERIES was the possibility of using the programs in related sport sociology areas. Some examples of the potential in these areas are listed below:

1. Black Athlete in Sport . . . . Afro American Studies Area
2. Religion and Sport, and the
   Psychic Side of Sport . . . . Religion related courses
3. Being Human in Sport and
   Humor in Sport . . . . Philosophy related courses
4. International Politics and Sport and the USOC
   and Olympism . . . . Comparative Sport Study Area

Regardless of how the VTR programs are used, they are basically designed for the sport sociologist to use in the curriculum of sport sociology and sport studies, and they offer much in the way of course enrichment.

The material presented in the following pages describes briefly the SERIES format, the annotated titles of each program, and a more indepth coverage of the use of each program in the curriculum.

THE SERIES FORMAT

The original Sport in Society series was developed in the Spring, 1979 for use by sports sociologists at the national level. In Fall 1981 seven of the original series are being revised and seven new tapes are being developed to comlete a 21-tape series.

Each tape is a ¾ inch, 30 minute, color video tape that follows an interview with a professional sport sociologist or sport related professional and uses some visuals for impact. The titles of each tape in the series and annotation plus the professional interviewed are listed below:

THE ANNOTATED TITLES OF PROGRAMS

Intercollegiate Athletics, NCAA, and Exploitation ...... Sage
A view of intercollegiate athletics in the United States and how the NCAA exploits athletes and eliminates basic athletic rights
(revised, 1981)

Municipal Politics and Sport .... Varnell
An analysis of how politics works in city and state governments to impact sport at the professional level and the taxpayer in the community   (1979)

Superbowl and Sport .... Paige
An analysis of the superbowl as a microcosm of our larger society and as a bigger than life extravaganza   (1979)

College Sport and Law .... Brody
An analysis of college sport as the area relates to law; particularly with regard to basic athletic rights   (1979)

Black Athlete in Sport .... Biffle
A view of discriminatory practices in sport, quota systems, centrality of position, and the role of minorities in sport   (revised, 1981)

Violence and Sport .... Lyle
A view of aggression and violence in sport and the relationship to larger society   (revised, 1981)

Religion and Sport .... Stavely
An investigation into the role religion plays in sport, religious organizations, and the role of prayer in sport   (1979)

Professional Sports and Antitrust Laws . . . . Brody
A legal look at the law as it applies to sport and in particular
how baseball has escaped the antitrust laws in the United
States   (1979)

Youth Sports Competition . . . . Coakley
An overview of youth sports and competition and the impact
competition has on youth   PART I   (1979)

Developmental Implications for Youth Sports . . . . Coakley
A specific analysis of spontaneous play, informal games, and
organized games   PART II   (new, 1981)

Professional Sports and Economics . . . . Kitchen
A survey of what controls professional sport economically
and how professional sport is business; in addition, a look at
players, salaries, contracts, etc.   PART I   (1979)

Professional Sports and Economics . . . . Mills
An indepth analysis of money, cartels, and control (new,
1981)

The Female Athlete in Modern Sport . . . . To be announced
A review of the place of the female athlete in the United
States and the cultural implications of her development and
participation in sport   (revised, 1982)

Socialization via Sport . . . . Sage
A view of sport values, deviance, inculturation, etc. (new,
1981)

Media and the Sports World . . . . Brown
An indepth analysis of the impact the media has on society
as the media relates to sport in American society (revised,
1981)

International Sport and Politics . . . . Frey
An investigation of how sport is used for propaganda stretch-
ing from communist block countries to the free world and
including the Union of South Africa, East Germany, Cuba,
the USSR, and the United States   (new, 1981)

USOC and Olympism .... Miller
An interview with Col. Miller, Director of the USOC, on site at the Olympic Training Center, Colorado Springs, Colorado. Discussion includes the Moscow Olympics, the Los Angeles Olympics, Olympic Sports Festivals, athletes' rights, government financing, etc.   (revised, 1981)

Humor and Sport .... McLaughlin
A survey of how humor is inter-related with sport and is used in the literature, the media, and in daily life   (new, 1981)

The Future of Sport .... Woods
A futuristic scenerio of what sport can be, possibly will be, and how sport in the future will impact society (new, 1981)

The Psychic Side of Sport .... Zinner
An extension of religion in sport to the investigation of feeling in sport and energy flow   (new, 1981)

Being Human in Sport .... Rhodes
A humanistic review of sport and how sport can be used in a positive aspect   (new, 1981)

CURRICULUM USES

There are several curriculum uses for the Sport in Society series at the undergraduate and graduate level. Three are specified below.

Viewing assignments. The series can be used quite successfully as outside assignments for either undergraduate or graduate courses in sport sociology. Basically, a viewing assignment is made as a reading assignment due the day of discussion or day of lecture. An option to insure student viewing, particularly at the undergraduate level, is to require student response to a study guide or to a specific assignment through the use of a study guide or a written assignment. This prior preparation expectation for the student encourages the student to identify the major aspects of a particular program.

Use of excerpts in class. The series can be used as part of the course within the course meeting time. Under these conditions selected portions of a tape that are most appropriate for specific topic areas in the organization of the course are used. If planned carefully prior to the course the integration of the VTR can be highly impacting at either the graduate or undergraduate level basically because the program is fresh in the minds of students and, in fact, can be repeated during any particular program sequence to enhance discussion.

VTR course in Sport in Society. A unique, perhaps innovative, approach to the use of the total program series is to incorporate the 21 tapes into a self-paced course. The scenerio for a course of this type incorporates a two semester credit, arranged time course that would include:

1. 10.5 hours of program viewing
2. 21 study guide question/answer responses
3. Arranged conferences with instructor in 3 formats: one to one-student/instructor, small group with instructor, total class meeting with instructor. Discussion and clarification would be a major aspect in any of the three formats
4. Final exam — conceptual

The incorporation of the viewing of each program, response to study guides, and instructor/student communication insure a learning experience appropriate for junior/senior undergraduates in particular. Availability of the instructor and sensitivity to the possible missing components that provide smooth transition and comprehension between subjects through the use of tapes are major ingredients of this type of course.

Final Comments. All programs are designed to encourage discussion on the part of students and study guides are developed to direct students through the concepts of each program. Used as a supplemental tool for a sport sociology course or as an innovative media-oriented course, the Sport in Society series can enhance a sport sociology curriculum and student learning experiences.

DESIGN AND GRAPHIC ART
FOR BOOK AND COVER BY
JUDITH OELFKE SMITH.
THIS BOOK IS SET IN
ELEVEN POINT GARAMOND #3
BY FORT WORTH LINOTYPING COMPANY
PRINTED ON NEKOSSA OFFSET AND BOUND BY
STAFFORD-LOWDON PRINTING COMPANY.